Praise for *How to Make a Killing*

"Tom Mueller illustrates how modern medicine could devise technologies to literally revive people dying of kidney failure and how such miracles became perverted and incentivized abuses. A sad, shocking tale."
—Ezekiel J. Emanuel, author of
Which Country Has the World's Best Health Care

"Tom Mueller goes deep, then wide, then straight for the jugular of the corporate predators who are getting rich by exploiting the poor and vulnerable. This book raised my blood pressure by at least thirty points." —Carl Elliott, author of *The Occasional Human Sacrifice: Medical Experimentation and the Price of Saying No*

"I loved Tom Mueller's beautifully written and fascinating account of both the miraculous possibilities of medical technology and the perils of poorly structured markets. There is universal medical care in the United States, but only for kidney disease. How a program started by Richard Nixon and corrupted by finance has saved lives, and cost them, is the story of modern America." —Matt Stoller, author of *Goliath: The Hundred Year War Between Monopoly Power and Democracy*

"Tom Mueller's *How to Make a Killing* is a rich and sweeping saga that is, sadly, a quintessentially American story: how a miracle medical machine transformed into profit machine, sick and suffering patients be damned." —Jesse Eisinger, author of *The Chickenshit Club*

"A terrifying story of profit before patients, and a chilling glimpse of what can happen when private companies are allowed to take charge of healthcare." —Gavin Francis, author of *Recovery: The Lost Art of Convalescence*

"[A] grimly fascinating and humane exposé."
—Steven P————

"We have accepted too much for too l————
say that the book exaggerates and that t————

Maybe they don't in some/most clinics, but even if they happen in a few clinics, we can do better." —Beth Witten, Home Dialysis Central

"We urge you to stop what you're doing, buy this book, and read it from cover to cover. The book presents nothing short of an indictment of rabid capitalism run amok, effectively turning what should be a life-saving branch of medicine into a criminal enterprise."

—Pam and Russ Martens, *Wall Street on Parade*

"*New York Times* best-selling author Tom Mueller very well could be rocking the foundations of many a corporate boardroom with this book." —DialysisEthics.org

"Mueller provides a cautionary tale that exposes an underbelly of greed in the medical industry, one where people willingly sell off ethics and care to the highest bidder." —Ron Sylvester, *Spokesman-Review*

"A brilliant expose of one of the darkest corners of healthcare. This story must be told—to protect some of America's most vulnerable of patients, but also the people who care for them."

—Kimberlee Langford, registered nurse and
vice president of clinical services at Specialty Care Management

"Tom Mueller does a fantastic job of meticulously categorizing and explaining all of the abuses of power. I highly recommend *How to Make a Killing*." —Dr. Eric Bricker, founder of AHealthcareZ

"A must-read for clinicians, patients, economists, policymakers, and anyone interested in improving healthcare. Through exhaustive research and simple yet dramatic language, Tom Mueller reveals some of the biggest, darkest secrets in US healthcare."

—Kevin Weinstein, CEO of Renalogic

"Insightful, infuriating, and inspiring. As both the family member of someone who has been on dialysis for more than a decade and a practicing physician, I am deeply grateful for the journalistic work of Tom Mueller." —Tyler Wellman, MD

ALSO BY TOM MUELLER

Extra Virginity

Crisis of Conscience

How to
Make a Killing

BLOOD, DEATH AND DOLLARS

IN

AMERICAN MEDICINE

TOM MUELLER

W. W. NORTON & COMPANY

Independent Publishers Since 1923

For information about permission to reproduce selections from this book,
write to Permissions, W. W. Norton & Company, Inc.
500 Fifth Avenue, New York, NY 10110

For information about special discounts for bulk purchases, please contact
W. W. Norton Special Sales at specialsales@wwnorton.com or
800-233-4830

Manufacturing by Lakeside Book Company
Book design by Brooke Koven
Production manager: Anna Oler

Library of Congress Control Number: 2024937839

ISBN 978-1-324-07905-7 pbk.

W. W. Norton & Company, Inc.
500 Fifth Avenue, New York, N.Y. 10110
www.wwnorton.com

W. W. Norton & Company Ltd.
15 Carlisle Street, London W1D 3BS

1 2 3 4 5 6 7 8 9 0

Of all the forms of inequality, injustice in health is the most shocking and the most inhuman because it often results in physical death. I see no alternative to direct action and creative nonviolence to raise the conscience of the nation.

—MARTIN LUTHER KING, JR.,
Chicago, March 25, 1966

CONTENTS

1 : Beginnings   1

2 : The Inner Sea   5

3 : Dialysis in America   13

4 : Who Lives, Who Dies   33

5 : Medical Miracles, Bioethics and Dialysis for All   54

6 : The Roll-Up   77

7 : On the Blood Floor   98

8 : Musketeers   137

9 : The Fox in the Hen House   163

10 : The Wisdom of the Kidney   180

Epilogue and Annotations   203
Notes   205
Index   265

· I ·

Beginnings

I ENCOUNTERED DIALYSIS six years ago, while writing a book about whistleblowing. Several people I interviewed had blown the whistle on large dialysis corporations where they had formerly worked. The industry, they explained, is dominated by two publicly traded multinationals, Fresenius and DaVita. These companies and several smaller competitors have faced repeated allegations of healthcare fraud and other serious wrongdoing, and have paid substantial legal settlements to extinguish these allegations. (The settlements won by just three of the dialysis whistleblowers I spoke with—a financial executive, a medical doctor and a registered nurse—totaled around $900 million.) Yet they continue to post massive profits, year after year, and the US government continues to do business with them. Who knew there was so much money to be made in dialysis?

Looking deeper, I learned that dialysis had once been considered a miracle cure, and had made medical, ethical and legal history. In the 1960s, it became the first therapy successfully to replace a vital organ— the kidney—with a machine, a technological breakthrough that helped prompt the birth of the field of bioethics. In the early 1970s, recognizing dialysis as a medical paradigm shift, Congress pledged to pay for the treatment of nearly all Americans with kidney failure, making dialysis

America's first—and to this day its only—major experiment in "Medicare for All."

I was also struck by the industry's odd blend of high-stakes emergency medicine and routinized care. Though risks of infection, cardiac arrest and other medical crises are high, much dialysis is performed by low-wage dialysis technicians with limited training. Patients need multiple treatments a week, each lasting several hours, yet most dialyze not in their homes, but in clinics in strip malls and business parks. Many patients I met spend much of their lives traveling to clinics (typically three times every week), waiting to dialyze, undergoing the hours-long treatment, recovering from its side effects, and bracing psychologically for the next session. Fifty years ago, dialysis was high-tech, cutting-edge medicine. Today, it embodies America's corporate healthcare at its most extractive.

As I learned all this, healthcare was becoming an ever more prominent issue in US national elections. As America's one universal health program, "Dialysis for All" surely held important lessons for the country's larger healthcare debate—but as a way forward, or a warning?

To write this book, I interviewed hundreds of members of the dialysis community. I spoke with patients receiving care at the major dialysis companies, and current and past employees of those companies—nephrologists, nurses, dialysis technicians, social workers, psychologists and dietitians. I interviewed patients at smaller dialysis firms and university medical centers, some of whom dialyzed at home. I consulted attorneys, economists, union leaders, experts in healthcare policy, as well as nephrologists and nurses in several countries outside the US. Gradually a disturbing picture of American dialysis came into focus.

Before publication, I shared passages from my book with a number of organizations, private and public, whose activities I had described. These included the dialysis companies DaVita, Fresenius and Satellite, as well as the Mid-Atlantic Nephrology Associates, a group of dialysis providers in the Baltimore area. I also sent excerpts to the federal healthcare agency known as Centers for Medicare & Medicaid Services (CMS), the dialysis oversight body called the ESRD Networks, the Washington University School of Medicine, and Tenet Healthcare. Most of these organizations either did not respond, or chose not to comment. A few organizations did answer, however; and one, DaVita, replied at great length.

I have referenced some of DaVita's specific responses in the text of my book. However, it seems useful to summarize here the business principles according to which, DaVita spokespeople told me, their company operates—principles which, they said, rendered many of my assertions incorrect, or downright impossible.

1. DaVita states that patient welfare is paramount in its facilities: "The first consideration in every decision we make is patient safety.... We are committed to providing a comfortable, therapeutic treatment environment for all patients."

2. DaVita claims that involuntary discharges of patients from their dialysis clinics are a rare event. "In the event such a discharge becomes necessary due to patient behavior, we are committed to supporting the patient's continuity of care and operating within the guidelines that CMS tightly monitors and governs."

3. DaVita maintains that the dialysis industry is strictly regulated by CMS, the ESRD Networks, and state healthcare surveyors, whose various standards of care DaVita meets or exceeds.

4. DaVita says that all aspects of care provided at its facilities are determined not by DaVita itself, but by the independent physicians who visit patients there, write treatment orders, and decide whether to offer treatment in the first place. "As a dialysis provider, we do not make decisions about the duration or other parameters of any given patient's dialysis treatments."

5. DaVita claims that it treats all patients equally, whether their care is funded by private insurance or by a government program like Medicare. "The services we provide, how we bill for them, and the reimbursement rate are specified either by the government or in our contracts with our health insurance partners."

6. DaVita stresses its leadership in the industry: "We remain a clinical leader in the government's two key performance programs,

the Centers for Medicare & Medicaid Services' (CMS) Five-Star Quality Rating System and the Quality Incentive Program (QIP)."

7. DaVita does not comment on the circumstances of individual patients, "due to patient privacy concerns."

This, in brief, is how the company characterized its operations and values. My book draws a picture of dialysis in America that is often very different, and casts the rise of corporate dialysis as a cautionary tale about for-profit medicine as a whole.

· 2 ·

The Inner Sea

WHEN A LOBE-FINNED FISH, the gilled and scaly ancestor of all terrestrial vertebrates, first hauled itself up onto the muddy bank of a Devonian stream some 375 million years ago, it carried within itself a pool of primordial sea. The creature's cells, blood and tissues contained a precise chemical solution that had been fine-tuned over previous eons, as its forebears swam the oceans. This concentration of salt water, electrolytes and assorted nutrients had been relatively easy to maintain in a marine environment, but as our new landlubber stumped on finny feet from waterhole to waterhole across dry land, preserving it became an enormous challenge. And failure to do so meant the creature's rapid demise: if the pH or water-salt balance or any of a dozen other equilibria shifted fractionally; if its metabolic wastes were not promptly cleansed away; then cell membranes degraded, nerve and muscle fibers stopped firing, organs failed.

Over subsequent hundreds of millions of years, these pioneers and their descendants ventured into every corner of a planet in constant flux. The Earth's rotation slowed and days grew longer, mountain chains rose and wore away, ice ages alternated with torrid interglacial periods, and the environment's basic chemistry changed. The bodies of the early wayfarers evolved endlessly into amphibians, reptiles, birds and mammals, as they colonized new niches, consumed new foods. Yet amid this outward variation, within themselves, the ancestral ocean remained. As it does to this day, in geckos, platypuses, peregrine falcons, hippos, and in humans.

Which is why we all need kidneys. Starting in early sea creatures as a tube to excrete metabolic wastes and excess salt, kidneys took on complex new biochemical tasks as creatures moved into freshwater and then onto land, where water, salt and other active ingredients of life, which had been plentiful at sea, now had to be jealously conserved. In the womb, all vertebrates pay homage to the basal importance of kidneys: in the early weeks of development, amphibian, reptile, bird and mammalian embryos all grow a pronephros and then a mesonephros, two throwback kidneys that first appeared in our marine ancestors, the jawless and the bony fishes. Only after the embryo reabsorbs these two proto-kidneys does a third, definitive kidney structure, the metanephros, become functional. These relics of our inner fish not only signpost major phases of our evolutionary journey, but also reveal just how strongly the biochemical requirements of humans still resemble those of our distant forebears.

The great French physiologist Claude Bernard developed the concept of the *milieu intérieur*: the delicately regulated fluid environment that surrounds our cells, courses through our arteries and veins, bathes every muscle and nerve, organ and bone in our bodies. Kidneys do many things to maintain the equilibrium, or "homeostasis," of this fluid environment. They remove substances of varying molecular sizes from our blood, which our body produces as it makes and burns energy—by-products that become toxic if they accumulate. (The liver removes other chemicals directly after digestion, including alcohol and drugs, while the bowels, lungs and skin perform additional excretory functions.) While sieving these toxins from our bloodstream and voiding them as urine, the kidneys also conserve scores of essential blood components, preventing their loss during urination. And kidneys manufacture a number of hormones and vitamins that control bodily processes like red blood cell production, blood pressure regulation and bone building.

Kidneys even have a sense of smell. To sift hundreds of blood and urine chemicals on the fly, expelling some and husbanding others in precise quantities, kidneys employ odor receptors similar to those found in the nose. "The kidney is sniffing the urine and the blood plasma as they go by," says Jennifer Pluznick, associate professor of physiology at the Johns Hopkins School of Medicine, who discovered the organ's olfactory gifts. "The kidney's attention to detail is astounding. I'm convinced it has many other long-held secrets which are waiting to be discovered."

Even for people who spend their whole lives studying them, kidneys are mysterious.

❑

THE HEART tells with every beat how vital the kidneys are. Twenty percent of the blood of every pulsation goes straight to the kidneys, which receive four times more blood by weight than the liver, seven times more than the brain, and fourteen times more than the lungs. A healthy pair of kidneys cleans one liter of blood per minute, which means that every five minutes they purify the entire blood volume of a 150-pound adult. As blood traverses the kidneys, the components it holds in solution dance back and forth across various membranes and gradients, in an intricate quadrille of filtration and reabsorption that ultimately produces two separate streams: hyperclean blood and fragrant urine. The blood resumes its restless rounds throughout the body, while the urine travels down the ureter into the bladder, and out through the urethra into the open air.

Blood pumps from the heart to the kidneys down the renal arteries, and diffuses throughout a series of microscopic tubular structures called nephrons, the kidney's functional unit; a healthy young kidney contains about a million nephrons. Each nephron is a filtration system consisting of a tuft of capillaries called the glomerulus, which drains into a long, convoluted tubule. The glomerulus performs "ultrafiltration": high-pressure arterial blood straight from the heart hits the cell walls of the glomerulus, a multilayered membrane with pores about four nanometers across. Larger blood components like red and white cells and the bigger plasma proteins are held back by the glomerular wall, while smaller molecules of waste, and much of the water they're dissolved in, press through the pores into the nephron tubule beyond.

The liquid that collects on the far side of the glomerular wall, the "ultrafiltrate," is the first phase of urine production, and henceforth travels through the kidneys independently from the blood. But this liquid, which resembles blood plasma without its proteins, still contains many substances that our organism has always craved—salt, glucose, amino acids, electrolytes and water, always and forever water. The glomeruli produce about 180 liters of ultrafiltrate a day; if we simply pissed this liquid away, we would dehydrate and die in minutes. To avoid this, the tubule into which each glomerulus drains, with its hairpin curves, ascending loops and other convolutions, recaptures these life ingredients and returns them to the blood. Of the original 180 liters of ultrafiltrate that our kidneys produce daily, we actually void only 1.5 to 2 liters of carefully concentrated, miraculously sterile urine, redolent of phosphates, urea and other wastes. And occasionally, of asparagus.

Kidneys fail for many reasons. Time itself wears them out: between our twenties and our seventies, most of us lose half of our renal function, through a gradual atrophy of the nephrons. Some people are born with hereditary conditions and developmental malformations that accelerate the natural renal decline. Inflammatory and autoimmune diseases can also damage our nephrons, as can a sudden injury, a heart attack, or any other mishap that cuts blood flow to the kidneys. Signs of these ailments have been found in the kidneys of Egyptian mummies, and among notables of later times. Mozart seems to have died of kidney failure after a severe strep infection, Buffalo Bill Cody lost his kidneys after prolonged use of headache powders (a similar analgesic, Bex Powders, caused a rash of kidney disease in post–World War II Australia), and George Bernard Shaw expired from acute kidney injury after falling from a fruit tree he was pruning. More recently, Veronica Lake's kidneys packed up after an extended bout of cirrhosis, Dexter Gordon lost his kidneys to cancer, and chess prodigy Bobby Fischer died when a urinary tract blockage, for which he refused medicine or surgery, led to kidney failure.

In the past few decades, diabetes, obesity and hypertension have become health epidemics in the West, and are now the three main causes and accelerators of renal failure, because each condition damages or increases strain on the kidneys (in the United States, more than 60 percent of all patients newly diagnosed with renal failure also have diabetes). Certain medications also harm our nephrons, the worst offenders being nonsteroidal anti-inflammatory drugs like ibuprofen—the modern-day successor to Bex Powders—as well as some antibiotics, blood pressure medicines and chemotherapy drugs. Today, about 37 million adults in the United States are estimated to have some degree of renal disease, and nearly 800,000 have kidney failure. These numbers were still on the rise in 2020, when COVID-19 decimated the dialysis population. In 2020, for the first time since the US government began recording statistics on renal failure in 1973, the number of patients on dialysis dropped.

To confront the ancient curse of kidney failure, medical science devised dialysis. From the end of World War II through the 1960s, doctors in Europe and North America built a variety of instruments that could rid the patient's blood of some of the wastes and excess fluid that healthy kidneys naturally remove. Teams of doctors and brilliant loners, many of whom were gifted engineers and tinkerers as well as healers, cobbled together blood-purifying gadgets from sewing machine motors, ice-cream makers, aircraft parts and sausage casings, and invented novel ways to connect them to the circulatory system of their patients.

In so doing, they made medical history. For the first time, doctors had managed to substitute a machine for a vital organ, halting the progression of a hitherto fatal illness, and sometimes postponing death for decades. A new branch of medicine was born, "nephrology," from *nephrós*, Greek for "kidney." Progress in dialysis went hand in hand with the evolution of kidney transplantation, and of allied therapies to suppress the immune system so that the recipient's body would more readily accept the donor organ. In 1954, doctors at the Peter Bent Brigham Hospital in Boston, a teaching hospital for Harvard Medical School that is now part of Brigham and Women's Hospital, performed the first successful transplant of a major internal organ, removing a healthy kidney from Ronald Herrick and grafting it into his identical twin brother, Richard, a victim of incurable kidney disease. Lung, liver, pancreas and heart transplants soon followed.

This was a heroic age of medicine, which saw revolutionary surgical procedures and novel devices gain ground on a host of once fatal conditions. It was a period of intense intellectual excitement, as polymath doctors armed with new technologies joined battle with some of humankind's most intractable enemies, and seemed to be winning. It was an international age, where physicians in medical centers in Seattle and Boston, Toronto and Paris, but also in small town hospitals in Sweden and Holland, created hubs of advanced kidney expertise, to which other doctors traveled from around the world like pilgrims to a shrine, to return home after absorbing the new wisdom of nephrology, and become disciples in their own right.

In New York, Leonard Stern, who founded the dialysis program at Columbia University, remembers his medical school training and residency in the early 1970s, in a fledgling specialization that had just received a name. "I took to nephrology immediately, because it fed into my need to know how things worked. It was the only specialization at that point where you could examine the metabolic condition of the patient, identify a disorder, and intervene in the hope of correcting it. If you went into gastroenterology back then, you had no idea how anything worked in the GI tract—it just happened. Or in dermatology, you had a thousand different conditions, yet no idea of the mechanism or the cause behind any of them. Whereas in nephrology, you could actually decide, 'Well now, this is what most likely happened. So the patient feels this, and then we can dissect how they got there.' For me, nephrology became a way of thinking about the world, and about the whole patient—not just the kidney."

In the same years, on the far side of the world in Melbourne, John Agar, who was awarded the Order of Australia in 2009 for services to renal medicine, remembers how he and his peers saw nephrology as "a field of infinite promise." After completing his nephrology training in Melbourne and spending an additional year at the University of Massachusetts Medical Center, Agar founded a dialysis unit at Geelong, southwest of Melbourne, whose methods and guiding philosophy helped to shape the practice of nephrology throughout Australia and New Zealand. He also spent a pivotal period of work at the University of Toronto, where he learned the latest techniques being used in home nocturnal dialysis, a groundbreaking treatment method.

"When I began my nephrology training in 1972, it was a thrilling field in rapid growth," says Agar. "This seemed like the future of medicine. We were streets ahead of gastroenterology and cardiology. We were the only specialty that could replace a vital organ. Not only could we replace it artificially, but we could replace it with a new, transplanted organ. I was racing around Melbourne with an Esky cooler that contained donor kidneys! We were also on the cusp, or so we thought, of xenotransplantation: we were going to be able to transplant pig organs, monkey organs, even to breed special animals that would provide us with an infinite number and array of transplant kidneys, without need for a human donor at all. And dialysis was about empowering the patients: not only saving their lives, but giving them the skills to take charge of their own care. When I started nephrology, all this was happening."

Since 1972, across the world, the original promise of dialysis has faded. The new technology used to treat individuals with kidney failure, which exhilarated young doctors like Leonard Stern and John Agar in the 1970s, has not evolved significantly in half a century. "What was infinite promise, is now infinite disappointment," says John Agar today. But if dialysis is stagnating worldwide, it is in crisis in the United States, where the incidence of infection, heart problems and other dialysis disasters is high, and patients are condemned to a grim round of treatments that are not only painful and debilitating but often medically harmful. "The survival rate in the United States, where around 22 percent of patients die every year, is the lowest in the industrialized world," says Leonard Stern. "The mortality in Japan is only 5 to 6 percent per year, and in Western Europe it's in the range of 9 to 12 percent per year. So what is the difference? Well, for a start, most dialyzing in the United States is done for profit, and the for-profit survival is always less than the not-for-profit."

After watching for decades the rise of for-profit dialysis in America and the steady degradation of care, many experienced nephrologists like John Agar and Leonard Stern have seen enough. "For many years now, I've been telling my American colleagues, 'You have to stop killing your patients,'" Agar says.

· 3 ·

Dialysis in America

IN A BUSINESS PARK near the intersection of Interstate 175 and State Highway 34, tucked in among McDonald's, Whataburger, Dickey's Barbecue Pit, the Euphoria Nail Spa and the enormous stadium of the local high school football team, the Kaufman Lions, is a clinic run by Fresenius, the North American subsidiary of a Fortune Global 500 multinational that, together with another firm, DaVita, dominates dialysis in the United States. Kaufman is thirty miles east of Dallas. The town's only historic landmark is the Kaufman County Poor Farm, a sprawling ranch founded in 1883 to house and feed the area's needy, after the Texas legislature decreed that each county was responsible to care for its indigent. The Kaufman County Poor Farm closed and turned away its last residents in the 1970s. Now the homeless sleep beneath the overpasses of I-175 and Highway 34.

David Kaufman, the town's nineteenth-century eponym, made his reputation killing Native Americans, and the community seems unapologetic about its past. The towering Civil War memorial at the county courthouse, topped by a musket-toting Rebel who sports the same wide-brimmed Stetson as the Kaufman police, salutes the Confederate soldiers who "Fought for Their Constitution, Homes and Firesides," and wishes them "Honor to Their Memory, Glory to Their

13

Cause." "The racism here is unquestioning, instinctive," says Carrie Brito, a resident of nearby Eustace, Texas, who inherited the high cheekbones, almond eyes and golden-brown skin of her Latino father. "A lot of people seem to think hating people for their race is very American, the most natural thing in the world."

Walking south from the courthouse toward the clinic, turreted Victorian mansions with ample porches and hybrids parked in circular driveways dwindle to wood-frame dwellings dwarfed by the long-bed pickups standing out front. As you approach I-175, the shade trees disappear; above the concrete arc of the interstate, a big Texas sky unfurls, an ever-evolving play of clouds and fierce sunlight over flat, dead modernity. Beyond the highway, the last traces of community melt away into strip malls and office parks and raw lots overgrown with dallis grass and bittercress. In this place, in a Fresenius unit, Carrie Brito dialyzes. "I have to psych myself up before every treatment, just to be able to walk through that door," she says.

Brito is reclining on a pale-gray chaise longue in the clinic, beside a tall medical device with a touch screen and multiple buttons and dials. Two tubes run from the machine to a port, or "fistula," in her left arm, a balloon-like bulge beneath the skin near her inner elbow, which was created when a vascular surgeon joined her cephalic vein and her radial artery. The fistula is the spot where two 15-gauge needles go in. Brito's blood leaves her body through one needle, passes through the machine, which filters out contaminants and excess fluids, and returns to her, cleansed, via the other needle. In the space of about three hours, her entire blood volume will exit and reenter her body twenty times. Her kidneys once performed this purification and fluid removal continuously and effortlessly. But they began to fail eighteen months earlier, in June 2015, due to glomerulonephritis, an inflammatory condition that impairs the kidneys' tiny filters, the glomeruli. Without regular dialysis treatments, a nephrologist told Brito, she would die within days.

But dialysis itself, at least as administered to Carrie Brito in this Fresenius clinic in Kaufman, Texas, may be threatening her life. The treatments are likely too short and fast—too brief in duration, at too high an ultrafiltration rate (UFR)—to be healthy, particularly for people of small stature like Brito, who weighs 120 pounds. Decades of medical research has demonstrated that, when administered this way, dialysis may shorten patients' lives by stripping off bodily fluids too fast, triggering sudden drops in blood pressure that can damage the heart, brain, gut, and lungs; and lead to stroke, congestive heart failure and cardiac arrest. "The first ten minutes, when the machine's pulling your blood out of your body, you feel like you're fading," says Brito with her north Texas twang. "Like part of you is gone."

High-speed dialysis can also exacerbate the side effects of the treatment itself—vomiting, fainting, leg cramps, headaches and a state of fatigue and disorientation often called "dialysis fog." All of which makes each session a physical and psychological ordeal for Carrie Brito, and taints her entire existence. "When I come off dialysis, I sometimes have to sit in the clinic for an hour or so to recover. I go home, and usually go straight to bed. By the middle of the next day I begin to feel better. But that evening I have to start getting ready for the next dialysis session the following morning."

In clinics where dialysis is slower and gentler—in high-quality, nonprofit centers in the United States, for example, and in many parts of Europe—patients live better and survive longer. The symptoms of the treatment are less burdensome, so their frequent trips to the dialysis clinic are less exhausting and frightening. For good medical reasons, in fact, nephrologists in other developed countries typically avoid the kind of treatment that Carrie Brito receives, and that her peers endure in clinics throughout America. Many condemn it as dangerous. Fresenius knows this. In a 2011 memo to clinicians, the company recommended "a minimum dialysis treatment time of 4 hours, while aiming for UFR at ≤ 10 ml/kg/hr." Nevertheless, both Fresenius and DaVita routinely provide shorter and higher-speed dialysis, which enables them to process more patients per day.

But Brito faces more immediate concerns. Shortly after her latest dialysis session begins, her blood pressure spikes to dangerous levels. Terrified that she's about to stroke out, she has a violent panic attack. Sobbing and stammering, she begs the clinic staff for help. Despite the acute medical danger she feels she is in, however, they don't take her off the machine. Nor do they call 9-1-1, or alert Brito's husband and care partner, William Sarsfield, to her condition.

Instead, she says a nurse hovering nearby tries to quiet her. Brito's weeping, the nurse says, is disturbing the other patients in the unit.

"These assholes are trying to kill me," Brito thinks to herself.

Brito is a forensic accountant and corporate controller. She has examined documents in bank fraud investigations, while working as a contractor for federal banking authorities. Despite the double debilitation of her kidney failure and the dialysis she is undergoing, for weeks now she has made secret recordings and videos with her cell phone, documenting what she and other patients consider malpractice and poor care. She has examined her medical charts and other records prepared by the clinic staff, and seen what looks to her experienced eye like forgery. Even now, as her blood pressure grows critical, she's filming her facility—filming what may be the last moments of her life.

Carrie Brito believes her ordeal started months earlier, when she noticed sanitation hazards in her unit: open vials of medicine abandoned on a counter, a crust of blood on her dialysis chair. In a workplace where long needles are threaded into large blood vessels, infections can kill. Then, Brito says, she saw a document with false statements concerning one of her prescription drugs, apparently made in order to turn a higher profit from her care; though she'd never seen the document before, it bore her signature in two places. In her opinion, it had been "robosigned."

When she asked the staff and managers of her clinic about these problems, she says they turned on her, and began to punish her for speaking out. She claims that dialysis technicians began jamming the dialysis needles roughly into her fistula, and shouting at her to be silent when she cried out in pain. A tech cannulated her improperly and then turned on the machine at high blood-pump speed, causing internal bleeding that swelled her arm to twice its normal size and damaged her fistula—her lifeline. After one treatment, she says, the staff removed the needles and left her to bleed for a quarter hour, in full view of the other patients. They also barred her husband, William, who provided essential physical and psychological support, from entering the facility, claiming he'd made racial slurs and threatened to go out to his pickup and fetch a gun. Brito says an armed security guard began to shadow her movements in the clinic, as if to signal to everyone present that she was dangerous. Clinic staff told her friends, both patients and workers, to avoid her.

Brito claims that soon after, a team of managers demanded that she sign a behavioral contract, a formal pledge to avoid disruptive or threatening behavior and to comply with staff instructions . . . all of which she felt she was already doing. Brito sensed by now that something had gone terribly wrong with her care, and that worse was to come. "I am signing under duress," she wrote in emphatic capitals across the bottom of the document. "I, Carrie Lynn Brito, request a forensic autopsy in the event of my death."

Not long after, in a letter signed by the clinic's manager, its medical director and the firm's regional vice president, Fresenius informed Brito that her care was being terminated, because of her "continued disruptive behavior of the clinic [sic] & verbal aggression towards multiple staff." Though Brito, like other renal failure patients, required about three dialysis sessions every week to live, the letter stated that, within thirty days, she would be denied treatment at her facility. "You may want to contact your nephrologist to discuss options for continued dialysis," the letter concluded. Trouble was, her nephrologist did not push back against her termination.

As she read the letter, Brito remembers, "I felt like I was on death row, and was reading the date of my execution. Which is probably why I had a panic attack during my next dialysis session."

Fortunately, in a situation where many distraught, exhausted patients merely succumb, Brito's forensic skills remained keen. She wrote memoranda to document the abuse she felt she was suffering and, after examining her medical records, identified instances where she believed false statements had been inserted by staff after the fact, to incriminate her as disruptive and threatening. Also, Brito had allies. Her husband, William Sarsfield, was well aware of the problems at the clinic, and the campaign of retaliation against her. When her blood pressure started to rise during her next dialysis treatment, Brito surreptitiously texted Sarsfield, who was sitting in his pickup outside the clinic. Sarsfield dialed the telephone number of an organization that he and Brito had discovered on the web, a small group of former dialysis workers, lawyers, and other professionals who volunteer their time to help dialysis patients in harm's way.

A woman answered, a small dog yapping in the background. Her melodious contralto filled the cab of Sarsfield's truck. "Dialysis Advocates," she said, "this is Arlene."

❑

SARSFIELD HAD reached Arlene Mullin in her trailer park home in Albany, Georgia, where she lives with a three-legged rescue Jack Russell terrier, Jumper, for company, and a cell phone pressed perpetually to one ear. When she turns on the phone in the morning the calls start rolling in, from patients in danger and from their anguished kin, and from dialysis workers who are outraged by the practices they see on the job but feel powerless to halt. Calls arrive in waves throughout the day, and are still coming in after dinner when she finally clicks off to get some sleep.

Mullin instructed Sarsfield to alert paramedics and the police, in order to extract Carrie Brito from the clinic before her surging blood pressure could cause long-term harm. Mullin then called the clinic's managers, and demanded that they safeguard Brito's health. Next, she contacted a healthcare attorney in New York who occasionally helps her pro bono. The lawyer spoke with clinic managers and state healthcare officials, as well as with Brito herself.

This routine repeats itself hundreds of times every year. Mullin receives an urgent call, speaks long enough to grasp the situation and attempt to stabilize the patient, then fires a volley of calls to clinics, nephrologists, attorneys and would-be regulators, while the patient's life clock ticks down, the need for dialysis intensifying by the hour. Mullin is, to my knowledge, the only full-time private dialysis advocate in America. She is doing the job that many government officials and contractors responsible for the safety of dialysis patients appear unable, or unwilling, to perform. She takes no money from patients, and lives on her meager Social Security checks. "Just look at this circus!" she says, waving at the file folders stacked throughout her office in the trailer home, each file a patient in apparent danger, an ongoing and potentially preventable tragedy. "Luckily Jumper, my little three-legged wonder child, is an ace at clerical work."

Mullin's emergency measures may have saved Carrie Brito's life. Paramedics entered Brito's clinic, detached her from the dialyzer, and rushed her to the local hospital, where her blood pressure was brought under control. She still had to dialyze, however, and the clinic terminated her care a short time later. The only other dialysis facility in town, run by DaVita, declined to treat her—not for medical reasons, the facility's staff explained, but on advice of their legal counsel. Evidently her recent involuntary discharge, together with accusations of disruptiveness and aggression contained in her medical records, raised red flags when other dialysis units considered admitting her. This created a serious problem for Brito, because like other dialysis patients, she required several treatments each week, and needed a clinic near her home. The two Kaufman units were the only facilities within reasonable driving distance from where she lived in Eustace.

From then on, Brito was forced to dialyze in the emergency room of a local hospital. Here the staff, per ER protocols, only put her on dialysis when her condition became an emergency—in other words, when her blood became so toxic and fluid-filled that her life was in danger. Sporadic dialysis of this sort is dangerous, even deadly. According to Robert Bear, a veteran Canadian nephrologist and former board member of Mullin's organization, Dialysis Advocates, who has reviewed numerous records of involuntary discharges, "For many patients, dialysis in an emergency room is a death sentence of six to twelve months."

Carrie Brito was stranded in a medical limbo. But then a surprising thing happened. She waited for the familiar symptoms: the shortness of breath, chest pains and swelling of her ankles that warned her she needed to dialyze. Days passed, and the symptoms didn't come. She was still making urine, because she'd maintained some residual kidney function throughout her dialysis. After a couple weeks, she saw a specialist at Baylor Medical School in Dallas, who informed her that, while her kidneys were far from perfect, for the moment at least they were working well enough that she didn't need dialysis at all.

At first this seemed a miracle. But the longer Brito thought about it, the more she wondered: *Did I actually need to dialyze in the first place?*

Arlene Mullin is a slender, striking woman of seventy-three, whose calm gray-green eyes and aura of knowing serenity contrast strangely with her rapid-fire rush of words, and the deep, fruity chuckle she can summon even while describing the worst abuses. She writes long, stinging emails and faxes at high speed with spell-check off, spewing typos and malapropisms that hoodwink her adversaries, the dialysis executives and regulators she deals with daily, as she tries to place involuntarily discharged patients in a new clinic. "A lot of them must think I have a fourth-grade education," she says with a low hoot. "One guy called me 'an orangutan in a bamboo forest.' When they underestimate my intellect, they let down their guard. That's when the fun begins! I start learning their secrets."

Mullin's office is one of the four rooms in her trailer home, which belongs to a friend. Out the window, an abandoned car rusts into the crabgrass beside the neighboring trailer home. Over the years, Mullin has met a handful of professionals who have become aware of the darkness in the dialysis industry, and now help her to dispel it. The spouses of several patients rescued by Mullin have driven to southern Georgia and bunked in her trailer for weeks at a time to assist with paperwork. By phone, dialysis technicians, nurses, and nephrologists whom she has never met, most of whom work at large dialysis firms and prefer to remain anonymous, alert her from behind the scenes about abuses, and advise her on how to combat them. Pat Reilly, a private detective in Nashville, Tennessee, has gone undercover in several dialysis clinics to chronicle the questionable treatment of Mullin's clients. Social activists have answered Mullin's call to action against endemic patient harm in dialysis: Chili Most, a recording artist, music producer, radio personality and civil rights leader in Los Angeles; Reverend Ronald Wright, the minister of a nondenominational, largely African American church in Dallas, Texas; former NBA center Clem Johnson, whose daughter was on dialysis before receiving a transplant; and dialysis whistleblowers and whistleblower advocates David Barbetta and Marcel Reid.

Mullin's patient files fill her desk and filing cabinets, and lie in tidy rows across the floor. We sit down among them, and Mullin passes me file after file, each detailing claims of abuse, endangerment or termination of a patient. Some of the accusations used to eject people from their facilities would be amusing if the outcomes weren't so lethal. James Kasiewicz was involuntarily discharged by his Fresenius clinic in Willowbrook, Illinois. The discharge letter claimed that Kasiewicz had threatened to bring a rifle to the facility, to harm staff members, and to run down the clinic manager with a car. In written statements and in communications with Arlene Mullin, Kasiewicz denied these accusations, and said he believed they had been made in response to complaints he had lodged with the Illinois Department of Public Health and with the ESRD Network, a dialysis industry regulator, in which Kasiewicz challenged the air quality in another Fresenius facility, where he previously dialyzed. In an anguished written statement, Kasiewicz denied menacing clinic employees, much less threatening to run them over: he hadn't driven in over a decade, he explained, since losing both legs below the knee to diabetes. Mullin remembered how nearby Fresenius clinics, and one DaVita unit, declined to treat Kasiewicz; one facility justified its refusal by citing reports in Kasiewicz's medical file that he had "behavioral problems" and was "disruptive and uncooperative." Kasiewicz died nine months after his termination.

Justin Charles Evans, a patient in Atlanta, was repeatedly informed by the staff of his clinic, often at the last minute, that the clinic was unable to treat him (the staff referred him instead to a local emergency room for dialysis). Evans and eleven other patients wrote a letter to Johnny Isakson, then US senator from Georgia, reporting this dangerous interruption in their care and asking Isakson to intervene. When clinic employees learned of this letter, Evans says they discharged him and harassed several of his co-signatories in reprisal. Evans also claims he was accused of carrying a gun in the duffel bag he brought when he dialyzed; whereupon the clinic manager called the local police, who escorted him off the premises. (A registered nurse at the facility later told me that she'd been ordered by the clinic manager to add the gun accusation to his medical file.)

Many such complaints reach Mullin from dialysis workers, who feel complicit in the harm done to their own patients. Mullin hands me a letter to Esperanza, a patient in a dialysis facility in Queens, New York, who was terminated after being accused of striking other patients and jerking the dialysis needles out of her arm, while her husband, Juan, was said to have threatened staff members with a knife and a gun. (I use assumed names for everyone involved in this incident, to shield Esperanza and Juan, as well as the clinic employee, whom I'll call Alice, from retaliation.) The letter, written by Alice, admits that the charges made against her patient Esperanza were false, and that she included them in Esperanza's medical records at the direction of a "Dr. O," a clinic nephrologist, who turned against Esperanza after she reported staff misconduct to New York State health officials. (I reproduce the note as Alice wrote it, with errors of spelling and grammar.)

> I am writing you this letter to let you know about the truth what exactly Doctor O tell me what to do with you. He tell me to put in the false report on the wrap [i.e. "rap"] sheet.... He said to me that I have to stick up for the staff other wise that will cause me my job.... Please don't be mad at me. I have to do that just to cover myself up because I have a family to feed. I hope that you cold forgive me for what I did to you. I bring you some Christmas gift plus this letter and please don't tell nobody that I am at your door.

Some nephrologists recognize this pattern, though few are willing to speak openly about it. Joanne Bargman, a research nephrologist at the University of Toronto, Canada, describes her conversation with a "very highly respected nephrologist" in the United States, whom she prefers not to name, who explained to her matter-of-factly his techniques for goading undesirable patients into acting out, in order to eject them from his facility. Another veteran nephrologist at a university medical center in the northeastern United States, Dr. Jesse Goldman, reports witnessing the termination of multiple patients at his facility, run by Fresenius, after they had argued with staff. "Once they want to terminate a patient they are skilled at having multiple employees document a one-sided story," Goldman wrote in an email. "The story is always exaggerated. Not only is the documentation used as 'evidence' for the ejection but it also makes more difficult to place patients in the future since the extreme narrative scares away future units from taking a chance."

In most cases I have examined, patients who were involuntarily discharged were on Medicare or Medicaid. Because private insurance companies pay higher reimbursements than does government insurance—sometimes ten times higher or more—privately insured patients are far more lucrative for dialysis providers than are patients with government insurance. Dialysis firms make no secret about the importance of private payors to their business model, and clinic staff members are routinely instructed to treat them as VIPs. Publicly insured patients, because they are lower-margin, are by contrast often considered second-class citizens. Those who question the quality of their care, require more time because of handicaps or additional illnesses, or otherwise slow the routine of the clinic, may become expendable. (DaVita disagrees: "We welcome feedback to continually deliver the best care experience possible and strive to be a place of belonging for everyone in our center.")

Involuntary discharge is not driven exclusively by financial considerations, however. Though a rarity, privately insured patients who challenge the expertise or integrity of their clinic managers may also be terminated. "The biggest mistake we ever made was asking questions," says Sherry Thompson, a 9-1-1 dispatcher and Air Force veteran in Memphis, Tennessee, whose husband, Gerald, began dialyzing in 2017. "My husband had been a utility worker for twenty-six years, and had great insurance. Cigna was paying $20,000 to $30,000 a month for his dialysis. But when I started questioning their billing practices, the care started to decline. I couldn't even get people on the phone." Soon, during his regular visits to the dialysis unit, Gerald Thompson was shadowed by a security guard. Clinic officials referred him for a psychiatric evaluation, and sent a medical assistant to his home on a surprise visit, during which, the assistant claimed, Thompson brandished a handgun. (Gerald Thompson confirms that he owns a handgun, but denies brandishing it. "Why would I do that? I needed their help!")

"All of this was part of building a case against us," Sherry Thompson says. The unit discharged Gerald shortly after.

"According to a culture that exists too commonly in the dialysis industry in America, patients are supposed to be dependent souls, passive recipients of treatment," says Robert Bear, the Canadian nephrologist, who obtained medical training in the United States and has done nephrology consulting there. "In some instances, when patients question the quality of their care, they are 'involuntarily discharged' from their dialysis unit, often without alternative dialysis arrangements being made." Leonard Stern, the New York nephrologist, formerly worked at a DaVita-run facility, where, he notes, certain managers "were exceptionally rigid and authoritarian—like prison camp guards. If a patient broke any even minor rules of behavior, they were demeaned, ostracized, and potentially thrown out."

Even patients who aren't discharged suffer from the business model of Big Dialysis, where the relentless pursuit of profits often compromises care. To increase earnings, some clinic managers feel pressure to cut corners on supplies, hygiene and water purification, which potentially leads to a higher incidence of infections and accidents. They may reduce payroll expenses, too, by replacing skilled staff with inexperienced dialysis technicians, an occupation that doesn't exist per se in most other countries, where highly trained dialysis nurses treat patients and perform the all-important "stick." Patients are often organized into strict shifts with minimal transition time between, and little scope for tailoring treatments to suit individual patient requirements.

This approach to dialysis contradicts decades of settled medical science. Most leading nephrologists worldwide agree that dialysis should ideally be delivered in long, frequent sessions at low ultrafiltration rates, and be carefully tailored to each patient's physiology. Large dialysis companies, by contrast, frequently employ what John Agar, the Australian nephrologist, calls "bazooka dialysis": treatment in brief, high-speed bursts following a one-size-fits-all protocol. Nephrologists who order longer treatments or make other customizations of their patients' dialysis prescriptions may encounter obstruction by clinic management.

Many dialysis workers are themselves victims of this regimented approach to medicine. Nurses, dialysis technicians and other staff are required to care for numerous patients simultaneously, and are pressured by managers to get shifts of patients on and off the machines as quickly as possible. "If you're working for patients, you have to protect them," says Megallan Handford, a former Los Angeles policeman who retrained as a dialysis nurse, and has worked for both Fresenius and DaVita. "Like we used to say in the police, I feel I'm here 'To protect and serve.' But right now, given how the industry operates, I'm not able to do either." Handford, who has since moved to Texas, says that his life on the "blood floor" in Los Angeles clinics was psychologically more draining than when he was a police officer, facing down drug gangs in the worst Los Angeles housing projects. "After I'd been involved in a shooting, I'd at least get the rest of the day off to recover, and maybe receive some counseling. In dialysis, even if two of your patients drop dead on the floor, you're supposed to keep grinding, keep working, keep putting them on and taking them off those machines. All the companies are concerned to do is dialyze."

The term "moral injury" was coined to describe the enduring psychological wounds of combat soldiers who, following the orders of their superiors, had taken part in extreme acts (such as the killing of civilians) that violated their basic moral principles. It has more recently been applied to doctors, nurses and other healthcare workers, who sense that their daily responsibilities on the job violate their commitment to healing. Many dialysis workers I've spoken with seem to suffer from this condition at some level.

Megallan Handford, who in California units says he was assigned as many as seventeen patients to watch over simultaneously while they dialyzed, describes the regular crises he faced—patients cramping, fainting, coding and bleeding out—which make his workplace sound more like a wartime field hospital than a chronic-care facility.

Handford evokes the atmosphere in such clinics: "I have to move fast from one patient to another. No time to ask them how they feel, how their family is, just 'Okay, you're still breathing,' and move on. My job is nursing people, but I can't do my job on this assembly line." More than once, he says, he and his coworkers had to leave the lifeless body of a patient in the dialysis chair, concealed behind a screen, while continuing to treat other patients.

Grim, exhausting work conditions and low pay lead to poor morale, shortened tempers and case-hardening among workers, which increases the likelihood of conflict with patients. "Dialysis workers are stretched so thin, they have to deal with so much pressure and suffering, with the death of patients with whom they often become very close," says Cass Gualvez, organizing director at SEIU-UHW, the largest healthcare workers' union in California. "Some people just have to go into survival mode." Others call the SEIU-UHW or Arlene Mullin, and reveal what they've seen.

Mullin says that trumped up accusations frequently precede involuntary discharges, providing the requisite paper trail to justify terminating patients, who are then routinely blackballed by other facilities. She hands me file after file documenting cases of patient denigration, mistreatment, involuntary discharge and blackballing, each following a similar script: Carrie Brito, Justin Charles Evans, Vanessa Winters, Gerald Thompson, Cornelius Robbins, Gregg Hansen, Pacita Coats-Simpson, Antonia Watson, James Stravino, Abelinda Ruiz, William Brown, Eric Pickens, Terry Thermutis Lee, Trina O'Cain, Tirsit Gidey, Louis Thomas, Kenneth Harris, Jose Carlos and many others. Nearly all of whom are Black and brown. Some are still struggling to secure good dialysis care, often in a hospital ER. A few have received transplants. The rest are dead.

❑

"FOR ME it's not about the patients, it's about the teammates [i.e., employees]," says Kent Thiry, the charismatic longtime leader of DaVita, one of the two firms that dominate the US dialysis market, during a speech at the UCLA Anderson School of Management titled "Energizing a Firm with Mission & Values." "And there are some doctors that hate it when I say that.... But to me that's just not it. If I had 1,400 Taco Bells and 32,000 people who worked in them, I would be doing all the same stuff." (Thiry resigned from the firm in 2020, after a twenty-year tenure as CEO and a brief stint as executive chair of the board of directors.)

How can the head of a healthcare multinational compare his patients to fast food, or suggest that his philosophy may be at odds with medical ethics? And what is this "stuff" Thiry says he'd be doing, whether treating kidney failure patients or churning out burritos and quesadillas?

Actually, Thiry's fast food analogy, though eye-catching in a medical pursuit like dialysis that provides life-or-death care, reflects a widely accepted approach in America to the business of medicine. In the 1960s, early for-profit hospital chains like Humana, Hospital Corporation of America (HCA), and National Medical Enterprises (NME), the parent company of the dialysis firm that would become DaVita, applied this same standardized, low-unit-cost business model to hospital care. Some entrepreneurs brought actual fast food experience to their new medical empires: before cofounding HCA, Jack Massey had built Kentucky Fried Chicken into a national franchise, and later played a leading role at Wendy's. Today, the private equity firms that are gobbling up medical operations like hot French fries apply similar management practices. Thiry was schooled in them during his years at Bain Capital, the private equity firm, where he was a vice president in the healthcare division.

Some of Thiry's "stuff," however, is more unusual. He calls his firm a "Village," of which he is the "Mayor." He refers to his employees as "Teammates" or "Citizens." Thiry builds employee devotion by borrowing practices from military units, tribes and sports teams, with generous doses of schmaltz and showbiz. He also draws on faith. "Think about religions across the world," Thiry told an audience at the University of Denver business school. "What do they do? They wear different clothing, they do 'call and response,' they do chants together, they sing together. They do it to remind themselves of the spirituality they aspire to achieving in daily life." In fact, the firm has called its guiding policies "Commandments," and featured nuns in black and white habits and angels with halos and snowy wings in its in-house communications. To shape the company culture, Thiry hired Doug Vlchek, a Catholic deacon who later studied theology at Oxford, and was known throughout the firm as "Yoda."

At "Nationwides," the annual retreats where employees celebrate their firm and its leaders in skits and synchronized dances, Thiry has made numerous grand entrances, riding onstage on a rumbling Harley, flashing in on a zipline, or circling the venue astride a longhorn bull. Nor are Thiry's theatrics limited to in-house gatherings: at business conferences and university symposia he has dressed up as a musketeer, a ninja, and Luke Skywalker, and led the audience in DaVita chants that transform these gatherings into pep rallies for his firm. Leonard Stern, the New York nephrologist, remembers attending a corporate function at which Thiry pranced around a stage waving a light saber. "And I almost vomited on the spot," Stern says. "It was the most unprofessional interaction I have ever seen as a physician. I could not imagine that this was the model of the corporation, this person dancing around discussing how, instead of partners in care, we doctors were 'teammates.' As if this were some football team we were playing on. I was beside myself."

Nevertheless, Thiry's corporate culture has helped to make DaVita a financial juggernaut. Under his guidance, the firm's share price soared; in April 2022 it was worth $11.7 billion. Warren Buffett's Berkshire Hathaway owns a third of its stock, thereby bestowing the coveted "Buffett Blessing" on DaVita. Thiry himself has grossed over half a billion dollars during his firm's storybook rise. His unusual management style has been extolled in case studies by Harvard and Stanford business schools, and he has long been the toast of Wall Street and the financial press. Writing of Thiry's leadership practices, journalist Bill Taylor calls him one of "the real heroes of business," a person who is "more concerned about unleashing freedom than amassing power." Thiry has taken an increasingly active role in politics in recent years, and has been mentioned as a possible future governor of Colorado, where he lives.

Things looked less rosy for Thiry back in 1999, when he became the CEO of Total Renal Care, the dialysis firm that he would soon rename "DaVita." Total Renal Care was on the verge of bankruptcy after an overly ambitious series of acquisitions, and a federal securities class action lawsuit, later settled without Total Renal Care admitting any wrongdoing, which alleged, among other things, that the company had manipulated its financial statements and artificially inflated its stock price. As a graduate of Harvard Business School and a former private equity executive, Thiry knew the financial basics required to turn his new company around, which included minimizing costs, increasing income, creating captive clients, leveraging economies of scale, and growing market share. The US healthcare industry was an ideal place to do all of these things, being fragmented, enormous and fast-growing. (In 2021, total healthcare expenditures topped $4.3 trillion dollars, or 18.3 percent of gross domestic product, and are still rising.) Dialysis in particular, Thiry knew, was an entrepreneurial sweet spot: kidney disease had reached epidemic proportions in America, where the rate of renal failure was among the highest in the world, driven by underlying surges in chronic conditions like diabetes and hypertension. The population of patients with kidney failure had grown twenty-eight times over the previous three decades. The industry was also highly fragmented, with many small, doctor-owned nephrology practices which Thiry knew he could buy up, to increase his firm's market share rapidly.

Better still, much of the company's cash flow was guaranteed by the US government. Back in 1972, Congress had passed a law that promised to pay for the treatment of Americans with renal failure—the nation's first, and so far its only, major experiment with "Medicare for All." But the best news of all, at least for medical entrepreneurs like Kent Thiry, was this: dialysis patients are about the most captive clients imaginable. Thiry calls them "sticky": knowing they will die without treatment, dialysis patients cling to their nephrologist and clinic staff as a sailor in stormy seas clings to a lifeline. Sign up a dialysis patient at one of your clinics, and she's normally yours for the rest of her life.

All the same, Kent Thiry knew from hard personal experience that business fundamentals alone were not enough to fulfill his outsized ambitions for Total Renal Care. He had already worked for seven years as the CEO of a dialysis company named Vivra, which, despite a high-quality management team, fast growth and high profit margins, had undergone a grand jury investigation for billing fraud, and flirted with bankruptcy before being bought out by a competitor in 1997. Success in the dialysis business, Thiry had learned, also required managers to take bold financial risks, and to fend off challenges by competitors, Department of Justice investigators, healthcare regulators, insurance executives, and all others who threatened the firm's profits. It demanded close attention to patient referrals, by employing the twin incentives of generous payments and noncompetition agreements to encourage nephrologists to funnel their patients into your facilities. It rewarded tight, top-down controls on key treatment decisions, which were to be made, whenever possible, not by doctors and nurses at individual facilities, but by your financial managers at headquarters. (Though of course, at least on paper, your chief medical officer and other staff MDs, together with prescribing nephrologists, would dictate patient care.)

But for Thiry, the real secret sauce for building a billion-dollar dialysis firm was the corporate culture. Dialysis is a grueling experience not only for patients but also for the doctors, nurses and other healthcare professionals who treat them. Thiry somehow had to make this job . . . well . . . *fun*. Actually, *more* than fun. Joining DaVita had to feel, for the right kind of employee, like being born again.

As Thiry has told the story, his inspiration for creating DaVita's new business culture came from *The Man in the Iron Mask*, a film drawn from *The Three Musketeers* saga, in which Leonardo DiCaprio plays both the wicked, profligate monarch Louis XIV and his good-hearted twin brother Philippe, whom Louis is holding captive because he is Louis's rival to the throne. As Thiry watched the musketeers gallop, swagger and swordfight their way to the rescue of king and country, tears filled his eyes. "The three musketeers were famous for their dedication to their mission and to each other," he observed later. "They were the Marines of their time." Here was the model of absolute loyalty and commitment to the firm, plus plenty of swashbuckling fun and flamboyance, that could help Thiry make a killing in dialysis.

Thiry says he phoned several of his former executives of the defunct Vivra and explained his idea for transforming Total Renal Care, by infusing it with the spirit of Athos, Porthos and Aramis. "Will you ride again?" he asked them. All agreed to saddle up. Together, they created a flashy new dialysis company, whose stated mission was to be "The greatest healthcare company the world has ever seen." Their firm would integrate vertically, profiting not just from dialysis but also from lab testing, vascular surgery and other services to patients, and above all from the liberal use of dialysis drugs. They would instill a powerful sense of team and community at their clinics, and stress the redemptive quality of their work. Their new firm, in fact, would be named "DaVita," which in Italian means, "It gives life."

In the Casa del Mundo, the firm's world headquarters in downtown Denver, hallways and open spaces are named like the streets and squares of an imaginary American hometown. Walls are emblazoned with inspirational soundbites by the Buddha and Vince Lombardi. On the ground floor is a large wooden bridge that new employees cross when they join DaVita, a rite of passage that symbolizes their physical and spiritual commitment to the firm. "We are very explicit about this decision," Thiry has said. "Each individual chooses for himself whether or not to cross the bridge, but . . . you have to decide—there is no non-decision option."

The atmosphere at a Nationwide, the firm's signature annual conference, blends Baptist tent revival, high school pep rally and spring break on Miami Beach. Thiry has directed enthusiastic call-and-response routines, while other senior executives have impersonated Elvis, or led choruses of DaVita boosters who sing songs honoring their firm, set to the tune of pop classics like the Village People's "YMCA."

Not everyone in the audience is impressed, however. Daniel Barbir, a former dialysis nurse in the Atlanta area, attended a Nationwide in California shortly after DaVita bought out the dialysis firm he worked for. He remembers Kent Thiry, dressed as a musketeer, sliding down a rope onto a floodlit stage.

"He shouted that he'd come to save the Village," Barbir says. "He started running like a maniac up and down the stage, huffing and puffing. Then he started crying."

Barbir pulls out his cell phone, and plays a video to show me what happened next.

"Yoh Daveeeee-*taaaaaa*!" Thiry in his musketeer hat sings out, like a drill sergeant exhorting his troops.

"Yoh Daveeeee-*taaaaaa*!" the crowd echoes back.

"*What* is this company?" Thiry calls.

"New!" the crowd responds.

"*Whose* is it?"

"Ours!"

"What could it *beeeeeeee*?"

"*Specialllll!*"

"All for one . . . !" Thiry howls, reaching a fever pitch.

"*AND ONE FOR ALL!*" the crowd roars back.

"Damn straight!" Thiry concludes, with an exaggerated fist-pump.

Barbir was stunned. "Pretty soon I was scared to look at the stage."

The floor show had triggered uncomfortable memories from his childhood. Barbir was born and grew up in Communist Romania, during the dictatorship of Nicolae Ceauşescu. Like most Romanian children of his generation, he was a member of the *Organizaţia Pionierilor*, or Pioneers, a weaponized version of the Boy Scouts and Girl Scouts that helped instill Communist beliefs in young recruits. "They forced us all to clap together and do certain rhythmic chants, to break up into groups and make our own chant, to stand and sing together. Chants, rhythmic clapping, slogans, all designed to control how you think, to get uniformity of thought." Barbir and his fellow Pioneers were required to attend mass rallies, where they experienced the power hierarchies of the authoritarian regime.

In 1982, to escape totalitarianism, a seventeen-year-old Barbir had fled with his family to the United States. But here was his CEO, leading an exercise that felt to him eerily familiar. "I said to myself, 'Oh my God, I ran away from Communism, and here it is again,'" Barbir remembers thinking. "I won't sell my soul for these people. I would rather dig ditches!"

· 4 ·

Who Lives, Who Dies

DESPITE THEIR COMPLEX and pivotal roles in preserving life—or maybe because of their complexity—kidneys have long been underappreciated. Epic poems, religious scriptures and early medical tracts routinely ignore or even scorn them, and celebrate other organs instead as the seat of our most admirable qualities. Even today, we praise people for their heart or brains, for their lungs or even their guts, but spare not a word for their renal fortitude. However, while the heart is primarily just a blood pump, the lungs a pair of bellows that inhale oxygen and expel carbon dioxide, and the stomach and intestines two bags that sort nutrients and wastes, our kidneys, those fist-sized, bean-shaped organs flanking the base of our spine, are the architects of homeostasis, without whom all the other organs, even our mighty brain, would swiftly fail. "Superficially, it might be said that the function of the kidneys is to make urine," wrote Homer Smith, a groundbreaking kidney physiologist, "but in a more considered view one can say that the kidneys make the stuff of philosophy itself."

Their role in producing urine may help to explain why the kidneys have received so little respect. Or maybe it's their out-of-the-way location in the body, which suggests the marginality, or at least the obscurity, of their function. When you clean a trout, most of the innards—the

33

stomach, heart, liver, swim bladder and so forth—pull away neatly in one ropy braid, leaving glistening ribs in view. Only the kidneys remain, a reddish film clinging stubbornly to the spine, which requires a determined scrape with your thumbnail and a long rinse to remove. Similarly, when you embalm a dead pharaoh, you'll be able to extract most organs through one small incision in the abdomen, as the ancient Egyptians learned to do. But not the kidneys, tucked away behind the peritoneal cavity, which require a good deal more digging. Their retro-peritoneal location seems to suggest some distinction from the other internal organs. What are these things *for*, anyway?

The Egyptians themselves were clearly intrigued by the kidneys. The *Book of the Dead* sings their praises together with those of the heart, and embalmers sometimes left both the heart and the kidneys in place when they mummified their pharaohs, while removing the other viscera and placing them in canopic jars for separate burial. Some scholars maintain that the Egyptians did this because they believed the deceased would have particular need of the heart and kidneys in the afterlife. Or maybe the embalmers found the kidneys too troublesome to reach, and let them be.

The ancient Greeks frequently linked kidneys with sex. Certain Greek medical writers stated that kidneys produced or channeled semen—somewhat confusingly, in both men and women—to the genitals. They also prescribed the kidneys of foxes, lizards and eagles as an aphrodisiac: dissolving them in aromatic wine created a potion that stimulated erotic desire and enduring love in everyone who drank it. Kidneys were also favored as offerings to the gods, possibly because these organs were somehow linked in the Greek mind with the sacrificial victim's life energies . . . or because nobody fancied eating kidneys at the post-sacrifice barbecue. Indeed, many Greek medical writers mention the kidneys' foul odor, and their ill side effects if eaten; Galen of Pergamos calls them "bad-juiced and indigestible, like the testicles of adult animals."

Galen himself recognized that kidneys cleansed the blood and helped produce urine, but there his understanding of renal function ended. Many other learned Hellenes had no idea what kidneys did, and downplayed their importance; Aristotle himself pronounced that they were not essential to life. Most Greek authorities identified the heart, the brain or the liver as the paramount organ, seat of the human soul.

The Hebrews saw kidneys in a more exalted light. The Old Testament and later commentaries speak of them as the source of our inmost emotions, intuitions and desires, as well as a repository of divine wisdom. "For you formed my kidneys," the Psalmist tells God gratefully, "you knitted me together in my mother's womb. I praise you, for I am fearfully and wonderfully made." (Later translators, likely squeamish about the kidneys' associations with urine and excretion, substituted renal euphemisms like "inward parts" or "reins." The original Hebrew word, however, is unambiguous: *kelayot*, "kidneys," appears more than thirty times in the Old Testament.) The Hebrew God even communicates with His believers through their kidneys. "My kidneys give me counsel in the night," says the Psalmist. The Midrash commentary on Genesis claims that the illiterate Abraham learned the Hebrew law from his kidneys, whereupon an understanding of God took shape within him.

Perhaps because this anomalous pair of organs is located deep within the body, and visible only to God, He is repeatedly seen passing judgment on people's souls by examining their kidneys, searching for clues to their virtues and vices. Likewise, a kidney injury in the Old Testament is the cruelest of wounds, almost a malediction. When the long-suffering Job, spurned even by his own family, reaches the depths of despair, he expresses his condition as a punishment by God: "His archers surround me. He pierces my kidneys without mercy and spills my gall on the ground."

The Hebrews were on to something. Because when our kidneys fail, the metabolic fallout is so sweeping that we would be forgiven for feeling cursed. Without the kidneys, our inner sea, that nurturing balance of fluids and chemicals we inherited from distant, slimy ancestors, dries up. Contaminants accumulate in our blood, and many of the body's basic processes break down. Because of the kidneys' intimate relationship with the heart and with blood pressure regulation, kidney disease frequently causes heart disease, as well as a spectrum of bone, endocrine, neurological and pulmonary disorders. People with bad kidneys are prone to anemia, hypertension, gastrointestinal problems, insulin resistance, muscle wasting, metabolic acidosis, hormone imbalances . . . and on and on and on. Kidneys play an important, though poorly understood, role in the immune system, which helps to explain why COVID-19 has taken such a toll on dialysis patients, particularly those who treat in dialysis centers, where they spend many hours each week in open-plan facilities, side by side with other immunocompromised patients. During the first wave of COVID-19, in the eleventh epidemiological week of the pandemic (March 8 to 14, 2020), 65 percent of patients with chronic kidney disease who were hospitalized for coronavirus either died or were discharged to hospice. In 2020 as a whole, almost 17 percent of dialysis patients on Medicare who contracted COVID-19 died within the first thirty days, nearly twice the mortality rate of Medicare beneficiaries not on dialysis (9.8 percent). Dialysis patients were also more likely to require emergency room care and to be put on a ventilator.

Conversely, COVID-19 has caused widespread kidney injury and failure, and forced many people to dialyze for the first time. The virus apparently targets kidney cells, starves kidneys of blood oxygen, and destroys renal tissues during extreme immune responses known as "cytokine storms." Recent studies have found that more than 30 percent of patients hospitalized with COVID-19 develop kidney injury, and more than half of patients in intensive care with kidney injury may require dialysis.

In the mid-nineteenth century, during the golden age of physiology, breakthroughs in chemistry and physics provided empirical corroboration for ancient Hebrew intuitions about the kidneys' decisive role in human life and afterlife. French physiologist Claude Bernard, a devotee of Descartes's reasoned skepticism, rigorously applied the scientific method to the study of medicine, helping to liberate the field from animal spirits, the four humors, and other time-honored fantasies. In Bernard's day, many medical doctors and natural philosophers subscribed to vitalism, the theory that living beings were intrinsically different from inanimate objects because of certain mysterious vital forces within them, which operated outside the bounds of physics and chemistry. Bernard and his intellectual allies objected: animal bodies were simply magnificent machines, whose every organ, cell and molecule faithfully followed the same laws that governed their constituent chemicals.

Bernard made his point through a lifetime of imaginative and often savage experiments on rabbits, dogs, horses and occasionally on himself, which must from time to time have produced disturbing noises from his dank cellar laboratory. (His wife, Fanny, whose dowry helped to fund his experiments, returned home one day to find that Bernard had vivisected the family dog. She left him in 1869, and, together with the couple's two daughters, became a vehement early activist against cruelty to animals.) Bernard's delicate ablations and painstaking poisonings revealed to him a stunning new vision of the internal organs, the major blood vessels and the digestive tract in higher animals, and how intimately they were interrelated. In his classic *Lectures on the Phenomena Common to Animals and Plants*, published in 1878, the year of his death, Bernard explained how our body balances fluids, chemicals and temperature to create an "internal environment" (*milieu intérieur*), "a veritable greenhouse" within which our organic processes continue unimpeded, however the conditions around us may change.

> *Higher animals are enveloped in an unchanging environment that creates, as it were, its own atmosphere within the ever-changing [milieu] of the world. . . . In reality, the animal has two environments: an external environment in which the organism is located, and an internal environment in which the tissue elements live. It doesn't actually exist in the external environment (the air for the air-breathing animal, fresh or salt water for aquatic animals), but in the liquid internal environment formed by the circulating organic liquid that surrounds and bathes all the anatomical elements of the tissues. . . . All the vital mechanisms, however varied they may be, have only one object, that of holding constant the conditions of life in the internal environment.*

Bernard recognized the crucial role of the kidneys in guaranteeing the stability of the *milieu intérieur*, that internal environment which, he wrote, is "the condition for free and independent life." In essence, he had explained why our ancestral fishes had troubled to bring the sea with them when they first crawled up on dry land, and how their kidneys maintained the original composition of this pool of life, wherever on earth they traveled. Bernard's discoveries also suggested an at least symbolic truth to ancient Hebrew claims that the inner wisdom of the human organism is incarnate in its kidneys.

If Claude Bernard built the conceptual framework for dialysis, Scottish physicist Thomas Graham helped to forge the tools to perform it. In the 1850s and 1860s, Graham employed ox bladders, parchment and other semipermeable membranes, which he termed "dialyzers," in a series of experiments that revealed how certain substances, when held in suspension, would leave their liquid host and diffuse across these membranes, into fluids on the far side with certain chemical properties. In a paper he read before the Royal Society in London in 1861, Graham demonstrated that sugar, sodium, potassium and other volatile, generally small-molecule elements and compounds, which he termed "crystalloids," would diffuse through his dialyzers into a water bath beyond, becoming isolated from their solvent. (Larger-molecule "colloids" like albumin, starch and gelatin, he found, did not readily traverse such membranes.) Another small-molecule crystalloid that Graham identified was urea, which he managed to extract from urine with the use of an ox bladder dialyzer.

Graham's experiments introduced dialysis as an important technique for the isolation and microanalysis of organic compounds, and it became a popular means of purifying chemicals in industrial laboratories. Between 1912 and 1914, at Johns Hopkins, John Jacob Abel devised one of the first medical applications for dialysis. Abel fashioned an apparatus of collodion, a membrane made from gun cotton dissolved in alcohol or ether, elegantly encased in blown glass, which he attached to the bloodstream of living dogs and rabbits. With this device, Abel was able to remove harmful substances like urea from their blood. (To prevent the blood from clotting, Abel used hirudin, the natural anticoagulant produced in the salivary glands of leeches, which was laboriously extracted from huge numbers of ground-up leech heads.) He called his blown-glass creation an "artificial kidney," and speculated that it might be used to clean the blood of human patients whose kidneys had temporarily failed, thereby "providing a substitute in such emergencies, which might tide over a dangerous crisis."

❑

WORLD WAR II brought a flood of soldiers whose kidneys had shut down because of battlefield injury, infection and shock—and a new urgency to finding a cure for "uremia," a term for kidney failure coined from urea, then the best-known of bloodstream wastes. Civilian casualties, too, underscored the urgency of improving the treatment of renal failure. During the Blitz in London, for example, scores of people survived serious injuries they'd sustained during the collapse of their homes, only to die weeks later from sudden, systemic kidney failure, a medical mystery that came to be called "crush syndrome." Doctors were desperate for some means of blood cleansing that, as John Jacob Abel had mused thirty years before, might tide over such dangerous crises, and keep crush syndrome victims alive until their kidneys resumed function.

In Nazi-occupied Holland, Willem "Pim" Kolff, a general practitioner who moonlighted in the Dutch Resistance, built the first machine for human dialysis. At the time of the German invasion of Holland in May 1940, Kolff was engaged in postgraduate medical studies at the University of Groningen under the supervision of Leonard Polak Daniels, director of the university's department of medicine, who was Jewish. When the Nazis arrived, Daniels and his wife committed suicide, and Kolff, refusing to continue his research under Daniels's Nazi-designated replacement, moved to the small town of Kampen in north-central Holland. Here he saved an estimated 800 people from deportation to concentration camps, including a ten-year-old Jewish boy whom he concealed in his home, and other fugitives who masqueraded as patients in his hospital, where Kolff coached them on how to simulate illness.

Like many doctors of the time, Kolff was troubled by cases of incurable uremia. Working within the medical world view of Bernard, Graham and Abel, and operating in secret during the night at a factory that the Germans had commandeered to produce cookware for the Wehrmacht, Kolff built an artificial kidney from materials foraged from the war-torn landscape: an enameled bathtub, a sewing machine motor, a bicycle chain and a water pump from a Ford Model T, all arranged inside a frame constructed from parts of a downed Luftwaffe fighter plane. He made a drum from large wooden slats resembling those of a picket fence, wrapped it with thirty meters of cellophane sausage casings, filled the casings with the patient's blood, and rotated the drum slowly in a dialysate bath of salt, bicarbonate and glucose. Gradually, drawn by the chemical gradient between the dialysate and the blood, small-molecule metabolites like urea left the blood and diffused through the semipermeable cellophane into the bath, while the larger blood molecules remained behind. Kolff used his rotating drum dialyzer to cleanse the blood of a few of his kidney failure patients long enough for their kidneys to restart. (Ironically, his first successful patient, Sofia Schafstadt, was a Nazi collaborator, whose kidneys had failed while she was in prison after the Liberation. Her first words as she emerged from her uremic coma were, "I'm going to divorce my husband," who despised the Germans.)

Meanwhile, in wartime Sweden, Nils Alwall, another gifted physiologist, performed dialysis experiments on rabbits, which demonstrated that the kidneys removed from the blood not just urea and other contaminants, but also excess water contained in the blood plasma, which could harm the heart, lungs and other organs if it accumulated. Like Kolff, with whom he had no contact until after 1945, Alwall put war salvage to good use: one of his early dialysis machines contained a piece of Plexiglas stripped from an American bomber that had crash landed in Sweden, after a mission over Germany. Alwall devised a way to reduce the water content of his patients' blood by creating higher pressure on the blood side of the membrane than on the dialysate side, which pushed water molecules through the membrane—a process that, like the natural function of the glomerulus in a kidney, is called "ultrafiltration." In September 1946, Alwall dialyzed a forty-seven-year-old man suffering from uremia and silicosis, substantially reducing the toxins and fluid in his blood and the telltale swelling around his eyes, though the man died of pneumonia a day later. Alwall impressed on the Swedish industrialist Holger Crafoord that a lot of money could be made in dialysis. In 1964, Crafoord founded AB Gambro, which became a leading manufacturer of dialysis machines and provider of dialysis treatments.

Though a significant medical advance, dialysis as practiced by Kolff and Alwall remained no more than an emergency technique to save people whose kidneys had halted temporarily. It was of little use to victims of permanent renal failure, because each time patients were connected to the dialyzer, a surgical procedure was required that destroyed one of their major veins and arteries. If their kidneys didn't resume function soon, doctors ran out of blood vessels through which to access the bloodstream. The survival rate among Kolff's and Alwall's initial patients was very low. (Uncharitable critics, noting that most of the Swedish doctor's dialysis patients expired during the procedure, coined a new term for their cause of death: they'd been "Alwallized.")

Further nephrological advances came after World War II, at the Peter Bent Brigham Hospital in Boston, a teaching hospital of Harvard Medical School. Here a surgical team led by John Merrill, a gifted researcher in cardio-renal disease, synthesized various medical advances made throughout the world, to improve the two known approaches to treating kidney failure, dialysis and transplantation. The Brigham invited Pim Kolff to spend 1948 as a sabbatical year at the hospital, where he and Merrill revamped Kolff's rotating drum machine.

During the Korean War, many soldiers stationed in the Han Valley suffered hemorrhagic "trench" fever with acute kidney injury, caused by a pathogen later identified as a hantavirus. A young US Army medic, George Schreiner, treated them with the new Kolff-Brigham dialysis machine, then being used by the US military and the Veterans Administration (now known as the Department of Veterans Affairs, or VA). After he left the military in 1951, Schreiner joined Georgetown University Hospital as chief of its newly formed division of nephrology. Here in Washington, DC, Schreiner played a salient role, as a doctor and later as a lobbyist, in bringing dialysis into the mainstream of American medicine.

John Merrill also spent a year at the Necker Hospital in Paris, working alongside Jean Hamburger, an early innovator in the experimental pursuit of kidney transplantation. Merrill was in Paris on Christmas Eve in 1952, when a sixteen-year-old carpenter's apprentice arrived at the hospital in critical condition. The boy's one healthy kidney had been mangled in a scaffolding collapse, and his distraught mother convinced Hamburger to remove one of her kidneys and transplant it into her son. The grafted kidney worked fine for three weeks, before the boy's immune system rejected it, and he died. Hamburger and Merrill learned much from the operation's initial positive outcome, and even more from its ultimate failure. Among other things, they saw that the challenges of kidney transplantation lay less in the surgical procedure itself than in slipping the new organ past the recipient's immune defenses.

Merrill returned to the Brigham to help lead America's first kidney transplant and dialysis program, together with the distinguished surgeon Joseph Murray. Their Boston team, which attracted brilliant young nephrology fellows like Constantine Hampers, Edward Hager, Eugene Schupak and Edmund Lowrie, performed a series of experimental transplants of kidneys taken from cadavers, often using the Kolff-Brigham machine to keep patients alive long enough to receive the new organ. Each of these transplants, like the 1952 attempt in Paris, was defeated after some time by the recipient's immune response. But Joseph Murray had ideas about how to overcome this barrier. During World War II, he had performed skin grafts on burn casualties, and had observed that autografts of these patients' own tissues often took and grew, while allografts—skin taken from other people—invariably melted away, though more slowly among patients with compromised immune systems. Murray and his colleagues theorized that the closer the genetic match between donor and recipient, the greater the chances that a graft or transplant would take—and that suppressing the immune system would further increase the odds. John Merrill himself had served as the flight surgeon to the crew of the *Enola Gay*, the US B-29 that dropped the first atomic bomb on Hiroshima, and had received state-of-the-art training on the effects of radiation on the human body, which included immunosuppression. The two men began to see that, if the action of the immune system on foreign tissue caused rejection, radiation might be used to reduce the immune response and thus facilitate transplantation.

In December 1954, combining their disparate experiences, Merrill and Murray performed the first successful kidney transplant—which was also the first successful human organ transplant in history—after Richard Herrick, an emaciated twenty-four-year-old recently discharged from the Coast Guard for ill health, arrived at the Brigham in convulsions, and received a diagnosis of critical kidney failure. Luckily, Richard had an identical twin, Ronald, who was willing to part with a kidney.

The two surgeons left little to chance. They performed seventeen different tests to ensure that the twins were genetically identical, including a graft of Ronald's skin onto Richard's leg, which healed after four weeks without even microscopic signs of rejection. They asked the Boston police to fingerprint the brothers, for further proof that they were identical, not fraternal, twins. (Journalists waiting around the police station for a scoop thus learned of the impending operation; that same evening, Murray heard on the radio that he was about to perform a daring procedure at the Brigham. From then on, the press followed the story eagerly.)

Just before the operation, the surgeons subjected Richard, the future transplant recipient, to 450 rads of full-body radiation, to blunt his body's immune response. They cleansed his blood one last time with their Kolff-Brigham artificial kidney, then set to work, in two operating theaters fifty meters apart. J. Hartwell Harrison, chief of urology, removed Ronald's healthy kidney and passed it to Murray and Merrill. As they inserted it into Richard's body, the tension was palpable. "The operating room fell silent," Murray wrote years later. "We watched—some with fingers crossed, some saying silent prayers—as the transplanted kidney gradually turned pink and plumped up, engorged by Richard's blood. Then urine began flowing briskly. There were grins all around."

Richard Herrick lived another eight years in relatively good health, before dying of a heart attack. After this triumph, the Boston team performed further kidney transplants, suppressing the recipients' immune system first with radiation, later with drugs. Groups of surgeons elsewhere began to transplant other organs, and continued to advance the science of immunology.

Though a crucial part of Harvard's kidney transplant program, dialysis remained a short-term treatment for renal failure, because doctors had not yet devised a way to access a patient's bloodstream for extended periods. The access problem became an obsession for Belding "Scrib" Scribner, head of the newly established nephrology division at the University of Washington Medical Center (UWMC) in Seattle. Scribner, like the Netherlander Pim Kolff, was a medical polymath and inventor who had long been both fascinated and appalled by the problem of kidney failure. After hearing John Merrill speak about the Kolff-Brigham machine at the Mayo Clinic in 1950, Scribner began to practice dialysis in earnest. He procured the most advanced blood filtration systems available—first a Skeggs-Leonards plate dialyzer built at Case Western Reserve University in Cleveland, then the even more effective (though unfortunately named) Kiil dialyzer, designed by Norwegian physician Fred Kiil. Instead of a rotating drum, the Kiil device ran the patient's blood and dialysate through semipermeable membranes sandwiched between plates of rubber or grooved plastic.

Scribner finally solved the access problem, after witnessing the disturbing death of one of his patients. "I cannot recall ever having seen a sicker patient survive on the artificial kidney," Scribner wrote of Joe Saunders from nearby Spokane, Washington, who arrived at the UWMC in January 1960. "He was in coma, and his heart failure was so bad that foam was oozing out of his lungs and mouth. Yet one week [after starting dialysis] Joe was up and about, feeling amazingly well as a result of several treatments on the artificial kidney." However, further testing revealed that Saunders's kidneys were irreversibly damaged. "We did the only thing we could do," Scribner concluded. "We had an agonizing conversation with Mrs. Saunders and told her to take her husband back home to Spokane where he would die, hopefully without much suffering." Two weeks later, Saunders passed away. "The emotional impact of this case was enormous on all of us," Scribner concluded. "I could not stop thinking about it."

A short time later, at four in the morning, Scribner awoke suddenly from a vivid dream. He groped for paper and pencil at his bedside, and sketched a rough idea: two tubes, or "cannulas," one fixed in a patient's artery and one in a vein, which between treatments would be joined together by a U-shaped connecting tube, allowing blood to continue to flow. Whenever doctors needed to dialyze the patient, they would simply remove the connecting tube, "uncorking" the arterial and venous cannulas, which could then be attached to the dialysis machine, and rejoined after treatment. (Unbeknownst to Scribner, Nils Alwall had experimented during World War II with a similar system of cannulas made from rubber and glass tubing, but his attempts had failed because of blood clotting.)

Scribner was still developing his idea on March 9, 1960, when Clyde Shields, a machinist at a local Boeing aircraft plant, was rushed to the UWMC with acute kidney failure. In hallway conversations with Loren Winterscheid, a heart surgeon, and Wayne Quinton, head of the hospital's medical instrument shop, Scribner described one serious problem with his idea: blood clots might form in the tubing. Winterscheid suggested using Teflon, a newly invented polymer whose nonstick, nonreactive surface might reduce the risk of clotting. Quinton bent a length of Teflon tubing over a Bunsen burner into a U, and plunged it into cold water to fix its shape. Using Swagelok fittings popular with plumbers, Scribner attached the ends of the U-shaped tube to cannulas inserted in the cephalic vein and radial artery in Clyde Shields's forearm. He now had a way to connect the same blood vessels to the dialysis machine time after time, without destroying them.

So the "Quinton-Scribner shunt" was born, and almost overnight, dialysis became a viable long-term treatment for kidney failure. Scribner obtained a grant from the National Institutes of Health and used it to open the world's first hemodialysis clinic, with Clyde Shields as its inaugural patient. Unlike Joe Saunders three months earlier, Shields's health stabilized; he eventually returned to work at Boeing, and lived another eleven years on dialysis before dying of a heart attack. Two other patients soon joined Shields in Scribner's care: plastic molder Rollin Heming, who survived on dialysis for fourteen years, and shoe salesman Harvey Gentry, who dialyzed for a decade before receiving a kidney transplant from his mother and living another eighteen years.

Nephrology, a discipline that had only just been named, was now a frontier of medical innovation. Dialysis and transplantation developed as sibling fields, in a worldwide race to build a better artificial kidney and to perfect the art of transplanting natural organs. Nephrology practices, transplant centers and dialysis units proliferated at university medical centers, led by innovators like Pim Kolff, who had emigrated to the United States and now worked at the Cleveland Clinic; Belding Scribner at the University of Washington; John Merrill at Harvard; and George Schreiner at Georgetown. Drawing on an array of technologies and designs, they built new medical devices with names like dragsters: the "Monster," the "Mini-Monster," the "Pressure Cooker." Nephrologists continued Belding Scribner's work of devising new methods to connect patients to these machines, which culminated in 1966 with the invention, by Italian American physicians James Cimino and Michael Brescia, of the arteriovenous fistula. This surgical union of an artery and a vein, which created an artificially enlarged and strengthened graft where needles could more easily be inserted, remains to this day the best vascular access for most dialysis patients. Medical device companies like Gambro and Baxter spent increasing budgets to develop new membranes and filter designs with better diffusion and convection properties. By the mid-1960s, the first disposable hollow-fiber dialyzers, the dominant design today, began to replace earlier membranes that had to be cleaned laboriously between treatments. The hollow-fiber design employed arrays of microscopic capillaries that had far greater surface area for filtration.

Nephrologists also experimented with new forms of dialysis. They filled patients' abdominal cavity with dialysate and used the peritoneum as a blood filter. This peritoneal dialysis became a viable alternative to hemodialysis, and the preferred method for children because its gentle daily administrations, typically done at home, caused fewer side effects and lifestyle disruptions than hemodialysis. (Because the peritoneum typically loses its efficacy as a filter within a few years, peritoneal dialysis is far less prevalent among adults than hemodialysis.) After a girl of fifteen was denied dialysis treatment in Seattle because she was too young to qualify for Scribner's program, nuclear engineer Les Babb, a friend of the girl's family, worked with Scribner to build a miniaturized dialysis machine that the girl and her parents could operate at home. The nephrology group at Harvard, and a team at the Royal Free Hospital in London led by Stanley Shaldon, also began training patients to perform hemodialysis in their homes. A program at the University of Toronto launched by Robert Uldall and later led by Andreas Pierratos developed nocturnal home hemodialysis: patients attached themselves to the machine at bedtime, dialyzed through the night, and awoke cleansed and renewed after eight hours of gradual purification.

Cutting-edge medical programs like these provided inspiration and formative training for nephrologists from around the world. John Agar's stint in Toronto with Andreas Pierratos produced a paradigm shift in his approach to dialysis, which he applied back home in Geelong. "Andreas opened up a whole new world for me," Agar says.

While treating Clyde Shields and other early patients, Scribner and his team learned indispensable lessons about the challenges of life on an artificial kidney. Patients developed mysterious lumps in soft tissues around their shoulders, which turned out to be caused by elevated phosphate levels in their blood. A gastroenterologist told Scribner to try an oral antacid, known to reduce phosphate, and the strange deposits disappeared. Not long after initiating dialysis, Shields's blood pressure rose so high that he nearly went blind. Like Nils Alwall before them, the Seattle team recognized that excess water in Shields's blood was to blame—few of us appreciate the momentousness of making urine, until our kidneys fail—and discovered that longer dialysis treatments were able to control it. Shields and other patients also experienced gout-like swelling in their fingers and toes, and peripheral neuropathy, a painful tingling in their arms and legs due to nerve damage. These symptoms, too, relented when the patients' time on dialysis was increased, though why longer treatments helped was unclear for the moment.

From a decade of such data, the Seattle team pieced together a fuller picture of the kidney's role in human physiology. They saw that healthy kidneys did a great deal more than just filter out urea: they also removed a wide array of other impurities, controlled fluid levels and secreted crucial enzymes. Scribner and his group noticed that patients who retained some residual kidney function were far less prone to peripheral neuropathy and several other harmful side effects of renal failure. So, too, were patients on peritoneal dialysis, although their blood routinely contained more small-molecule wastes like urea and creatinine than did the blood of most hemodialysis patients. These discoveries led Scribner and colleagues to formulate the "middle-molecule hypothesis," according to which many negative symptoms suffered by their early patients weren't due to excess serum urea or creatinine, but to larger, middle-molecule toxins that conventional dialysis had a hard time removing from the blood. Scribner believed that these symptoms were absent among patients who had residual kidney function because, though compromised, their kidneys still cleared some middle-molecule substances. Peritoneal dialysis patients, too, were spared these adverse symptoms, because the peritoneum, more permeable than artificial membranes, allowed the middle molecules to pass through and exit the bloodstream. Scribner and his team concluded that the removal of urea and creatinine, the most widely recognized measures of dialysis efficacy at the time, ought not to be the only—and arguably not even the main—aim of good dialysis. They also inferred that long, slow dialysis treatments, and careful attention to fluid management and the preservation of residual renal function, were best for their patients' health and quality of life.

The Seattle team also recognized the many benefits of home dialysis. In the short term, dialyzing in the home saved lives, since far more patients could be treated in their dwellings than could be accommodated in Scribner's small dialysis center. But home dialysis also facilitated longer, gentler treatments that were tailored to the patients' individual bodies, which produced cleaner blood and fewer side effects. Home dialysis was cheaper than in-center treatment, because patients provided the real estate, paid for water and power, and often had their family members serve as unpaid medical assistants. Psychologically, too, patients who dialyzed at home had more control over the dialysis schedule, and a greater sense of independence. Such patients, the Seattle doctors saw, were more likely to return to work and resume much of their normal lives. "If the treatment of chronic uremia cannot fully rehabilitate the patient, the treatment is inadequate," Belding Scribner pronounced.

❑

IN SEPTEMBER of 1959, Nancy Spaeth, an athletic seventh-grader from Seattle, began to struggle at track practice and on the ski slopes. She felt a crushing and inexplicable exhaustion, and her race times plummeted. Before long she could barely sit up, or comb her thick, sandy-blond hair. Her urine turned cola brown, she vomited constantly, and her eyes swelled almost shut. After a series of blood tests and medical exams, her doctors gave Spaeth a diagnosis of glomerulonephritis, which they attributed to multiple wasp stings Spaeth had recently suffered. They prescribed extended bedrest, and reductions in sodium and protein in her diet, which her kidneys were now hard pressed to process. For a time, Spaeth's condition improved. She enrolled in a college in Seattle. But in early 1966, when she was eighteen, her health collapsed once more. This time, the doctors said, her kidneys were failing for good.

Despite her terrible misfortune, however, Spaeth was in luck. Until recently, her uremia would have been a death sentence without reprieve. Her parents and doctors would have watched helplessly as wastes accumulated in her blood, turning her skin a chalky yellow-gray. Excess fluid would have swelled her ankles and legs, and accumulated in her lungs, causing increasing shortness of breath and strain on her heart. She would likely have suffered from headaches, extreme fatigue, and inability to concentrate. Dusky-white crystals known as "uremic frost" would have appeared around her lips. Within weeks, even days, she would have slipped into a coma and expired, killed by the by-products of her own metabolism.

Death by uremia made hard memories for many doctors, who were forced to stand by helplessly as otherwise healthy patients succumbed to an inexorable condition they had few medical arms to combat. Seattle internist Belding Scribner described his own "grim personal experience" with uremic patients like Joe Saunders, and the "slow, agonizing death" to which they were condemned, "sometimes involving many months of intense suffering and great expense." However, by 1966, when Nancy Spaeth fell ill, Scribner and his team at the University of Washington Medical Center had been practicing dialysis for six years in the Seattle Artificial Kidney Center, a small clinic they had opened in the basement of a nurses' residence at the nearby Swedish Hospital (their own UWMC administrators had refused to house the clinic). At the time, they had forty-seven patients under care. Yet far more uremia victims were applying for treatment than could be accommodated. In response, Scribner and local health officials formed an "Admissions and Policy Committee," to help determine which patients would be allowed into the clinic, and which would be turned away.

Nancy Spaeth remembers the screening process, which she viewed through the increasingly foggy lens of her kidney failure, as less traumatic than baffling. "I had to do two days of psychological testing, and my mother met with social workers and finance specialists," Spaeth says. "They met with my brothers, too. We never actually saw the Committee, and our names were blacked out on all documents they received. Everything was done anonymously. I'm sure the review process was a lot harder on my family than it was on me. They must have worried that I might not be chosen, which of course would mean that I'd die. But I was only eighteen. At that age, death doesn't seem like something that will ever happen to you." (Spaeth died in 2022, shortly before this book was completed.)

Her fate was being decided by seven people—a minister, a housewife, a lawyer, a union representative, a banker, a state government official and a doctor not involved in dialysis care—whose identities remained secret. The trustees of Scribner's hospital had established this panel, intended as a microcosm of society, because they believed that the questions surrounding patient selection for dialysis were grave and unprecedented, and that every segment of society should share their burden. The committee assessed each candidate's fitness for the dialysis program with a series of criteria that included net worth, emotional stability and perceived contribution to the community. Patients with other chronic conditions such as diabetes or hypertension were excluded a priori, as were applicants under sixteen and over forty-five, the former because they were not yet self-sufficient adults, the latter because their health was, in actuarial terms, less robust. Participants were also required to have sufficient medical insurance to cover the costs of the experimental treatment, or to put up $30,000 in cash (more than $250,000 in 2022 dollars).

During its first thirteen months of existence, the committee evaluated thirty candidates and accepted ten. The other twenty died. Nancy Spaeth and her family faced a final judgment, without appeal, before this group of seven people, which informally had come to be known as the "Life and Death Committee," or the "God Committee." "Fortunately I got the thumbs up," she says.

Coming under Belding Scribner's care in 1966, Nancy Spaeth became the beneficiary of six intense years of medical creativity and experimentation in the Seattle program, as well as in Boston and other medical centers across the world. Her first treatments, in the clinic at Swedish Hospital, employed the old-style Kiil flat-plate dialyzer; she dialyzed three times per week, for eight hours each session. After two years, Scribner and his staff trained Spaeth and her mother to run a modified Kiil machine at home, and she began dialyzing at night, lying on a cot in her basement. "Nocturnal dialysis at home was the perfect solution," Spaeth says. "I got my life back." She was able to complete her undergraduate degree at Seattle University in 1970. Two years later, she received a transplant from her brother, which gave her a seven-year respite from dialysis. She married, and had two healthy children.

When her transplant failed in 1979 after an incident of food poisoning, Spaeth resumed dialysis. (Though transplanted kidneys often continue to function for a decade or more—organs from living donors typically last longer than those from cadavers—they can fail due to immune rejection, infection or disease.) There had been much technical progress in dialysis since she'd last undergone treatment seven years earlier; the machines ran faster, allowing shorter treatment times of four hours' duration. Tellingly, however, she found that she preferred her old treatment method, dialyzing at low pressure all night long. "I often felt sick and washed out after a dialysis session, and the daytime treatment schedule broke up my day."

Spaeth continued dialyzing at home and in-center, with interruptions of several years at a time after she received a new transplant. (Spaeth had four transplants in all, the last in 2000.) Nevertheless, she says the first treatments, between 1966 and 1972, gave her the fewest side effects and the greatest well-being. This may in part be explained by her youth when she began to dialyze, and her decreasing tolerance for the treatment as she aged. But it probably has more to do with the beneficial effects of extended, low-speed dialysis. Writing in response to a 2008 article by California nephrologist Thomas Depner, in which Depner catalogued the common side effects of dialysis—lethargy, poor appetite, nausea, inability to concentrate—Christopher Blagg, one of Belding Scribner's closest associates in Seattle, remarked, "In the 1970s, with the advent of more efficient dialyzers allowing shorter dialysis at greater blood flows, the rapid proliferation of dialysis units with the Medicare End-Stage Renal Disease Program, and the rapid decrease in the use of home hemodialysis, the symptoms described by Depner became commonplace in patients dialyzed in US centers. Because almost all present-day US nephrologists started practice years after the late 1960s and early 1970s, they have no knowledge of the experience at that time and have accepted and expected that the symptoms described by Depner are 'normal' for many patients." Somewhere, Blagg realized, dialysis in America had taken a wrong turn.

Back in 1966 when Nancy Spaeth entered the Seattle Artificial Kidney Center, Blagg, Scribner and the other members of the University of Washington team had ample reason for optimism about the future of their medical brainchild. What worried them, rather, were the larger questions being raised by dialysis. Their program had already drawn national media attention, and launched a vigorous discussion in the press and on Capitol Hill about the ethics of distributing scarce medical resources—and about who should pay for such costly, high-tech treatments. Over the following two decades, the debate over dialysis grew into a confrontation between two opposing philosophies of medicine. Was dialysis, and healthcare more broadly, a privilege to be sold in the financial marketplace, or a fundamental right of citizenship?

· 5 ·

Medical Miracles, Bioethics
and Dialysis for All

"I HAVE DECIDED to discuss this subject at the risk of making both you, my audience, and myself uncomfortable, because I feel with great sincerity and great urgency that we must bring these problems out in the open and try and face them squarely," Belding Scribner told an April 1964 gathering of medical doctors engaged in organ replacement and transplantation. "I believe that the specific problems I am about to relate to you will recur again and again as other new, complicated, expensive, lifesaving techniques are developed. Hence, these matters, although presented as special problems of the present, may become general problems of the future."

Scribner then described some of the difficult questions that he and his colleagues in Seattle had faced during the first four years of their dialysis program, each a pressing and unresolved medical dilemma. According to what criteria should patients in need of a rare, expensive therapy be accepted for treatment, or turned away? Could their care be terminated without their consent? Should they themselves be able to end their treatments, a form of suicide? And how could a complex and grueling new cure like dialysis, which some doctors and patients viewed as a fate worse than death, be administered in such a way that patients retained some control over their own fate, and, in the end, could die with dignity? Scribner concluded with an appeal to his audience to help him draw up a new code of ethics—"a modern Hippocratic Oath if you will"—to guide doctors in the application of high-tech medicine.

Scribner's unease and sense of urgency were understandable. Since World War II, research and technology were transforming medicine. X-rays and ultrasound were providing powerful new diagnostic tools, while the extensive use of artificial respirators, advances in general anesthesiology and the appearance of the first "shock wards"—early intensive-care units—enabled doctors to save countless lives. Medical science had even begun to impinge on the beginning and end of life, through the introduction of oral contraceptives, improvements in surgical abortion techniques and early progress in genetic engineering. Dialysis and transplantation broke further barriers: by substituting or replacing a vital organ, these therapies were extending human lives for years, even decades, that until recently would have ended in days.

Shortly after the Seattle Artificial Kidney Center opened on January 1, 1962, the national press, the US Congress and society at large began asking pointed questions about this medical "miracle," and the underlying ethics of life and death with which it was being applied. Unlike earlier medical breakthroughs such as penicillin and the polio vaccine, which became widely available soon after they were invented, long-term dialysis treatment was so scarce and expensive that only a fraction of patients could access it. Scribner's innovation had raised unprecedented moral dilemmas, which, as he predicted in his 1964 address, previewed many of the questions that society would confront with the rise of high-priced, life-altering technologies in other medical fields. Leading medical ethicists like David Rothman and Albert Jonsen have identified the dialysis program in Seattle, and allied advances in kidney transplantation, as decisive forces in the birth of the new field of bioethics.

In the 1954 kidney transplant performed on identical twins at the Brigham, Merrill and Murray had subjected Ronald Herrick, the healthy twin, to the multiple risks of surgery—threats of infection, hemorrhage, harm to other organs, and the hazards associated with general anesthesia—in order to give his organ to another person. Hence the procedure had, at least in regard to Ronald's health, violated a central Hippocratic tenet, "First, do no harm." Before the operation, realizing that what they were about to attempt exceeded the bounds of conventional medicine, Merrill and his team had sought the views of other physicians regarding transplantation, and had consulted attorneys and clergy of several religious denominations. This practice of reaching beyond the medical profession for answers to modern medicine's latest conundrums would be repeated frequently in the coming years.

Some fellow MDs condemned the procedure outright, accusing Merrill and Murray of wanting to "play God." Others compared organ transplantation to "cannibalization," the scavenging of parts from one machine in order to repair another. Pius XI, in a papal encyclical, had rejected such acts by healthy people as "self-mutilation," and his successor Pius XII confirmed the Catholic church's position at a symposium on transplants not long after the Herrick operation. For an ardent Catholic like Joseph Murray, such pronouncements were not trivial.

The "artificial kidney" created even thornier moral dilemmas. In 1961, after Clyde Shields and two other trailblazing patients had survived on dialysis for more than a year, Belding Scribner asked the University of Washington Medical Center for permission to start more kidney failure patients on this novel therapy. Hospital administrators refused, observing that the center could only accommodate a handful of patients, and that building and staffing new dialysis stations would be expensive. (Dialysis treatment in their clinic cost about $15,000 per patient annually—three times what the average US household spent on goods and services in a year.) But the real trouble was, the cure appeared to be working. Administrators pointed out that if the federal government, which was then supplying crucial funding, decided to end its support for the program, the hospital and the state of Washington would have to foot the bill for the patients' care, for an indefinite period. The hospital declined to take this risk.

In response, Scribner organized a fund drive in the Seattle area, secured grants from national foundations, and used the proceeds to found the Seattle Artificial Kidney Center in the nearby Swedish Hospital. On January 1, 1962, a team of registered nurses under his direction began administering dialysis, twice a week for eight hours at a stretch, to a handful of patients. The Veterans Administration (VA) announced plans to open thirty dialysis centers of its own throughout the nation, and the Public Health Service (PHS), an arm of the Department of Health, Education and Welfare (now the Department of Health and Human Services), began issuing grants to units nationwide. The first of these grants went to Scribner, which enabled him to expand his center to ten stations that could treat about fifty patients.

But demand for dialysis continued to dwarf the number of available stations, and the Seattle doctors found themselves accepting certain patients while denying care to others, a situation which violated another Hippocratic precept: that physicians must preserve the life of each of their patients, without hint of favoritism. Though Scribner helped to institute the triage-by-committee system as an emergency response to this predicament, he nevertheless considered the God Committee's decisions not to treat certain patients to be a form of killing. Scribner continued to grapple with the issue of who should make the fateful choice of patient selection—and who should pay for the care of those who were chosen.

❑

SCRIBNER EXPRESSED his misgivings about dialysis at a time when modern medicine and science as a whole, once widely considered paradigms of human progress, had taken on somber new overtones. With the nuclear explosions over Hiroshima and Nagasaki, society began a searching reassessment of science. Splitting the atom had shown with searing clarity the ambivalence of technology, which could kill as well as heal, destroy or create, and had produced devices that could instantly end human civilization. President Eisenhower included academics along with military leaders and defense contractors in his "military-industrial complex," which he identified as a dire threat to American democracy. (Senator William Fulbright rebaptized this sinister brotherhood the "military-industrial-academic complex.") And Nazi Germany had shown the world how utterly some doctors had forsaken medical ethics. During the so-called Doctors Trial, held before the International Military Tribunal at Nuremberg, twenty Nazi MDs were prosecuted for murder, torture and gruesome medical experiments on concentration camp inmates. Analysis of their monstrosities led to the promulgation of the Nuremberg Code in 1947, a landmark statement on the ethics of human experimentation, which stressed the necessity of obtaining voluntary informed consent from test subjects, forbade researchers from causing unnecessary harm or suffering, and underscored science's obligation to undertake only those experiments that seemed likely to benefit society.

Like Belding Scribner, many doctors began to explore the mortal threats to their professional ethics posed by modern technology and by political ideology. Among the first and most trenchant of these internal critics was Leo Alexander, a Vienna-born Jewish doctor who had emigrated to the United States in 1933. Immediately after World War II, Alexander traveled extensively in Germany and met with numerous doctors of the former Reich, many of whom attempted to rationalize to him their actions under Hitler's regime. He aided the prosecution during the Doctors Trial, and helped to write the Nuremberg Code. In a harrowing 1949 article in the *New England Journal of Medicine* (NEJM), "Medical Science Under Dictatorship," Alexander chronicled the phases by which German medicine had fallen under the spell of Nazi eugenics, beginning with the widespread adoption in the early 1930s of the view that the chronically ill were needless drains on society; progressing to programs of sterilization and euthanasia aimed at preserving the "genetic purity" of the German race; and ending in the lethal pseudo-scientific experiments and wholesale genocide of the 1940s. Under a dictatorship, Alexander wrote, the health of citizens is viewed "merely in terms of utility, efficiency and productivity. It is natural in such a setting that eventually Hegel's principle that 'what is useful is good' wins out completely." The corruption of German medicine began, Alexander observed, with the acceptance by German physicians "of the attitude, basic in the euthanasia movement, that there is such a thing as life not worthy to be lived."

Some physicians, however, had avoided this sinister ethical decay entirely. Alexander noted that doctors in occupied Holland (he might have mentioned Pim Kolff as an example) had categorically refused Nazi orders to dispatch chronically ill patients to camps, where they would no doubt have been killed. When the Germans threatened to punish these intransigent Dutchmen by revoking their medical licenses, they surrendered their licenses voluntarily. And when the enraged Germans made an example of 100 Dutch doctors by packing them off to concentration camps, the doctors who had been spared stood firm, while looking after the widows and orphans of their missing colleagues. "Thus it came about that not a single euthanasia or non-therapeutic sterilization was recommended or participated in by any Dutch physician," Alexander wrote. "They had the foresight to resist before the first step was taken. . . . It is the first seemingly innocent step away from principle that frequently decides a career of crime. Corrosion begins in microscopic proportions."

Alexander concluded his disturbing chronicle of the fall of German medicine by observing that American doctors themselves had already taken the first fatal step away from the purity of their medical calling, and begun to follow the same cold-blooded doctrines that had ultimately led their German counterparts into murder. The advent of sophisticated medical tools in America, he said, was unmooring the practice of medicine from its moral, ethical and religious values— from time-honored norms such as compassion for patients and an unwavering commitment to alleviate human suffering. Instead, many doctors now practiced medicine according to novel calculations based on rationalism and efficiency, and suffered dark new "delusions of omnipotence."

In America's competitive, money-driven and increasingly utilitarian society, Alexander wrote, "physicians have become dangerously close to being mere technicians of rehabilitation." As had occurred in Germany, the chronically ill patient in America "carries an obvious stigma as the one less likely to be fully rehabilitable for social usefulness," and is "looked down upon with increasing definiteness as unwanted ballast." The growing stream of public funds into US medicine only accentuated this utilitarian perspective, Alexander observed, and led many doctors and policy makers to ask, "Is it worth while to spend a certain amount of effort to restore a certain type of patient?"

Alexander concluded his article with a plea to American doctors not to lose sight of human compassion or divine law, and never to reduce their profession to a mere economic calculus. "From the attitude of easing patients with chronic diseases away from the doors of the best types of treatment facilities available to the actual dispatching of such patients to killing centers is a long but nevertheless logical step."

Alexander's misgivings about American physicians were more apt than he knew. During the infamous Tuskegee Study, which began in Macon County, Alabama, in 1932, some 400 poor Black sharecroppers suffering from syphilis were intentionally left untreated for decades, while being assured that they were receiving proper medical care, in order to study the natural evolution of the disease "in the Negro male." This experiment, funded by the Public Health Service—the very organization that helped to pay for Belding Scribner's Seattle dialysis clinic—was only halted in 1972, after a whistleblower's denunciations reached the newspapers. As with syphilis, so with radiation: from 1944 through at least 1974, under a cloak of Cold War secrecy, unsuspecting Americans—poor Blacks, disabled children and other vulnerable patient populations—were fed, irradiated or injected with radioactive substances by doctors, many employed at prestigious academic health centers like MIT, Berkeley and Massachusetts General Hospital. Researchers exploring the effects of radiation on human reproduction irradiated the testicles of inmates in Oregon and Washington penitentiaries, and later vasectomized them, for fear they would produce mutant offspring. (Berkeley physician Joseph G. Hamilton, who participated in plutonium experiments on humans, remarked in a 1950 memo that radiation experiments on prisoners "had a little of the Buchenwald touch.")

❑

FOR ALL the humanity and good intentions of Scribner and his Seattle team, their God Committee suggested the validity of Alexander's fears about the ascendancy of utilitarianism over compassion in American medicine. The "Seattle experience," as Scribner's dialysis program and its selection committee came to be called, struck a nerve in the nation. In November of 1962, only months after the Seattle Artificial Kidney Center opened, *Life* magazine ran a feature article by Shana Alexander entitled "They Decide Who Lives, Who Dies." Alexander's title was taken from the Unetaneh Tokef, the traditional Hebrew prayer recited on the high holy days of Rosh Hashanah and Yom Kippur, which says that God alone decides "Who shall live and who shall die; who shall attain the measure of man's days and who shall not attain it." Her article examined the workings of the Admissions and Policy Committee in Seattle.

In Alexander's interviews, members of the committee echoed diverse aspects of the manifold unease that America had begun to feel about modern medicine. The banker worried about the high cost of the treatment, while the state official feared that medicine had advanced faster than society's ability to comprehend its implications. The lawyer, for his part, said he wasn't overly troubled by the plight of patients whom his committee didn't select, because "the ones we do choose have an awfully rugged life to look forward to. Not all men would wish it." Alexander also implied that, despite Scribner's compassion and concern, he was using Clyde Shields and other early dialysis patients as human guinea pigs for his experimental treatments. (In fact, the glee with which Scribner exhibited them to Kolff, Merrill, Schreiner and other luminaries at medical conferences can make for uneasy reading.)

Further high-profile coverage of the Seattle program followed. NBC aired the documentary *Who Shall Live?* narrated by Edwin Newman, the famed anchorman. Newman explained that each applicant to the program was judged by a "jury of their peers" on the basis of his medical, psychological and financial record, but also "on his record as a member of this community—on his record as a responsible human being. In a word, is he *worth* saving?" To objections that the nation could not afford to subsidize such expensive treatment, Newman and some of his guests countered by pointing out how much the nation was already investing in space exploration and the arms race with the

USSR—and that America's health should come first. "We're spending billions of dollars to get to the moon," Melvin Laird, a Republican congressman from Wisconsin, said during the transmission, "and it seems to me that these human problems [i.e., kidney failure and high-priced dialysis], which we have right here on earth, need to be solved." Newman agreed. "A medical miracle has been achieved, and we refuse to face its implications," he concluded. "We continue to argue where the money is coming from. And we *have* the money."

These and subsequent news stories drew national attention to the life-and-death nature of dialysis, and to the perplexing new decisions being prompted by medical innovation. It also alerted Washington, DC, that dialysis was becoming a hot-button issue for American voters.

Just as the initial response of Scribner and the trustees of his hospital to the problem of patient selection had been to form a selection committee drawn from many areas of society, so he and other nephrologists reacted to the growing national attention to dialysis by consulting with experts in fields outside medicine, seeking perspective on the broader moral questions their work was raising. Transplant specialists reacted similarly. In response to a 1964 editorial in the *Annals of Internal Medicine* that bemoaned the lack of serious debate about the ethics of organ replacement, William Bennett, a young Oregon internist, called for a systematic analysis of the issue by a panel of distinguished philosophers, theologians, biologists and social scientists, because, he wrote, "few physicians are sufficiently grounded in these disciplines to bring to bear the wisdom of the ages on such questions."

A series of interdisciplinary conferences—the first sponsored by the American Medical Association (AMA) in June 1963, eighteen months after Scribner opened his Seattle clinic—did just what Bennett asked, bringing together theologians, psychologists, attorneys and philosophers as well as physicians from diverse specialties, to hash out the moral implications of dialysis and transplantation. Leading nephrologists like Kolff, Scribner, Merrill, Schreiner, Jean Hamburger and Carl Gottschalk, all of whom had experienced the shadowy side of the "New Medicine" firsthand, took part. The Penn State College of Medicine, founded in 1967, became the first medical school in the nation to include a humanities department tasked with exploring bioethical issues; by 1974, 97 medical schools out of 107 surveyed in that year offered courses in medical ethics. The first full-fledged research centers in bioethics appeared, beginning with the Hastings Center in 1969, founded jointly by Catholic philosopher Daniel Callahan and psychoanalyst Willard Gaylin, and the Kennedy Institute of Ethics formed two years later at Georgetown University.

Probably the most urgent and contentious question raised by bioethics remained patient selection. Some of Scribner's illustrious peers condemned the Seattle approach to rationing care; George Schreiner and Pim Kolff declared that their programs had never employed anything like the "God Committee," and never would. A paper cowritten by a lawyer and a psychiatrist denounced the Seattle methodology for its "prejudices and mindless clichés," and the hopelessly subjective, bourgeois nature of metrics like "public service" by which it purported to quantify a person's absolute worth. The authors concluded that such an approach inevitably "rules out creative nonconformists . . . who historically have contributed so much to the making of America. The Pacific Northwest is no place for a Henry David Thoreau with bad kidneys."

Belding Scribner was startled. Instead of applauding his new treatment for kidney failure, which almost overnight had transformed a condition with 100 percent mortality into one with a 95 percent survival rate over the first two years, the world had fixated on the bureaucratic process of selecting eligible patients—when, in any case, there were far more eligible patients than could be treated in existing dialysis facilities. "In retrospect, of course, we were terribly naive," Scribner admitted years later. "We did not realize even then the full impact that the existence of this committee would have on the world." He also observed that, since only a few hundred of the many thousands of Americans with kidney failure were receiving dialysis, "obviously rigid selection of one sort or another must have taken place." Doctors like Schreiner and Kolff, despite their high-minded condemnation of the Seattle selection committee, had their own ways of deciding who would live and who would die.

Dialysis also challenged how success was to be defined in a technology-driven therapy. Because kidney failure had, until recently, always led to death, doctors tended to view a patient's mere survival as a triumph. Barring a transplant, however, dialysis shackled patients to a machine for the rest of their lives. The treatment created a novel kind of patient, who was completely dependent on an invasive technology. Psychologists observed the crippling sense of helplessness that could arise from "life on the machine," a psychic pain that many doctors ignored or even amplified with their high-tech thaumaturgy. Transplant pioneer Jean Hamburger at the Necker Hospital in Paris used the phrase "therapeutic relentlessness" to capture the brave new blend of technology, specialist knowledge, ethical compassion and clinical detachment that he saw to be implicit in modern medicine, which deprived patients of any control over their own fate, and placed them entirely at the mercy of their caregivers. "In its commitment to the preservation of life," sociologist Paul Starr wrote of this moment in history, "medical care ironically has come to symbolize a prototypically modern form of torture."

Dialysis programs in Seattle and elsewhere also revealed with painful clarity that even seemingly straightforward financial choices in healthcare had far-reaching ethical dimensions. To open and operate his clinic, Scribner repeatedly solicited money from regional and national foundations, and directly from Seattle residents. (In 1963, when his unit ran low on funds and faced closure, Scribner's efforts received a boost from the *Seattle Times*, which ran photographs of the nine patients then dialyzing there, under the headline, "Will These People Have to Die?") But most patients had to cover about half of the cost of their treatment. Some, like Ernie Crowfeather, a Washington resident of Sioux descent, organized fund drives to pay for their treatment; those who failed to generate enough attention, and cash, did not survive. Crowfeather himself, after watching his dialysis nest egg dissipate, decided to discontinue his treatment, an act that was widely viewed as suicide.

One last ethical question posed by dialysis, arguably the thorniest of all, tormented Scribner: Should nephrologists be allowed to profit directly from providing this lifesaving care? The Seattle Artificial

Kidney Center, which in 1970 was renamed the Northwest Kidney Center, remained stalwartly nonprofit, and derived its operating income from local and national fundraising as well as from patients. Scribner and his colleagues received a fixed salary from the University of Washington Medical Center, regardless of how many dialysis treatments they administered.

In Boston, the Harvard nephrology team led by John Merrill and Joseph Murray had faced the same financial quandary as their Seattle counterparts, but had resolved it differently. They too had asked their managers at the Brigham Hospital to increase the size of the dialysis unit to accommodate more patients, and their request was likewise refused because of concern about the program's future costs. In response, in 1966 Merrill's younger protégés Constantine Hampers, Edward Hager and Eugene Schupak opened an outpatient dialysis clinic in Normandy House, a small rehabilitation facility in Melrose, a north Boston suburb. Instead of Seattle's community-funded, nonprofit approach, the Harvard MDs ran their dialysis clinic as a for-profit concern, charging $160 per dialysis session. The more patients they treated, the more money they made, which supplied working capital to build more facilities and save more lives. The for-profit model also made the founding doctors rich.

In these same years, America began a heated debate about money in healthcare. Though tensions between profit motive and the practice of medicine were hardly new—the American Medical Association (AMA) had denounced "fee splitting," or paying a doctor for referrals, back in 1912—the problem of financial conflicts of interest in healthcare had scarcely arisen in professional or popular writing before the 1960s. The AMA had long condemned for-profit medicine in general terms; until 1980, the association's ethical code stated that "the practice of medicine should not be commercialized, nor treated as a commodity in trade." However, after a series of landmark legal judgments challenged the right of professional organizations to limit their members' income, the AMA removed this stipulation from its code.

Contemporary shifts in the public perception of business, government and society also favored the rise of for-profit medicine. America grew disenchanted with the social programs of the New Deal and the postwar era, and developed a hostility, exacerbated by decades-long geopolitical confrontations with the USSR and China, to virtually anything that could be labeled "socialism." These shifts were accompanied, and accelerated, by the rise of neoliberal economic theory. In academia, business and the Beltway, self-regulating markets came to be celebrated as the ideal mode of human interaction; and private enterprise was increasingly credited with the ability to produce uniformly better and cheaper goods and services than Big Government ever could. Such changes in attitude contributed, from the late 1960s, to a boom in for-profit hospitals, diagnostic laboratories, nursing homes, ER centers and other medical facilities. By 1980, such structures were collectively earning an estimated $40 billion per year.

Flush with the triumph of Normandy House, Constantine Hampers, Edward Hager and the other members of the venture left Harvard Medical School and, in 1968, founded National Medical Care (NMC), a for-profit dialysis company whose aim was to build more such clinics across the country, and to buy out or form joint ventures with existing nephrology practices. Soon NMC was the nation's largest dialysis firm. To fund further growth, Hampers and his associates took their company public in 1971. Earnings skyrocketed, and NMC became one of Wall Street's favorite stocks, consistently rewarding investors with high returns.

In 1972, the ethical and financial controversies within American dialysis came to a head in hearings on Capitol Hill, where leading Republicans and Democrats had been debating for years how—and whether—to fund this breakthrough therapy. Lawmakers now heard a tale of two cities, Boston and Seattle, two opposing visions of healthcare. These hearings marked a turning point in dialysis, and a watershed in the practice of American medicine.

❏

ON NOVEMBER 4, 1971, Shep Glazer, a traveling salesman and father of two from upstate New York, whose kidneys had failed a year earlier, dialyzed before the House Ways and Means Committee. Arriving late at the hearing, a senior congressional aide looked out over the floor of the committee room at Glazer, seated beside his gleaming machine with its blood-filled tubes, and blurted, "What the *fuck* is going on here?"

The aide's perplexity was understandable. Though Ways and Means, chaired by the influential Arkansas Democrat Wilbur Mills, had a tradition of allowing interested members of the public to address the committee in person, until that day no one had undergone a potentially fatal medical procedure as part of their testimony. George Schreiner, the Georgetown nephrologist and former president of the National Kidney Foundation who for years had been lobbying Congress to fund dialysis for all Americans, had advised against the stunt, fearing a bloody accident that would sour Washington on the therapy. In fact, minutes after Glazer's session began, he went into ventricular tachycardia, forcing James Carey, a Georgetown nephrologist who was attending Glazer, to clamp the bloodlines and stop the machine.

Despite opposition from doctors and political strategists, Glazer was determined to show Congress what his strange new life looked like. In the end, his instincts proved correct. Though of negligible medical value to Shep Glazer, this first dialysis procedure in Congress helped politicians and journalists present that day to see kidney failure as an existential threat to the American dream.

After dialyzing, Glazer told the rapt lawmakers how renal disease had progressively deprived him of his job and much of what he loved in life, until this wonder cure had enabled him to return to work and become a productive citizen and happy family man once more ... provided, of course, that he could continue to pay his crushing medical bills. Glazer explained that dialysis had driven him to the verge of bankruptcy—and therefore of death.

I am 43 years old, married for 20 years, with two children ages 14 and 10. I was a salesman until a couple of months ago until it became necessary for me to supplement my income to pay for the dialysis supplies. I tried to sell a non-competitive line, was found out, and was fired. Gentlemen, what should I do? End it all and die? Sell my house for which I worked so hard, and go on welfare? Should I go into the hospital under my hospitalization policy, then I cannot work? Please tell me. If your kidneys failed tomorrow, wouldn't you want the opportunity to live? Wouldn't you want to see your children grow up?

News stories on life-and-death panels in Seattle had made dialysis a political issue, and an emblem of technology's triumph over nature. "The kidney dialysis machinery had become for the 1970s the epitome of medicine's ability to turn away death with advanced machines that could substitute for critical biological functions," observes MD and medical historian Stanley Joel Reiser. "Politicians found support of such innovation attractive and, in the end, easy to give—as long as their cost was not prohibitive." Dialysis also became a political concern at a grassroots level. Around the country, as desperate patients and their families fought for access to the treatment and the money to pay for it, local patient advocacy groups proliferated. One such group was the National Association of Patients on Hemodialysis, of which Shep Glazer was vice president.

To evaluate the medical viability and the financial implications of dialysis and kidney transplantation for the federal government, President Lyndon Johnson's Bureau of the Budget formed yet another interdisciplinary committee, this one operating in secret and composed of physicians, economists, statisticians, theologians and ethicists. The position paper they produced is known as the Gottschalk Report, for its chairman, the influential nephrologist Carl Gottschalk. The report asserted that dialysis and transplantation were no longer experimental therapies but proven treatments, and moreover that the federal government should fund them.

The debate over who should pay for dialysis was part of a larger dispute about federally funded healthcare, which had a long and contentious history in America. Franklin Delano Roosevelt had expressly omitted healthcare coverage from his Social Security Act of 1935, part of his New Deal legislation to heal the ravages of the Great Depression, largely because the AMA had threatened to mobilize nationwide and block the entire law if Roosevelt included a national health insurance plan. After World War II, when countries around the world were instituting universal healthcare programs (Germany had led the way in 1883 under Chancellor Otto von Bismarck, ironically a staunch anti-socialist), Harry Truman formed the Committee on the Nation's Health to promote federal health coverage for all Americans. This too was blocked by special interests, including the AMA, which branded Truman's plan "pink-tinged" and "socialistic." (In his memoirs, Truman wrote that his failure to pass national health legislation was his greatest regret from his time as president.)

"Harry Truman was the first president to formulate and work hard to pass national health insurance," says Max Fine, a senior healthcare advisor to John F. Kennedy and Lyndon B. Johnson. "The AMA called Truman's initiatives an intolerable intrusion by the federal government on the doctor-patient relationship, which the AMA held sacrosanct. Little did the AMA foresee the real intrusion that was coming, by corporations."

When the Democrats under Kennedy began once more to push for a national healthcare plan, as an extension of Social Security, the AMA returned to the attack. This time the association enlisted Ronald Reagan, a B-list actor and former FBI informant against supposed communist sympathizers in Hollywood, who was beginning a new career in politics. Reagan recorded a florid diatribe against Medicare, which he called "a government invasion of public power," and "the most evil enemy mankind has known in his long climb from the swamp to the stars." Wilbur Mills, chair of the House Ways and Means Committee, likewise opposed Medicare and other federally sponsored healthcare plans, because he feared their costs would grow unmanageable.

Nevertheless, the combination of Kennedy's determined groundwork, the shock and sadness at his November 1963 assassination, and the canny political maneuvering of his successor Lyndon Johnson, ultimately led in 1965 to the creation of Medicare and Medicaid, as extensions of FDR's original Social Security legislation passed thirty years earlier. These Democratic healthcare initiatives were part of the momentum of Johnson's Great Society legislation, and the New Deal, programs aimed not only to improve US health, but also to reduce poverty, increase affordable housing, revitalize education and the arts, and, most radically, to break down systemic racism, through the landmark Civil Rights Act of 1964 and subsequent laws.

Modern healthcare reform and the civil rights movement were in fact interconnected. In March 1966, before addressing the Medical Committee for Human Rights about the inferior medical care received by African Americans, Martin Luther King, Jr., stated, "Of all the forms of inequality, injustice in health is the most shocking and the most inhuman because it often results in physical death. I see no alternative to direct action and creative nonviolence to raise the conscience of the nation." King spoke from personal experience as a Black man from the South. Here hospitals routinely refused to treat Blacks, causing many unnecessary deaths during medical emergencies, and condemning countless African Americans to low-grade, segregated care. Throughout the 1960s, Black and white physicians periodically picketed AMA headquarters to protest the association's tacit tolerance both of healthcare segregation and of racial discrimination in state and local medical organizations.

Recognizing the essential link between health and racial justice, and attempting to channel the energy of healthcare reform into the civil rights movement, the Johnson administration found innovative ways to enforce civil rights laws. Shortly after LBJ created Medicare in 1965, Max Fine, one of his top healthcare advisors, went to Mississippi to implement racial integration in the state's hospitals. Fine traveled with a small team of healthcare workers, one of several such teams funded by the Public Health Service. "The Public Health Service knew that the old-school AMA members wouldn't go along with it, they knew they needed new blood," Fine remembers today. His team included a Black MD and a white nurse, who later married. "Years later they used to joke, 'We were miscegenating all over Mississippi!'" Fine says.

Though the Civil Rights Act of 1964 had prohibited segregation in federally funded hospitals, nevertheless, many hospitals in the South continued to follow Jim Crow policies. "They had different ways of segregating, some blatant, others more subtle," Fine remembers. "There might be a flower pot in the middle of a ward, and it was understood that Blacks were to stay on one side, whites on the other. Blacks had to sit at one end of waiting rooms. We were visiting hospitals and telling them, 'If you don't integrate, you're not going to be able to participate in Medicare.' Which would mean they'd receive no federal dollars."

Fine and his colleagues traveled with an FBI escort. Not long before they went south, three civil rights activists had been abducted and murdered by the Ku Klux Klan and local law enforcers in Neshoba County, Mississippi. "Two or three times the FBI told us, 'Don't leave your hotel room,'" Fine remembers. Violence against Blacks and civil rights activists was part of the political transformation of the South, triggered by the passage of the Civil Rights Act of 1964 by a Democratic administration, which saw this longtime Democratic bastion swiftly become a stronghold of the Republicans—the party of Abraham Lincoln.

By November of 1971, when Shep Glazer dialyzed before the House Ways and Means Committee, the nation had reached a fleeting moment of bipartisan support for universal, single-payor healthcare for all Americans. Healthcare was a pivotal issue in the coming election of 1972. Calling the nation's skyrocketing medical expenditures a "massive crisis" that demanded "a new national health strategy," Richard Nixon put forward his National Health Insurance Partnership Act, which included a federal health plan for unemployed and low-income citizens, mandatory insurance for workers, and provisions for coverage of catastrophic illness. Democratic leader Edward Kennedy likewise demanded urgent healthcare reform, and proposed his own Health Security Plan, a federal insurance system that would supersede existing public and private health coverage, and provide free medical care for all citizens. The AMA, the insurance industry and the hospital lobby, three historic opponents of "socialized medicine," had, by late 1971, all come to support some version of a comprehensive national health program. Wilbur Mills himself had had a change of heart. Sensing that the passage of Medicare in some form was inevitable, Mills had chosen to take part in its creation, so he could have a hand in limiting its costs.

At this moment of national consensus in favor of comprehensive healthcare, Congress took up the issue of dialysis. Shep Glazer's bold gambit helped convince many lawmakers that funding dialysis for all Americans represented an important first step toward the creation of a universal healthcare system.

❑

In October of 1972, Richard Nixon signed Public Law 92-603, the first "Medicare for All" provision in US history, which instituted universal insurance coverage for nearly all American citizens with kidney failure. For patients without private insurance, costs of dialysis would be paid by a government program such as Medicare or Medicaid; while privately insured patients would retain their coverage for a period of time (currently set at thirty months), then transition to coverage under a government plan—a mandatory shift designed to shield health insurers from the heavy, open-ended financial burden of dialysis. The new law also obligated the government to pay some of the costs of transplants, including organ procurement, the operation itself, and one year of immunosuppressive drugs to help avoid the rejection of the new organ. Because few dialysis facilities existed at the time, and thousands of kidney failure victims were dying every year, Congress offered financial incentives to hospitals and individual nephrologists to build facilities and treat patients. It also gave dialysis units a helping hand, by allowing them to collect government reimbursements for medications at higher rates than they paid to pharmaceutical companies for those medications.

At the time, most observers in Congress and in America assumed that the passage of the dialysis amendment was paving the way for universal health coverage. The Democrats under Edward Kennedy continued to push their all-encompassing national health plan. Nixon, announcing before Congress in February 1974 that "comprehensive health insurance is an idea whose time has come in America," proposed a health insurance plan that was even more generous and equitable than his previous proposal of 1971, this time mandating both private and government-secured insurance coverage for the entire population. The United States seemed about to join the long list of developed countries that were making government-sponsored healthcare the birthright of all citizens.

But dramatic events derailed the movement. Already distracted by the war in Vietnam, Richard Nixon was consumed by the conflagration of Watergate, and resigned the presidency in August 1974. The OPEC oil embargo in October 1973 had dealt a sledgehammer blow to the US economy, opening a season of inflation and economic stagnation so extreme that it received a new name, "stagflation." National attention turned increasingly from providing medical care for all Americans to containing the growing costs of government programs, healthcare in particular. "Nixon had proposed the best plan for national health that Republicans have ever formulated," says Max Fine sadly. "Watergate and the oil embargo took that away from us."

Amid oil shocks, stagflation and the unending global confrontation with Communist forces, the optimism and altruism of the New Deal and the Great Society faded. Instead of the expansive social welfare programs and strong federal regulation of the economy that, since the Great Depression, had been championed by many in Congress and the White House, lawmakers and the general public alike increasingly supported a neoliberal agenda, aimed at removing government regulation from many areas of the economy, and allowing free markets and private enterprise to shape society. In healthcare as in other industries, neoliberal pundits maintained, this approach would yield optimal services at optimally low prices.

The passage of "Dialysis for All" in 1972 injected a stream of tax dollars into dialysis that has grown ever since. In fact, Congress approved the plan without fully understanding what it would cost. Initial estimates worked out by the National Kidney Foundation put the price tag of dialyzing America's renal failure patients at $75 million for the first full year of treatments. Two years later, however, the annual government bill for dialysis had already reached $250 million, and by 1980 it exceeded $1 billion, while the patient population grew from 10,000 in 1972 to almost 60,000 in 1980. In a political and social environment dominated by the economic recession, these ballooning costs were a constant source of criticism and concern. Throughout the 1970s, in a series of often heated congressional hearings, members of the dialysis community argued about the best ways to perform and pay for treatment, and how Congress should ensure their implementation. Two schools of thought emerged, led by the Seattle and Boston nephrologists, which reflected profoundly different philosophies of medicine and social responsibility.

Belding Scribner, Christopher Blagg and other Seattle nephrologists made their case for long, low-speed dialysis, preferably at home, as being cheaper, healthier, and sure to save many lives at a time when few clinics existed. They identified transplants as the ultimate goal for most renal failure patients, and insisted that dialysis should be provided strictly on a nonprofit basis, for medical and ethical reasons alike.

The Boston nephrologists, by contrast, urged Congress to espouse for-profit dialysis, which also happened to be the business model of their thriving new firm, National Medical Care. In their congressional testimony and in the press, Constantine Hampers, Edmund Lowrie and Eugene Schupak used several arguments to promote in-center dialysis. First, they stated that the spread of self-funding dialysis clinics would quickly make treatment more widely available, thus saving countless lives. Second, they maintained that in-center treatment was a better option for most patients, because few patients were capable of dialyzing at home. Finally, in the spirit of American entrepreneurialism, they declared that for-profit dialysis would produce better care at lower cost.

Congress's original conception of dialysis in 1972 was a hybrid of the Seattle and Boston models. Early legislation stressed the importance of rehabilitating patients and allowing them to return to work, so they would become productive citizens and taxpayers once more. Many lawmakers thus favored home dialysis as more compatible with holding down a job, and, pragmatically, because home treatment provided nearly every patient with his or her own dialysis unit. Transplantation remained Congress's ultimate stated aim for end-stage renal disease (ESRD) patients who could tolerate the operation.

Yet the 1972 law, paradoxically, had created financial disincentives to home dialysis and transplantation. Home dialysis patients faced delays in starting treatment, and were saddled with substantial co-pays for equipment and supplies, while nephrologists received very low reimbursements for treating patients at home. Kidney transplant patients lost their Medicare coverage one year after their operation (coverage was later extended to three years), and Medicare only paid for one year's worth of the expensive immunosuppressive drugs they needed take for the rest of their lives—at least until their donated organ failed, which could happen at any time. And no provision was made to cover the many incidental expenses involved in transplantation, including travel to and lodging at a transplant center, and loss of income while recovering from the operation. These economic barriers, together with an organ procurement system in the United States that since its inception has consistently supplied far fewer viable organs than Americans need—in 2022, twelve people died every day waiting for a new kidney—caused transplantation in the United States to languish.

The original ESRD legislation of 1972, inadvertently or by calculation, tilted the playing field in favor of in-center dialysis. The NMC nephrologists, who maintained a permanent staff of lobbyists and lawyers in Washington, DC, strove to perpetuate the tilt. When Congress considered removing financial disincentives to home dialysis, and even mandating dialysis at home wherever possible, NMC hired John Sears—Nixon's former political advisor and Ronald Reagan's campaign manager during his landslide election victory in 1980—and launched an all-out assault on the bill. Testifying under oath before Congress, Edmund Lowrie actually accused the Seattle nephrologists of lying about the benefits of home dialysis, and of endangering their patients' lives by insisting on this form of treatment. "Our analysis indicates that the cost of self-care dialysis is not significantly less than limited care dialysis," Lowrie stated, "and that the indiscriminate use of home dialysis may lead to unacceptable patient mortality." Lobbyists also urged lawmakers not to mandate home dialysis or any other specific form of treatment; Congress, they opined, should never dictate the practice of medicine to doctors, who must be free to prescribe the best individualized care for each of their patients.

Scribner, Blagg and other experts pointed out that Lowrie's data

were misleading: the cost figures he had cited were inflated, and his purported mortality rates for home dialysis patients also included deaths
among in-center patients and among patients with other chronic disease besides renal failure, all of which should have been excluded. They
also observed that if lawmakers knowingly left the existing disincentives to home dialysis in place, they would, de facto, be dictating the
practice of medicine.

But the damage to the Seattle cause was done. Congress issued a
tepid, nonbinding statement in favor of dialyzing at home. (One Social
Security official summed up the fate of the home dialysis law succinctly:
"The lobbyists gutted the hell out of it.") Though costs to Medicare and
Medicaid continued to soar, NMC had convinced Congress to maintain high reimbursement rates for in-center dialysis, while leaving in
place the financial disincentives for home dialysis and transplantation.

"I raise the question as to why the only physicians testifying that
the cost of home dialysis is almost as high as that of in-center dialysis
and that home dialysis has an inferior survival rate have been representatives of National Medical Care," Chris Blagg told the Senate Finance
Committee's Subcommittee on Health, "the largest company owning
outpatient dialysis units in the United States."

Belding Scribner was disconsolate. "As the years have passed, I have
become deeply troubled about what has happened to my 'brainchild,' "
he testified in 1977. "What started out in 1960 as a noble experiment
gradually has degenerated into a highly controversial billion-dollar program riddled with cost overruns and enormous profiteering.... In addition, the present regulations have encouraged the rapid expansion of a
very profitable business, selling in-center dialysis to the Government."

In the end, Congress and the nation forsook Seattle, and embraced
the Boston model, in dialysis and in healthcare overall. Today, although
numerous studies have since reaffirmed the positions of Scribner and
his colleagues, the dominant form of dialysis in America remains in-
center and for-profit. Not coincidentally, the United States has only 1.9
percent of patients on home hemodialysis, the lowest patient survival
rate among major industrial nations, and an annual expenditure on
dialysis, from Medicare alone, of almost $38 billion.

· 6 ·

The Roll-Up

In April of 1983, Alonzo Plough, a freshly minted PhD in anthropology from Cornell University, entered an office with commanding views over Boston Harbor, high in the John Hancock Tower, a mirror-sided I. M. Pei skyscraper. Plough had been summoned to a meeting with Edmund Lowrie, a senior vice president at National Medical Care (NMC). "In retrospect, I realize the meeting was an attempt to steer me away and intimidate me," he says today, "around the impact that my research was going to have on their business, and the impact that they could have on my career."

Plough had done extensive fieldwork in a dialysis unit in inner-city New Haven, Connecticut, where he examined the ethical and psychological implications of this fast-evolving new therapy. He was now writing an explosive article about the dialysis industry for the prestigious *New England Journal of Medicine* (NEJM), which would allege that for-profit dialysis centers like those run by NMC were "cream skimming"—homing in on healthier and more profitable patients, while avoiding the treatment of sicker, lower-profit cases, who would end up in nonprofit hospitals. (Healthier patients are typically more profitable because they require less additional, unpaid care and assistance, and because they live longer, which typically produces a longer revenue stream.) But his study hadn't been published yet, and only a handful of researchers knew of its existence. What, Plough wondered, could Edmund Lowrie and NMC want with him?

Lowrie was a leading nephrologist and research scientist, whose work had helped to set the standards of care in the emerging practice of dialysis. He was lead author of the report, published in the NEJM in 1981, on the National Cooperative Dialysis Study (NCDS), the first randomized control trial of the dialysis "dose," which attempted to establish targets for good dialysis. The NCDS identified Kt/V_{urea} as the definitive measure of dialysis quality, and so it remains today. Kt/V is based on the assumption that urea, which is abundant in the blood and easily measured, accurately models the behavior of other bloodstream toxins during dialysis, and that it is one of the more harmful of those toxins. Because urea is water-soluble and is dialyzed away relatively swiftly, the NCDS concluded that length of treatment was not a significant factor in determining patient outcomes.

This identification of Kt/V as a yardstick for dialysis quality was a valuable step in the early days of dialysis, when physicians were still mastering the elementary physiology of renal failure, and groping for ways to evaluate their success in treating it. But subsequent research over several decades has revealed that Kt/V is actually a poor measure of comprehensive dialysis quality. Fixation with this factor is part of a pattern of treatment that can shorten lives.

In reality, the toxicity of urea is minimal at concentrations normally encountered in the blood of dialysis patients. Numerous other small solutes—phosphate, parathyroid hormone, β_2-microglobulin, phenols, indoles, p-cresol, and many more besides—are at least as injurious as urea. Nor does urea provide an accurate model for these other molecules: some are protein-bound and not water-soluble, and do not move or behave like urea. Still other, middle-molecule solutes, including cytokines, adipokines, and growth factors, behave differently from urea because of their greater molecular mass. Crucially, a single-minded focus on Kt/V also leads many caregivers to ignore the extreme importance of fluid balance: the ebbs and flows of our inner sea, whose tides a healthy kidney so deftly controls. Downplaying all of these other factors, each more important for a patient's health than urea clearance, routinely leads to heart failure, organ stunning (damage to the heart, brain and other organs due to oxygen deprivation) and dialysis sessions plagued by cramps, nausea, headaches and other debilitating symptoms, created less by renal failure itself than by the way it is treated.

The thing about Kt/V is, it's convenient: a single target for a complex treatment, easy to work out with a hand-held calculator. A fixation with urea clearance also meshes well with the short treatment times and high ultrafiltration rate (UFR) favored by large for-profit corporations. "Since nephrologists got themselves mired in solute clearance back in the 1970s, by the seductive bit of maths that is Kt/V_{urea}, all that has mattered in the US since then has been the removal of small solutes, like urea, in truth the least significant solute of all," says Australian nephrologist John Agar. "The faster and more brutal the dialysis, the quicker these can be removed. But who cares? Solutes are not, and have never been, the main game. But time is money, and shorter treatment time means greater profits. And Kt/V provided such a convenient stop point! If you are an unthinking doc who has been brainwashed to think 'small solutes,' then all you have to do is ramp up the machine, rip off urea, ignore the other (more important) stuff, and when you reach your target Kt/V of 1.3, turn off the machine. Next you turf the treatment-sickened patient out—no matter you have nearly killed him/her in the process—he/she will hopefully recover in time for the next bazooka treatment in two to three days—and roll in the next victim. Kt/V is the corporate golden goose."

In 1983, when Alonzo Plough met Edmund Lowrie, a decade after Congress had begun pouring Medicare dollars into dialysis, corporate nephrology had become a mammoth money-spinner—a "self-proliferating giant," as one NEJM editorialist called the field. The population of patients on dialysis had grown 800 percent, and free-standing, for-profit dialysis units, whose numbers were increasing at 13 percent a year, were swiftly replacing hospital-based, nonprofit dialysis facilities. Treatment methods had also shifted dramatically. Despite the recognized advantages of home dialysis, the percentage of patients dialyzing at home had shrunk from 40 percent when the Medicare End-Stage Renal Disease (ESRD) Program started, to 10 percent a decade later. Most patients now dialyzed in for-profit clinics, because that was what was available near their homes.

At the same time, the cost of dialysis to the federal government had skyrocketed. By 1983, ESRD Program costs had reached $1.9 billion a year, and they have continued to rise ever since. In 2019, dialysis patients represented only 1 percent of the Medicare fee-for-service population, but dialyzing them consumed 7.2 percent of the entire Medicare budget.

Riding the wave of this growth, NMC had become the nation's leading dialysis firm. It had integrated vertically, opening subsidiaries that manufactured dialysate, performed lab tests, and did vascular surgery, as well as diversifying into unrelated medical fields including psychiatric clinics and respiratory centers. NMC succeeded by applying the methods and metrics of financial management, including tireless cost minimization, to the practice of medicine. "National Medical Care is the largest, and most efficient single provider of artificial kidney services in the country...through the applications of sensible, carefully controlled business procedures," a 1976 NMC annual report announced complacently. "We have achieved this through techniques such as standardization of supplies, volume buying, better personnel utilization, etc, procedures well-known to industry but heretofore rarely used in health care." For a profession whose governing body, the AMA, had long forbidden doctors to practice medicine as a "commodity in trade," these were strange new words.

But these were indeed strange new times for medicine. Ronald Reagan entered the White House in 1981 with a vigorous new economic agenda, and began rolling back regulations, outsourcing government activities and privatizing federal programs. ("Government is not the solution to our problems," Reagan announced in his inaugural address, "government is the problem.") Reaganomics was imbued with the philosophy of University of Chicago economist Milton Friedman,

Reagan's economic advisor, who characterized the years between 1945 and 1980 as a period of "galloping socialism" in America. To heal the economy after this aberrant period, Friedman favored free markets, which he said provided the optimal, ideology-free means of organizing human relations more efficiently and fairly. And the lifeblood of markets was money: financial incentives were crucial drivers of human behavior, as well as the corporation's raison d'être. Friedman famously declared that the corporation's only social responsibility was to increase its profits. He also branded national healthcare based on Medicare and Medicaid "a socialist-communist system."

NMC and its managers enthusiastically espoused the Friedman ideology. To increase their profits and grow their business, the firm's executives learned to flex their scientific and political muscle. NMC cultivated strong ties with prominent Republicans in Washington, DC. Still more consequentially, at the local level, wherever NMC opened a new clinic, the firm's distinguished Harvard MDs made the most of their academic pedigrees, forging close, lucrative alliances with leading doctors, researchers and policy makers. This was "a virtual prescription for gaining political power in the medical community," said one observer at the time. "Once NMC comes into an area it is difficult for local doctors to oppose it, for it is backed by the most influential nephrologists in town." NMC's clout in dialysis research was likewise considerable. Edmund Lowrie, the company's senior vice president, had led the team that published the National Cooperative Dialysis Study, which established industry benchmarks for quality dialysis.

In an influential NEJM editorial from October 1980, Arnold Relman, a leading Boston nephrologist and editor of the journal, singled out NMC as a prime example of what he called "the new medical-industrial complex," a burgeoning network of for-profit healthcare concerns that also comprised private hospitals, nursing homes and testing laboratories, which had proliferated since the creation of federally funded health insurance. The profit motive in these fast-growing new businesses, Relman said, created serious risks of overuse of medical services, excessive reliance on technology, and cherry-picking of healthier, higher-margin patients. For-profit medicine also generated severe new conflicts of interest for doctors, which could easily warp their medical ethics.

Relman criticized Wall Street for accentuating these problems. Borrowing once more from Eisenhower's noted speech, Relman warned of the "unwarranted influence" that large financial investors were exerting on Congress's healthcare policies. "If we are to live comfortably with the new medical-industrial complex we must put our priorities in order: the needs of patients and of society come first," Relman concluded. "We should not allow the medical-industrial complex to distort our health-care system to its own entrepreneurial ends. It should not market useless, marginal, or unduly expensive services, nor should it encourage unnecessary use of services. How best to ensure that the medical-industrial complex serves the interests of patients first and of its stockholders second will have to be the responsibility of the medical profession and an informed public."

In response, Lowrie and Hampers, also writing for the NEJM, penned a full-throated manifesto for free-market, for-profit medicine, which, they contended, would optimize care and costs not just in dialysis, but in all areas of American health. Lowrie and Hampers flatly denied that for-profit medicine invited harmful conflicts of interest. On the contrary, they argued, the profit motive actually benefited medicine: doctors who managed and invested in their own facilities could effectively control costs and increase productivity, and even enjoyed a more ethically transparent relationship with their patients. By contrast, Lowrie and Hampers condemned nonprofit medicine as both inefficient and clouded by harmful incentives. They rejected out of hand the practice by national health systems around the world of putting doctors on a fixed salary, irrespective of the number of patients they treated, to encourage them to attend to medicine rather than money. Such a system, in their view, merely induced doctors to avoid work and maximize their leisure time. Similarly, Lowrie and Hampers condemned nonprofit hospitals, which are tax exempt, as wasteful, oversubsidized burdens on taxpayers. For-profit medicine with cash incentives, they maintained, was the only approach that reliably ensured that doctors did their job efficiently and well.

At NMC, Lowrie and Hampers practiced what they preached. Nephrologists who were named directors of NMC facilities also became investors in those facilities, and received a share of the profits, determined in part by their skill at cost management: the lower they held the operating costs of their units, the higher their personal gain. (The legality of offering physicians a share in the earnings of their own facilities was called into question in 1993, with the passage of the so-called Stark II law against financial conflicts of interest in medicine, though subsequent criminal and civil proceedings against NMC suggest that the company may have continued the practice after Stark II.) Constantine Hampers himself became a 1980s financial swashbuckler in the Michael Milken mold, waging savage boardroom battles, selling a majority stake of NMC shares to chemicals giant W. R. Grace (later to become infamous, and then insolvent, for allegedly poisoning local communities with carcinogenic waste), and then attempting, in vain, to regain control of the firm in a hostile takeover. Hampers, Lowrie and NMC's other executives were top practitioners and theoreticians of investor-owned medicine, and their arguments carried great weight in the press and in Washington, DC. They were highly visible exemplars of a thriving new species: the doctor-entrepreneur.

This, then, was the temple of for-profit, free-market, Wall Street–fueled medicine that young Alonzo Plough entered on that day in April 1983. Edmund Lowrie offered him coffee, then came straight to the point. As Plough remembers their conversation, Lowrie said he knew about Plough's forthcoming article in the NEJM, because he had obtained an early manuscript (he didn't explain how). Lowrie challenged the statistics behind Plough's piece, and questioned its thesis: that for-profit dialysis facilities, most of which were run by NMC, were cherry-picking high-margin patients. Lowrie also observed, says Plough, that publishing this article in a prestigious journal could harm NMC financially.

For years now, in fact, the firm's directors and lobbyists had been fighting a running battle against a congressional plan to reduce the reimbursements that Medicare paid to outpatient dialysis centers. Though NMC refused to disclose cost reports from its facilities to the government, claiming they contained competitive information, the company nevertheless avowed that Medicare's per-treatment rate, then set at $138, was the bare minimum reimbursement required to turn a fair profit from providing dialysis. To strengthen its bargaining position, though in evident tension with the Hippocratic Oath, the company threatened to close certain clinics if Medicare cut reimbursement rates. Lowrie told Plough that his forthcoming NEJM article, which suggested that NMC facilities were gaming the government payment system, might encourage healthcare policy makers to reduce reimbursements, thereby cutting NMC profits.

"I was sitting there listening, and was just flabbergasted by all this," Plough remembers. "By the fact that Lowrie had somehow obtained an early manuscript of my as yet unpublished paper. By the bluntness of the arguments he used to defend his profits. But most of all I was stunned by his hubris. Here was the Harvard Medical Complex in full panoply. 'We are doing good, and we're doing it in volume,' Lowrie seemed to be saying. 'How *dare* you confront us with doing something wrong, when we are the apex of medical science?' "

Plough had experienced medical hubris in dialysis before, on the blood floor of an inner-city dialysis center in New Haven. He had spent several months embedded in the clinic, observing with the eyes of an anthropologist and an epidemiologist the evolving psychological dynamics of this new area of medicine. Plough recognized that the life-threatening nature of kidney failure, and the techno-centric character of dialysis, placed new strains on the relationship between patients and their caregivers. "I saw how the central role of the machine in treating kidney failure tended to dehumanize care, and make doctors define success as patient survival, without really taking into account their well-being. And dialysis was one of the first technologically driven, transactional, 'assembly line' kinds of procedures. Where you could run people through, and the per-unit costs are not that great, so it was set up to be exploited, if that's what you wanted to do. And that was precisely the NMC approach."

He also observed how dialysis revealed, and amplified, certain authoritarian tendencies in American medicine. Despite the acknowledged principle in the treatment of chronic conditions that a patient's self-reliance and sense of control over her treatment is essential to her well-being, both physical and psychic, Plough saw time and again how dialysis patients who suggested improvements or reported medical errors in their care were punished by their caregivers. Such criticism by patients was perceived as a challenge to the authority and the prestige of the nephrologists, nurses and other staff who treated them. "It's characteristic of a chronic disease, particularly a relatively well-managed chronic disease, that the patient knows the subtleties and what's going on quite well, often better than the provider," Plough says. "And in the more advanced forms of empowered medical practice, like a shared care model, that precept is accepted. But what I saw in that New Haven clinic, and what often is the default in American healthcare, was this sense of confrontation, of challenge to the patient: 'Who's in charge here? *We're* in charge.'"

Plough remembers one patient in particular, whom he identifies as Mr. O, a supervisor at an engineering firm, who researched his treatment extensively and developed a considerable understanding of how dialysis affected his body. After the clinic began buying dialysate from a new supplier, Mr. O felt weak, dizzy and nauseous during each session, and blamed the new solution. The facility staff rejected his assertions as absurd, and continued using the same dialysate, though to silence Mr. O's complaints—as staff members admitted to Plough—they changed the label on the dialysate containers. His symptoms continued nonetheless, only to disappear abruptly eighteen months later, when the clinic finally changed the solution.

"Ninety percent of the people would not listen to me, or they would try to make me [feel] like I was stupid and didn't know what I was talking about," Mr. O told Plough. During one dialysis treatment, he begged his caregiver to keep the pressure (apparently either the blood pump speed or the UFR) low, because high-pressure treatments made him sick— which is medically correct for many patients. Instead, "she looked at me and ... put the pressure right up to the maximum. This made me real, real sick for about six weeks, this one treatment." Mr. O made several other objections that evinced a sound grasp of nephrology and his own physiology. Nevertheless, Plough says, the staff categorized him as a "difficult personality," and suggested referring him to a psychiatrist.

"Patients who spoke out about their care were typologized as 'acting out,' as 'trouble-makers,' even as mentally ill," Plough says. "And this ultimately harmed their survivability." He saw several patients refused treatment at the facility, after verbal clashes with clinic staff. "Caregivers seemed to think that if patients didn't 'behave themselves,' they could legitimately be denied care."

Plough also noted that the unique status of dialysis as a universal entitlement, paid for by tax dollars, created among some clinic workers "a series of implied judgments. That dialysis was a form of public charity. That the patients had brought this condition upon themselves through bad lifestyle or diet. That perhaps they didn't deserve treatment in the first place."

A short time after his meeting at NMC headquarters, Plough received a follow-up letter from Edmund Lowrie—written, Lowrie said, on advice of his attorney—which reprised concerns about Plough's "distorted" results, and predicted "irreparable harm" to NMC if they were published. "Please be advised that we intend to submit your study for detailed statistical consultation, evaluation and review and will seek the appropriate remedies if our perceptions are confirmed." In a subsequent phone call, Lowrie advised Plough to retain a lawyer. Lowrie also wrote a series of letters to the Health Care Financing Administration (HCFA), the predecessor of the Centers for Medicare & Medicaid Services (CMS), which had funded Plough's work, and to the editors of the NEJM. Plough says these letters were an attempt to discredit his research.

Plough did publish his paper on dialysis cherry-picking, in the May 31, 1984, issue of the NEJM. But pressure from NMC, he observes, "resulted in an overly cautious (even deferential) tone in the editing of the final manuscript." The continued and expanded funding that HCFA had promised Plough for further dialysis research abruptly disappeared.

Plough later wrote a fascinating analysis of the politics of dialysis, *Borrowed Time*, and went on to play leading roles in health systems in Boston, Seattle and Los Angeles. He is currently the chief science officer at the Robert Wood Johnson Foundation, the nation's largest healthcare philanthropy. "They didn't stop my work—they didn't quench my spark," he laughs, without much humor. "But they did block my grant."

❑

AFTER THE creation of Medicare and Medicaid in 1965 and of other government insurance programs in later years, Wall Street began to target healthcare as a unique investment opportunity: an industry that was backstopped by the federal government, growing in value as advanced medical technologies led to higher treatment costs, and virtually immune to economic downturn, since in bull and bear markets alike, people get sick. Financial investors poured capital into many areas of healthcare, enabling growth-minded firms to expand rapidly, both by new building, and by acquiring smaller competitors in a process of industry consolidation known by financiers as a "roll-up." The rising share prices of big healthcare firms fueled this expansion, by creating an ever-expanding war chest from which the firms could pay for further acquisitions. Growth meant more revenues, which in turn drove still higher share prices—here, in many areas of healthcare, was the "self-proliferating giant" that the NEJM editorialist saw in the nephrology business.

Wall Street funding was a boon to many companies, but also a devil's bargain: bankers and other investors demanded high, consistent returns, creating intense pressure on firms to increase their earnings and share price every single quarter. For healthcare companies, this emphasis on financial metrics often distracts from, or actually impedes, the work of healing.

But healers were less and less in charge. Giant hospital chains like the Hospital Corporation of America (HCA), National Medical Enterprises (NME), Humana, Columbia and HealthSouth gobbled up hundreds of local medical structures, consolidating small, independent entities into larger for-profit chains that were run by the same financial rules which NMC executives had described. The original heads of these local entities often received large payouts, which helped convince them to allow the public goods they administered, built with the tax dollars and elbow grease of generations of city elders, to pass into private hands. Day-to-day management of these hospitals was removed from the doctors who once ran them and the local municipalities and charities who'd built and owned them, and was placed in the hands of financial managers: at the helm were venture capitalists and marketing gurus like Jack Massey, creator of the Kentucky Fried Chicken franchise and cofounder of HCA. Massey and his peers applied a fast food business model to medicine, which aimed to provide medical treatment in quick, cheap, standardized bursts, much as fast food chains served up tacos and burgers.

As the twin processes of privatization and consolidation continued, the economics and ethics of healthcare changed. The AMA excised that part of its code of conduct which forbade for-profit medicine, and old-school medical ethics swiftly yielded before a new conception of the doctor as manager, marketer and entrepreneur. Even conspicuously charitable institutions began to think more like financiers. Sister Irene Kraus, member of the Daughters of Charity of St. Vincent de Paul, a Catholic religious order, earned an MBA, and ran a $6 billion not-for-profit hospital organization with an iron hand on costs, in keeping with her maxim, "No margin, no mission."

Today, many Americans—and many American MDs—no longer consider medicine a higher calling, merely the job of providing medical services in a free market: healthcare as commodity. Many of us accept without qualm the objectively odd notion that a healthcare firm's success can be measured primarily by such metrics as market share, stock price and profitability, rather than by the well-being of its patients.

As the for-profit movement accelerated, other private healthcare industries emerged, including plastic surgery, pain management, rehabilitation, emergency medicine, ophthalmology, eldercare and hospice. These facilities were often sited not in hospitals, where medicine had traditionally been practiced, but in strip malls and industrial parks. Here real estate and operating costs were lower than in hospitals, healthcare regulations were less intrusive, and legal loopholes in medical conflict of interest laws enabled doctors to refer patients to themselves for further treatment, prescribe in-house procedures and diagnostic tests, and sell products made by their own organizations. Fast food medicine spread to malls and office parks across America.

❑

DIALYSIS CLINICS became a visible new presence in strip malls. After the 1972 law made dialysis a federal entitlement, the surge of Medicare dollars caused a proliferation of local and regional providers. Some, like the nonprofit clinic in Portland, Oregon, where Arlene Mullin got her start treating dialysis patients, provided excellent care. Betty Smith, a registered nurse who later became a dialysis executive and a leader at the ESRD Networks, the group of regional, not-for-profit contractors that regulate the industry on behalf of CMS, was the head nurse at a publicly funded safety-net hospital in northern California, which had an in-patient acute dialysis center, two chronic dialysis units, and a self-care unit where patients were trained to perform their own treatments. (She prefers not to be identified, so I'm using a pseudonym.) "Self-care was big back then," says Smith. "Patients could come in, do their own assessments, set up their dialysis machines, pretty much run their dialysis, and we were there to just support them. Which is a wonderful, *wonderful* way of allowing and encouraging people to take charge of their own care, that are not in a position to be able to do it at home."

Other mom and pop dialysis shops provided dreadful care. Veteran nephrologists tell horror stories from these frontier days of the industry, of nephrologists treating patients in improvised trailer-home dialysis clinics, and of units infamous for refusing to place their patients on transplant waitlists (because transplantations would have reduced their customer base). "There were plenty of bottom feeders formed mainly to gobble up government funds, and these were genuinely dangerous to patients," says Brent Miller, a respected academic nephrologist at Indiana University. Steven Bander encountered some of these "bottom feeders" when he toured the Deep South as chief medical officer at Gambro, the Swedish company born of Nils Alwall's wartime innovations that was an industry leader in American through the

1990s. Bander was charged with inspecting units that his company had recently acquired, and often was unimpressed. "Going through the facilities in backwaters of Mississippi, Alabama, Georgia and Florida, I couldn't tell you the number of problems I found in the water delivery systems, bicarbonate holding tanks that had biofilm problems, bacterial growths leading to serious endotoxin reactions."

A few large dialysis companies also emerged to compete with NMC, the market leader. These included the Swedish firm Gambro; the German medical supplies and devices giant Fresenius, which also manufactured dialysis machines; Total Renal Care, which had spun off from the scandal-torn hospital group National Medical Enterprises; and the California-based Vivra, headed by a young private equity whiz named Kent Thiry. These firms all applied some version of the business model introduced by NMC, centered on rigorous cost-control and centralized, top-down management. They also mimicked NMC's technique of securing the support of influential members of local medical and academic communities, by forming lucrative joint ventures with university medical centers, and paying substantial directorship and consulting fees to nephrology luminaries and senior academics. "These distinguished academic nephrologists felt entitled to massive payments," Steven Bander remembers. "We were paying them hundreds of thousands of dollars each to be 'regional directors' over dialysis centers where they never set foot, and merely funneled their patient referrals into the company. I couldn't believe their hubris." Brent Miller agrees. "Dialysis centers have historically been huge revenue generators for many American universities," he says, "but not much money seems to go back to the care of patients—it doesn't get reinvested in the clinical programs. Too often, it becomes a de facto expense fund which the nephrology division chiefs use at their discretion."

The mid-1990s saw successive waves of consolidation, as larger dialysis firms bought out smaller players, and then began to acquire one another. Fresenius purchased the storied NMC in 1996, after NMC was prosecuted for a kickback scheme and multiple frauds, for which Fresenius, as its new owner, paid civil and criminal fines of nearly half a billion dollars, at that time the largest healthcare fraud settlement in American history. In 1997, Gambro bought Kent Thiry's old firm, Vivra, which had also faltered after falling afoul of the law. "When we took over Vivra, it was like a pig in a poke," says Steven Bander. "It seemed profitable and robust, but in reality the profits were being made on fraudulent billings. The water systems were terrible, poorly maintained and antiquated in design. Many of the physical plants were not in good condition. And the clinical outcomes were not being reported correctly." In 2004, however, Thiry got his revenge, when as the new CEO of Total Renal Care, which he'd renamed "DaVita," he announced the acquisition of the US dialysis operations of Gambro, which had suffered poor financial performance and crushing fraud charges of its own. Fresenius's takeover of the Renal Care Group in 2006 and of Liberty Dialysis in 2012 completed the intense phase of the dialysis roll-up, and produced the highly consolidated market we see today.

Many acquisitions made during the roll-up took place well below the radar of federal antitrust authorities, through a process that economist Thomas G. Wollmann has termed "stealth consolidation." Between 1996 and 2017, dialysis companies attempted 4,000 acquisitions, half of which were never reported to antitrust watchdogs because their dollar amounts were below the threshold for mandatory disclosure to the Federal Trade Commission (FTC). Wollmann argues that, had these deals been reviewed by regulators, most would have been blocked on monopoly grounds: given the highly regional nature of dialysis, where patients require a facility near their home, many such acquisitions produced de facto monopolies in local markets.

The ultimate outcome of this extended period of consolidation is the current dialysis duopoly of Fresenius and DaVita. Of the 6,900 clinics scattered around the 3,100 counties in America, about 80 percent are run by these two companies, which collect about 80 percent of the industry's total net revenues. What happens to patients and caregivers when Big Dialysis takes over a small, independent facility often suggests a swift change in priorities, from patients to profits.

❏

IN JUNE of 2000, with the roll-up of the dialysis industry well under way, Chuck Grassley's Senate Subcommittee on Aging held a hearing entitled "Kidney Dialysis Patients: A Population at Undue Risk?" A driving force behind this hearing was Arlene Mullin, who had quit her dialysis job and blown the whistle on what she considered systemic patient harm in her Oregon clinic two years earlier, and had been advocating for patients ever since. Among the witnesses who testified were two patients she had represented, Kenneth Bays and Brent Smith, who had also become her friends. (The mobile home in southern Georgia where Mullin was living when I met her belonged to Kenneth Bays's widow, Jamie.)

Bays and Smith both confirmed that dialysis patients certainly *were* at undue risk. In fact, they said, the mere fact of testifying about the industry's endemic corruption might put them in harm's way when they returned to their clinics. Many other patients had been afraid to appear at the hearing.

Senator Grassley seemed upset by this news. Why, he asked, would patients be hesitant to testify? What could their caregivers do to them?

"You are on the verge, the end, you realize that if you miss two or three dialysis treatments, you are going to die," explained Bays, a retired dentist. "You do not want to make them mad, because they have this needle as big as a 10-penny nail. They can make you behave."

Bays stopped, and looked uncertainly at Grassley. "I do not know if this makes sense to you or not," he added. "Until you are in this position, you really cannot understand."

Brent Smith described what he called the "intimidation factor." Most patients, he testified, "are so afraid of what the technicians are going to do to them that they just do not say anything." He had been harassed and retaliated against numerous times, he said, for reporting unsafe medical practices in his unit.

Smith described the dramatic change that had taken place in the industry between the late 1970s, when he first dialyzed, and 1990, when his transplant failed and he had to resume treatment after a decade away from dialysis. In the 1970s and 1980s, he said, all caregivers on the blood floor were registered nurses and other healthcare workers with advanced medical training. The consolidation of the industry into a few for-profit chains had changed all that. "Today I see technicians with only a high school diploma," Smith said. "In Arizona a manicurist is subject to more licensing than a dialysis technician is. When I first returned to dialysis, I had technicians handle my blood and my life who were convicted criminals, strippers and refrigerator technicians." The ratio of patients to techs had also risen dramatically, leading to serious treatment errors. "This is not safe and it does not work," Smith concluded.

Kenneth Bays said he shared Smith's sense of helplessness within the US dialysis system. "I was appalled to find that dialysis patients have no right of self-determination," he said. "Never before had I been in a position where treatment options were not offered, much less explained." He stated that, because nephrologists enjoyed certain exemptions from the Stark laws against self-referral and other financial conflicts of interest, dialysis companies routinely sold patients to each other, as if they were livestock. "I was just another money cow with a market value of $100,000." He also compared dialysis patients to concentration camp victims. "They are very easy to control," he said. "Their main thrust is on keeping alive."

Bays paused once more, clearly still concerned that his words weren't getting through to the senators at the bench. "I know this sounds strange to you that this would happen in this country," he told them, almost wistfully.

More witnesses added their damning views. The deputy inspector general of Health and Human Services, and the public health director at the General Accounting Office (which became the Government Accountability Office in 2004), both reported the results of the progressive deregulation and defunding of oversight bodies that had occurred in the dialysis industry over the previous several years. They cited recent investigations which revealed that the percentage of clinics inspected each year had dropped from 52 percent of all clinics in the year 1993 to only 11 percent in 1999, while the incidence of serious violations detected during these inspections had more than doubled over the same period. Even when violators were caught and ordered to correct their deficiencies, investigators often returned to the same facilities months later to find that patients were still in harm's way. The current level of regulation and enforcement, the public health director observed laconically, "does not provide strong incentives for dialysis facilities to stay in compliance with Medicare standards."

Senator Ron Wyden of Oregon said that the proliferation of for-profit chains and the growing demand for dialysis had produced "a recipe for disaster" in his home state. A recent investigation, he said, had revealed serious, sometimes life-threatening problems in a quarter of Oregon dialysis units. Senator Pete Stark, author of the landmark conflict of interest laws, was even blunter. "Poor centers are killing people, Mr. Chairman," he told Grassley in a written statement. Stark concluded his testimony with a letter he had written to the head of HCFA (the federal agency that administered Medicare, now called "CMS"), Nancy-Ann DeParle, demanding better regulation of dialysis clinics. "People are dying needlessly," he told DeParle. "What do we do about this?"

Stark also criticized some members of the ESRD Networks, the chain of nonprofit regulators, for failing to do their job. Jay Wish, a distinguished academic nephrologist and president of the umbrella organization that oversaw the ESRD Networks, disagreed. Leading nephrologists who served on ESRD Network boards, he said, commanded respect in the medical community, and had improved patient health as measured by dialysis adequacy, anemia management and other metrics, working with dialysis units "in a nonpunitive, collegial, quality improvement mode." The ESRD Networks also dealt with patient grievances and concerns, Wish pointed out.

Kenneth Bays, who had served as a patient advocate on the board of his local ESRD Network 6 in Georgia, was having none of it. After joining Network 6, he said, he quickly saw that the organization served dialysis companies, not patients. "That Network was constructed for the betterment of the industry." Patients were afraid to identify themselves to the Network when filing complaints, he found, because Network policy was to pass the names of complainants back to their facilities—to the very people about whom they had complained—thus exposing them to reprisal. And Bays called the ESRD Networks' data-gathering activities "a joke," because they relied on the honor system, trusting dialysis clinics to report their own performance accurately rather than taking the data directly from the dialysis machines. Other witnesses agreed with Bays's assessment. "Too often the ESRD Networks side with the dialysis providers to ease the . . . strife on hand," said Dale Ester, a patient from Arizona. "Who really currently stands up for the dialysis patient when they have a legitimate complaint? No one."

Several times the testimony touched on the growing practice of involuntary discharge. Senator Pete Stark demanded that deficient centers "be terminated from the [Medicare] program and not permitted to 'terminate' patients." Brent Smith, Kenneth Bays and another witness, California dialysis patient Frank Brown, all reported being pressured to leave their facilities after calling out unhealthy practices. "Common clinic policy is to get rid of the minority who will speak up, rather than to solve problems or make changes they might find inconvenient," Brown said.

Chuck Grassley, famed for his support of whistleblowers and of laws to protect them, was visibly irritated by the thought that patients might be punished for speaking out, all the more when they did so before Congress. "I want to make it clear that retaliation against congressional witnesses is a crime," he told Smith and Bays. "I intend to use all tools available to me to ensure that there is no retaliation against either of these witnesses for their testimony today."

Near the end of his testimony, Brent Smith shared a sinister detail. When his clinic managers learned that he was going to testify, a vice president of the company that owned his unit, Total Renal Care, called to ask what he planned to say. This vice president insisted, against Smith's wishes, that they speak while Smith was dialyzing. "I am not sure if there was a subliminal threat of some sort," Smith told the senators, "but she then went on to say that the chairman of the board of the company would be calling me Wednesday when I get back. So I do not think they are going to be congratulating me on this."

Chairman Grassley seemed to grasp for the first time the extent of Smith's vulnerability.

> *The Chairman.* And being in the situation where you are, without dialysis, obviously death is just around the corner and then being intimidated about that is even further stress that, I presume, causes some health problems?
>
> *Mr. Smith.* Absolutely. But personally, after 20 some years, I am not intimidated easily. So it is not just me; it is the other patients. The other patients get intimidated very easily and it does affect their care.
>
> *The Chairman.* In my opening statement I talked about the law that protects congressional witnesses, so I hope if there is any retaliation against you that you will inform me.
>
> *Mr. Smith.* Absolutely.

All of which makes for stirring congressional theater. But in day-to-day life on blood floors across America, moral indignation and promises of protection from a distant senator count for very little. For Brent Smith, in fact, they appear to have counted for nothing at all.

After testifying in Washington, Smith returned to his home in Arizona and continued to dialyze at his facility in Scottsdale. Possibly as a result of what he revealed during his testimony, in early 2001, state healthcare officials inspected his facility and found numerous deficiencies: violations of sterile procedure, fruit flies in the dialysis solution, and so forth.

A few months later, in September of 2001, Smith suffered a series of cardiac arrests during dialysis. His sister, Brenda Smith, says he had complained before starting his run that something about his dialysate mixture wasn't right. Brent Smith was rushed to the emergency room at a nearby hospital, where he died five days later, without having regained consciousness.

Brenda Smith remembers arriving at the ER, and encountering the manager of Brent's clinic. "What the hell was he doing there?" she wonders today. "Brent always told us, 'If something happens to me on dialysis, you better investigate.' I think he was right. I think they killed him."

Like all dialysis patients, Smith was in fragile health. He stated during his Senate testimony that he had already suffered a cardiac arrest in 1994, while on dialysis, apparently caused by abnormal potassium levels in his blood, which he attributed to deficient potassium management at his clinic. Hence foul play in his death is impossible to prove. Brenda Smith nonetheless notified Chuck Grassley, and one of her US senators from Arizona, John McCain, of her brother's sudden death. She shared her suspicions with the senators, and demanded that they take action against the company.

"Grassley promised to protect federal witnesses from retaliation," she says. "But Grassley did shit. McCain did shit."

· 7 ·

On the Blood Floor

LEONARD STERN WAS raised in the Brownsville and Flatbush neighborhoods of Brooklyn, by Jewish parents who had survived the Nazi invasion of Poland, the horrors of the Warsaw Ghetto, and imprisonment in a Soviet forced-labor camp in Siberia. In 1941, after Germany had invaded the USSR and the Russian camp guards were abruptly called away to the front, abandoning the internees, the Sterns began a 4,000-mile trek that ended in northern Iran, where a group of Muslim farmers concealed them from the Germans. After World War II, the Sterns spent four years in Allied camps for displaced persons, before finally relocating to America, with the help of a Jewish aid organization and of an elderly widow in Buffalo, New York, who acted as their sponsor. Stern was born in Buffalo, and moved to Brooklyn with his family when he was two years old.

"An aura of residual trauma hung over my household growing up. My parents didn't go out, they didn't go to restaurants or movies, they didn't celebrate birthdays, they never hugged. My father was so turned off by everything he grew up with that he abandoned all religion, although his father, who died in Warsaw or in the camps, had been a rabbi." Seeking escape from this restrictive atmosphere, Stern became a voracious reader. "Astronomy, biology, music, theater, you name it—I explored constantly. I was very curious, and needed to know how things worked."

Stern's parents instilled in him a strong sense of the sacred in daily life, and of the immense responsibility of the professional classes, particularly doctors, to serve the common good—and never to abuse it like Dr. Josef Mengele, whom some of Stern's relatives may have seen as they passed through the gates of Auschwitz. Stern has long believed that doctors bear a particular responsibility to the poor. "We have to change the way we think about health in America. We should add to our Bill of Rights that when you are a US citizen, you have the right to health care."

Each morning, Stern recites an oath attributed to Moses Maimonides, a twelfth-century Jewish physician, through which he asks God to inspire him with love for his patients and respect for the medical arts, never to thirst for profit or fame, and to protect the sick from false physicians who cause their death. "The Oath of Maimonides means much more than the Hippocratic Oath, which is often summed up as, 'Do no harm.' Maimonides reminds physicians that we have a moral obligation to be the best physician we possibly can be, in body, mind and soul, in caring for our patients."

When Leonard Stern opened his outpatient dialysis unit at Columbia University, in partnership with Gambro, he handpicked and trained his nursing staff, and oversaw the installation of a state-of-the-art water purification system (water purity is essential to high-quality dialysis). He also made his clinic as aesthetically satisfying as possible for patients, installing large windows that overlooked the Hudson River, and hanging paintings by prominent modernist artists on the walls. "The emotional aspect of a chronic condition like dialysis is often decisive," he says. Above all, Stern ensured that he and his staff spent extensive time getting to know each patient's unique biology and psychology.

Stern was also adamant that all of his patients, whatever their financial status or skin color, deserved high-quality care. He saw many Dominicans in his clinic, most from the Washington Heights neighborhood of Manhattan, which is home to a large Dominican population that includes many undocumented immigrants. The incidence of renal failure among Dominicans is far above the national average, because of genetic predisposition and poor diet. Stern says that when he conducted a simple written survey among patients at his clinic, to better understand their nutrition, "We learned to our shock that at least half of our Dominican patients were completely illiterate. Which meant that all the brochures the dietician was handing them about what to eat, all the consents and agreements they were signing—they were signing their lives away, without understanding a word. We found these people had hidden their illiteracy, because they were afraid they'd be turned away from the clinic if they couldn't read. They were afraid because of their undocumented status. They fear the whole system."

DaVita concluded the acquisition of Gambro in 2005, and took over the management of Stern's facility. The results Stern says he witnessed should by now be familiar: fewer skilled RNs, more low-wage techs, more patients per caregiver. Workloads grew overwhelming, employee turnover rampant. The firm's efforts, Stern says, seemed directed more at recruiting new staff than caring for patients; he sometimes didn't recognize any of the workers who were treating his patients, because they had all been hired since his last visit to the clinic. To increase profits, DaVita managers instituted four shifts of dialysis per day, with strict thirty-minute transition periods between shifts—hardly enough time to get one group of patients off their machines and stabilized, sterilize the dialysis station, cannulate the next shift of patients, and resume dialyzing. (DaVita responds that "extra shifts are instituted to address patient convenience and evidence-based practices," and that "there is no evidence that current transition times pose a threat to patient care.") Stern says that DaVita managers declined to pay the insurance coverage on the modernist paintings displayed in the clinic, which had to be removed. "The managers seemed to view the emotional state of our patients as a secondary concern," Stern says.

Stern found that his orders—the medical prescriptions he wrote for each patient—were being blocked by corporate managers because they were too individualized. "DaVita would tell me that the patient needs a fixed amount of care, but I know this is wrong, and I'd write orders differently. They would prevent my orders from being enacted many times, because they wanted a fixed thirty minutes between each shift. They wanted to adhere to their rigid schedule, which meant that I couldn't tailor the treatment to fit a specific patient. So if I ordered a five-and-a-half-hour treatment, or a fifteenth treatment that month, there would be a lot of pushback. And ultimately the answer was no." Stern says the company only bought one brand of dialyzer, the filter of hollow synthetic fibers at the heart of the machine; if some patients suffered an adverse reaction like itching, cramps or a sudden drop in blood pressure with that dialyzer, they simply had to make do. "It was one size fits all," he says. "Because in their financial model, it was cheaper for them to buy a large quantity of one brand of dialyzer." (DaVita denies that they would only use one brand of dialyzer, or prioritize scheduling over patient care. "As is standard in the healthcare industry, non-formulary requests are reviewed. While not all requests can be granted, each one is reviewed for medical value and appropriateness.")

Stern also observed that vulnerable patients often seemed to receive worse care. He claims that his Dominican patients, though uniformly courteous and cooperative, were often treated less favorably than other demographics, at least in part because they spoke little English. "Those are the patients that are brutalized. Those are the target patients. Because they are innocent, soft. Ignorant, easy marks. They're like the simple child in the Passover Seder, the one that doesn't understand." (DaVita's response: "We are committed to ensuring that every patient and teammate in our community is safe and feels valued and respected within an inclusive environment.")

Eventually Stern resigned. "I absolved myself of any responsibility for dealing with DaVita," he says. "Part of my frustration was the total vulnerability of the patients, particularly the Dominicans and other low-income patients. I couldn't protect them." He believes that corporate dialysis as practiced by DaVita and Fresenius is incompatible with ethical medicine. "The concept that you would minimize the care to generate more revenue is the wrong way of thinking," he says. "This is a systematic, facilitated pattern of abuse. Yes, they're keeping them alive, but at what cost to their quality of life?"

Brent Miller experienced similar pressures when Gambro and then

DaVita entered joint ventures with several of the clinics they co-owned with his employer at the time, Washington University in St. Louis. On multiple occasions, Miller says, the dialysate flows he had prescribed for his patients were altered without his knowledge; and he was pressured to approve higher dosages of calcimimetics and vitamin D analogs than he wished to prescribe—dosages that seemed to be determined by corporate medication algorithms. Miller felt that these modifications of his prescription, though done with the support of each clinic's medical director, were made in order to benefit DaVita financially. (DaVita disagrees: "We rely upon clinical experts to design evidence-based protocols that physicians may choose (but are not required) to use to assist in optimal dosing of medications.")

Miller was incensed. "These are my patients!" he remembers saying. "I write dialysis orders on my patients!" He also objected to patients being segregated according to their insurance coverage, with more valuable private-payor patients being flagged as "HIPPERs" ("high-paying patients"), and to the practice of submitting monthly capitation bills even when physicians hadn't actually seen patients. (DaVita denies that they treat privately and publicly insured patients differently, and that monthly capitation bills are submitted even when physicians haven't seen patients.) But his repeated complaints to corporate executives and to his university colleagues who managed the joint venture, he says, fell on deaf ears. "I went to everyone. I told both the division administrator and the division chief, who were the board members of the joint venture, 'If this doesn't change, I will file a complaint.' I went to the chair of medicine. I went to the CEO of the practice plan. I was able to impact individual problems as they arose, but not the structure that allowed these practices to occur again and again. Simply put, the university's financial investments in the dialysis centers and the individual benefits to several senior faculty members at the time were too valuable to allow any disruption to the business model."

Miller eventually retired from Washington University and moved back to his home state of Indiana, where he accepted an endowed professorship, and now leads the clinical arm of the Nephrology Division at the Indiana University School of Medicine.

Leonard Stern explains how the consolidation of the US dialysis industry led many practicing nephrologists to shirk their responsibilities to their patients. During the roll-up, large dialysis firms bought out individual nephrology practices across the nation. The owners of many practices instantly became millionaires, and continued to receive yearly salaries for serving as medical directors in the facilities they formerly owned. In return, Stern says, the majority entered a Faustian bargain with their new employer. On paper, these MDs remained responsible for the individual treatment plan of each of their dialysis patients, just as they had been before they sold their practices. In reality, they tacitly accepted the blanket use, on all of their patients, of a corporate treatment protocol designed to maximize revenue, not health. Today, only exceptionally confident and experienced nephrologists are likely to buck the system, given that Fresenius and DaVita control more than three-quarters of the nation's clinics, and nephrologists who refuse to play by the rules risk career suicide. "Like patients, doctors get blackballed too," says Brent Miller. "If a dialysis company says you were a pain in the ass as medical director, you're not likely to be offered that position again in the industry."

Nevertheless, Miller, Leonard Stern and a handful of other senior nephrologists have begun to speak out. Of Kent Thiry, Stern says, "He's recruited a group of physicians who were reputable, who have then bought into his stuff, and are no longer reputable, in my mind. Even the company name 'DaVita,' 'giving life,' is disingenuous, because their corporate purpose is primarily financial. They give life as a secondary goal, and disregard the impact of their care on the quality of the patient's life."

Miller blames his fellow MDs. "Nephrologists are the real problem— not the patients, not even the LDOs [large dialysis organizations]. And nephrologists really have to take this industry back. Where is the ASN [American Society of Nephrology], the NKF [National Kidney Foundation]? Where are the academic leaders of nephrology—the chairs of the Ivy League divisions? Where are they speaking out about it? True, after hearing criticism from nephrologists and patients, the ASN has recently launched promising new initiatives on kidney health, dialysis safety, novel treatments for kidney disease and added patient advocates. And the NKF has changed their KDOQI [Kidney Disease Outcomes Quality Initiative] guideline governance and composition. But these remain incremental changes. By and large, the professional societies like the ASN have gone too corporate, and are all about raising money, funneling grant money amongst themselves, appointing each other rather than a diverse group of nephrologists including non-academic clinicians. A small group of people controls the whole thing, and they don't primarily focus on advancing care or furthering the industry, because they're too dependent on the status quo."

Miller shakes his head in disgust. "Many nephrology divisions of a lot of universities have built up massive revenue streams and even endowments based on dialysis revenue. Yet almost none of that money seems to be put back into research, patient care, or anything related to dialysis. The leaders may use it for buying lab animals, for refurbishing their office, for first-class travel—whatever they want. A lot of big-shot nephrology researchers, they won't admit this, but a lot of their research has been directly or indirectly funded by revenue from dialysis centers. Look, my former bosses [at Washington University in St. Louis] manage a joint venture with DaVita and have a multimillion-dollar endowment largely based on dialysis revenue. Other universities received tens of millions of dollars for selling their dialysis centers. When revenue from an entity like Fresenius or DaVita helps fund a department of medicine, nobody's interested in developing disruptive technology or changing reimbursement. Few are really serious about changing the system, because no one wants to risk harming the cash cow. That's one of the reasons why there's a crisis in nephrology."

❏

FOR WORKERS on the blood floor, the results of the roll-up were even more tangible and disturbing. Arlene Mullin founded Dialysis Advocates in 1998 after witnessing the degeneration of the industry while working as a dialysis technician in Portland, Oregon. When she'd joined a not-for-profit clinic there three years earlier, the atmosphere was humane. "I loved the work," she says. "You spent so much time with dialysis patients, you got to know their families, their children and grandchildren. Some of them treated you like part of their own family. It was a very nurturing environment. Patients were still people." Several of her patients had been on dialysis for ten years or more.

Then, in 1998, her unit was bought out by Renal Care Group, a for-profit dialysis company that would be purchased, in turn, by Fresenius. Overnight, cost cutting seemed to become the mantra. Mullin recalls that her new managers rationed syringes, medical tape, and gauze, and forbade giving ibuprofen to patients who were in pain, because they considered the drug an optional expense. The reuse of sterilized dialysis filters became standard procedure, despite the health risks that this practice created. Many registered nurses were fired and replaced by low-wage dialysis technicians. Mullin and her coworkers went from dialyzing three patients at a time to treating ten or more, even as the company slashed their wages and health benefits.

The human costs of fast food dialysis soon became clear. Patients began losing consciousness, Mullin says, and having heart problems during treatment. She recalls that there was a spike in infections and hospitalizations. Tensions between workers and patients rose, leading to angry confrontations; the once steadfast solidarity between caregiver, patient, and family members withered. Mullin's breaking point came when two patients whom she'd been treating for years died suddenly within months of one another.

As Mullin left the clinic after learning of the second death, her hands shaking, she saw a blackbird standing on the sidewalk before her, its head cocked, fixing her with one black, glossy eye, as if asking her a riddle. The bird watched as Mullin approached, then turned and hopped down the pavement just ahead of her. Mullin instinctively followed.

"I'm no mystic, but that bird seemed like the spirit of those patients, leading me away from the clinic." By the time they reached a nearby park and the bird took wing, Mullin felt that the universe had sent her a message. "My job had been about caring for people. But now I was milking them for money, using them up. My new managers were trying to make dialysis as streamlined as Jiffy Lube. This wasn't what I'd signed on for. In fact, it was the *opposite* of care."

Mullin reported what she had witnessed at the clinic to a whistleblower hotline run by the Health Care Financing Administration (HCFA, now CMS). Though the hotline was supposedly anonymous and confidential, the next day, she says, her managers announced that the clinic would be undergoing a "surprise" government inspection. Mullin says they also berated her for having blown the whistle. She resigned, and, three weeks later, founded Dialysis Advocates.

But corporate dialysis wasn't created by financial managers alone. After all, the Harvard MD nephrologists who founded and ran NMC were famous for their emphasis on top-down managerial control and efficiency, which, according to a series of government investigations and lawsuits, often led to inferior care and patient harm. At Betty Smith's nonprofit hospital in northern California, doctors bought out the nephrology practice, and promptly shut its stellar self-care program, because it wasn't profitable enough. "The physicians' group . . . sent those patients into the chronic [dialysis] unit, and basically told them, 'Sit down and shut up. We're not doing self-care anymore.'" Smith watched as patient-staff ratios soared and costs were slashed throughout the facility. "We even stopped having linens," says Smith. "I remember one time there was an elderly woman with diabetes, who almost always became nauseous and vomited on dialysis. . . . So she vomited, and it went all over her clothing and the chair and everything. I'm standing there saying, 'How can you run a dialysis unit without some linens? You know, I need a washcloth. I need a sheet. I'm a nurse, and I need something to actually take care of—to *nurse*—this woman with.'"

Steven Rosansky worked as a nephrologist and researcher at a Veterans Affairs (VA) hospital in Columbia, South Carolina, until his retirement in 2012. Because the VA, a government agency, pays its staff a fixed salary regardless of the number of patients they treat, Rosansky and his colleagues were spared the divided allegiances between patients and profits that many nephrologists feel. "The VA was the Cadillac of dialysis. We were funded reasonably well, and we had lots of staff, with a very low patient-to-staff ratio. And we had only RNs. We had a couple of technicians, and they were primarily involved with machines—the RNs mostly stuck the needles." In many ways, VA workers have the same goals and financial incentives as doctors in foreign countries with universal healthcare systems. Unsurprisingly, patient outcomes at the VA are consistently better than in for-profit centers. A study from 2018 found that elderly veterans with kidney problems who were being treated in non-VA facilities (which were predominantly for-profit) were 28 percent more likely to be started on dialysis than those treated at the VA, and 5 percent more likely to die over the same time period. A paper from the following year found that veterans treated outside the VA were nearly twice as likely to die in the first two years of dialysis than those who dialyzed in a VA unit.

When Rosansky considered entering the for-profit dialysis arena, and made a bid to buy a dialysis unit in Elizabeth City, North Carolina, he says he could feel his own medical mindset changing. "I remember looking at numbers, because when you go into a dialysis unit, you looked at numbers. And the money was outrageous, it was absolutely astounding. You start looking at the numbers, and thinking, 'Okay, I've got a dialysis unit with this number of chairs. And I could do one shift, two shifts, or three shifts.' Then you start calculating what the fees are for the different pieces—for the facility, the physician and the director. And you multiply the fees by the number of patients that you have, right? But at one point I stopped and thought to myself, 'You're like a cattle rancher. You're thinking about these patients like you're raising a herd of cattle.' And that just didn't sit right."

In the end, the unit was purchased by NMC. "I've always felt I was spared," Rosansky says.

Assembly-line care can also make patients themselves feel like livestock, as Kenneth Bays observed during the congressional hearings of 2000. "We're nothing but a number," says Cornelius Robbins, a patient from Hephzibah, Georgia. "We're just like cows—they don't have identities, or names, just a tag in their ear with their number on it. You bring them in, you do what you got to do with them. The ones you want to keep, the big, healthy steers [privately insured patients], you keep them over here nice and off by themselves, fed up, looking pretty. The other ones, the little frail cattle you don't really want [government-insured patients], you're not gonna make a fuss about those, just make a few dollars off of them, and get them gone as fast as possible."

Gregg Hansen, a patient in San Rafael, California, uses a different analogy to capture his plight. The dialysis firms, he says, "don't care about us, because we don't pay their bills. Their real customers are Medicare and Medicaid, and the insurance companies. Dialysis patients are just the dogs at the pound."

❑

A GRAPHIC illustration of how financial conflicts distort the practice of dialysis in the United States is the story of erythropoietin, a hormone produced by the kidneys that stimulates the production of red blood cells, which carry oxygen throughout the body. The red blood cell volume (also called "hematocrit") of dialysis patients, whose kidneys no longer produce enough of the hormone, is typically low; most are anemic, and suffer symptoms such as fatigue, irregular heartbeat and difficulty breathing. To remedy this, many patients receive doses of a synthetic pharmaceutical substitute for erythropoietin. The most popular of these substitutes is produced by Amgen, the pharma giant, and sold under the trade name "Epogen," often abbreviated as "EPO." Introduced in 1989, EPO was used in modest quantities until 1991, when the Medicare reimbursement policy for the drug changed from a blanket fee, irrespective of dose, to a per-dose reimbursement. Since dialysis and other healthcare companies could buy EPO at prices well below the rate at which the government was reimbursing them for the drug, the spread between price and reimbursement produced a tidy profit on every dose of EPO.

Predictably, use of the drug shot up, and EPO became one of the first billion-dollar biotech drugs. Amgen aggressively promoted its use in dialysis (as well as in chemotherapy), suggesting that higher doses of EPO improved a patient's quality of life. The drug's packaging pledged that once target hematocrit levels were achieved, patients would enjoy "statistically significant improvements" in "energy and activity level, functional ability, sleep and eating behavior, health status, satisfaction with health, sex life, well-being, psychological effect, life satisfaction and happiness."

At least in part to increase its sales to the dialysis industry, Amgen funded the first advisory panel to formulate best practices for dialysis care; many of the experts who drew up the guidelines for EPO use were paid Amgen consultants. The panel did not consider some of the more serious problems faced by dialysis patients, such as heart disease and infection; instead it crafted guidelines to address other matters, including low hematocrit among patients, and how increased doses of EPO could help. (Dori Schatell, a veteran dialysis advocate and educator who participated in the anemia work group in the mid-1990s, wrote years later, "At no time was there ever a conversation that started out, 'What are the leading causes of preventable death in dialysis, and how can we address those?'") In 1997, nephrology experts who participated in the Dialysis Outcomes Quality Initiative (DOQI; later renamed the Kidney Disease Outcomes Quality Initiative, or KDOQI) published the first generally accepted clinical practice guidelines in nephrology. Among other things, these guidelines recommended a higher hematocrit target for dialysis patients—and therefore more generous EPO use—than that endorsed by the FDA. Many dialysis firms, particularly the LDOs, adopted higher EPO doses in their corporate treatment protocols.

Again EPO sales rose, and Amgen and the dialysis firms prospered. EPO became Medicare's largest single-drug expenditure, and by 2007, represented nearly half of the cost of dialysis treatments paid by Medicare. The drug also generated a large portion of the profits of dialysis companies. These were the heady days of the roll-up, and it is interesting to examine the changes in EPO dosages that typically occurred when a large dialysis firm bought out an independent facility. A 2019 study found that, on average, EPO use rose 129 percent after the change in ownership.

Between 1989 and 2010, Medicare spent more than $40 billion on EPO. Congress, smelling a rat, began to probe the overuse of dialysis drugs and to debate how to contain their cost. The Department of Health and Human Services Inspector General and the Department of Justice launched investigations into the EPO practices of Big Dialysis. Several lawsuits were filed against Amgen and the dialysis companies for overuse of EPO. Throughout, two of Amgen's major customers, DaVita and Fresenius, insisted that their dosages of EPO were determined solely by medical doctors, for the exclusive purpose of improving the well-being of their patients. In 2007, Kent Thiry declared in a *New York Times* interview that he would welcome the removal of financial incentives to overprescribe EPO. "Do that tomorrow so we get rid of the taint," Thiry said. "We're still going to use the same amount of EPO."

Meanwhile, however, clinical evidence was accumulating that high doses of EPO could have deadly side effects. Elevated hematocrit, though increasing oxygen uptake, also increased blood clotting, and therefore created a higher risk of stroke, cardiac arrest and thrombosis. Already in 1996, a major clinical trial of EPO use was halted, when the high-dose population suffered significantly more heart attacks than the low-EPO group. In 2006, the FDA issued an alert about potential risks of EPO use, and the following year applied its most restrictive, "black box" warning to the drug. Despite these mounting medical concerns, most dialysis companies continued to administer elevated doses of EPO to their patients. In 2010 alone, they billed Medicare $2 billion for EPO.

In January of 2011, Medicare eliminated reimbursement for individual EPO doses, and bundled the drug into its blanket payment, or capitation, for basic dialysis care. Each dose of EPO, which until the 2011 bundle had represented a profit, suddenly became a cost. Dialysis companies, switching to cost-cutting mode, abruptly changed their policy, and reduced the doses of EPO they were injecting into their patients. In that year, Fresenius decreased its annual EPO usage by 29 percent, and DaVita by 47 percent. So abruptly did the dosages fall, in fact, that a spate of emergency transfusions ensued, as patients suddenly deprived of EPO experienced severe anemia.

Kent Thiry's earlier claim that DaVita set its EPO dosages purely on the basis of patient well-being, and that the firm would maintain these dosages regardless of the government's reimbursement policies, may not have been entirely truthful.

Another disturbing aspect of the EPO saga was the role of the nephrologists who actually wrote prescriptions for the drug. At least in theory, every aspect of dialysis care, including how much EPO the patient receives, is the responsibility of his or her nephrologist. True, lawsuits and testimonials by nephrologists and workers have emphasized the lengths to which large dialysis companies sometimes went to increase their usage of EPO and other dialysis drugs—according to one billing fraud suit, which DaVita settled in 2015 for $495 million, the company developed a firm-wide software application, Snappy, that automatically maximized the dosages of certain dialysis drugs, in order to maximize Medicare reimbursement. (As part of the settlement, DaVita denied these allegations.) Yet in the final analysis, nephrologists hold the prescription pad for their patients.

"Dialysis providers realized, 'Hey, we can really make money with this drug,'" Brent Miller says of the EPO boom. "But the order comes from a nephrologist. After 2008, when definitive studies came out, we [nephrologists] couldn't hide from the truth. But EPO use didn't go down until the drugs were bundled in 2011. It is all in the public domain. Strokes, heart attacks, death in dialysis . . . nephrologists contributed to killing their patients, for money."

❏

"People who write the guidelines should not be in a position to profit from them," says Steven Rosansky, the former VA nephrologist and researcher, who has authored scores of peer-reviewed publications, primarily on kidney disease, as well as a book, *Learn the Facts About Kidney Disease*, which he wrote as a guide for patients and their families. "If they are, you've really let the fox into the hen house."

Rosansky's concerns with the corporate funding of the KDOQI guidelines go beyond high EPO dosages, to the underlying definition of kidney failure that those guidelines enshrined. In 2002, KDOQI established five stages of kidney disease by reference to a patient's estimated glomerular filtration rate (eGFR), a commonly used measure of how effectively the kidneys are removing waste products from the blood. (GFR estimates are typically based on levels of creatinine, a chemical by-product that appears in the blood when muscles burn fuel.) KDOQI defined normal kidney function as an eGFR of 90 or higher, with increasingly more serious kidney disease as the rate falls, from stage 2, mild kidney damage at between 60 and 90, down to stage 5, end-stage renal disease, at an eGFR of less than 15.

This five-stage model, which became the industry standard, provided the first commonly accepted definition of kidney failure. Although the KDOQI guidelines have evolved since then, an eGFR that drops below 15 remains, at least in the United States, a frequent starting point for dialysis. Rosansky and many other nephrologists say this approach is simplistic, and that many people with low eGFR are put on dialysis who could, and should, have avoided it. "But this sure got nephrologists a lot more customers," Rosansky says. The KDOQI guidelines and their handy scale of chronic kidney disease, written in large part by people who were involved in the business of researching or providing dialysis, are another feature of the self-licking ice-cream cone that is Big Dialysis.

Rosansky says putting people on dialysis by rote, using an algorithm like eGFR, is mistaken for several reasons. First, patients should be diagnosed and treated according to their actual symptoms, not from one number in their bloodwork—all the more since eGFR is merely an estimate, and can be inaccurate. Moreover, many older adults with an eGFR of 45 may have normal kidney function for their age; Rosansky has seen patients who seemed to be doing fine with an eGFR of 15, and others at that level who were deathly ill. Second, of more consequence than a patient's current eGFR is its rate of decline, something that the chronic kidney disease scale doesn't take into account. People over age 65 with a low eGFR may well never need dialysis. "At that age we are losing kidney function very slowly. The trajectory of decline in renal function is a critical but overlooked piece of data." Third, Rosansky points out that more conservative treatments are available to manage kidney disease without dialysis, such as diuretics to control fluid overload and binders to help lower potassium.

"After all, dialysis isn't a walk in the park." Rosansky tells the story of his longtime friend, whom we'll call Frank, who against his advice started dialysis at stage 4 kidney disease, with an eGFR of about 20. Six months later, Frank's vascular access became infected, and he was hospitalized. Then the catheter that the hospital staff used to dialyze him went septic, which led to an eye infection. "When his wife called me, he was in the hospital," Rosansky remembers. "They'd taken out his infected eye. And I said, 'How much urine is he putting out?' She said he was putting out about a liter [per day]. So I told her, 'You tell Frank, the best thing for him to do is get off dialysis right now. He's got enough kidney function, and the best way to eliminate bloodstream infection is remove that catheter." Frank and his wife apparently ignored Rosansky's advice once more. Frank died shortly after.

Rosansky flips through a series of PowerPoint slides from presentations he's given at medical conferences in a score of countries around the world, which summarize medical publications and clinical trials that support his contentions about problems in American dialysis. Bright graphs and bar charts reveal a steep rise, since the formulation of the KDOQI guidelines, in "early start" dialysis—the practice of beginning treatment on patients who have a better eGFR than patients in many other countries have when they start dialyzing. One slide shows that mortality among early-start dialysis patients actually increases with their eGFR: healthier patients, in other words, seem to die earlier when put on dialysis prematurely. "For patients who start dialysis at an eGFR above 10, their provider should be required to give a reason for starting dialysis that early," Rosansky says simply.

I mention how Carrie Brito feels she may have started dialysis before she needed to, and how Cornelius Robbins believes he was being "groomed for dialysis" by his nephrologist. "There's no way for me to know without seeing their medical history," Rosansky replies, "but that's a scenario my research suggests, and it worries me." Rosansky describes another of his concerns, the increase in dialysis starts that happen in hospitals as a result of acute kidney injury (AKI). He points out that AKI, like kidney disease itself, is a poorly defined disease state. Kidney function routinely drops when a patient is hospitalized for a serious condition like congestive heart failure or, more recently, for COVID-19. "Here's the study by Crews at Johns Hopkins," Rosansky says, flashing up a slide. "See? Fifty-three percent of dialysis initiations started with an acute event. And I think a lot of these may have been reversible, but we don't know." Nephrologists don't typically monitor renal function, he says, to see if the kidneys are recovering on their own; many don't even know how to measure residual renal function. And they rarely offer patients a clear choice about when, or whether, to start dialysis. "You just plug the patient in, they're easy to manage, the money's rolling in. Why look back?"

Rosansky's comment reminds me of the case of Gerald Thompson, the dialysis patient in Memphis, Tennessee. His wife Sherry, the 9-1-1 dispatcher, told me how Gerald was rushed to the ER one evening with shortness of breath, and was diagnosed with kidney failure. While still in the ER, and even before Sherry herself was allowed to visit him, Sherry says that Gerald was approached by a member of Satellite Healthcare, a dialysis company that has 90 centers in 5 states, and treats about 8,300 patients. "I was there waiting for updates, waiting to get into his room, waiting to see him," Sherry remembers. "However, Gerald woke up with a lady sitting at his bedside, who told him, 'You're in kidney failure, you're going to need dialysis, Satellite is going to take good care of you.' She gave him great promises. He was in the ICU trying to recover, his vitals were still unstable, he was barely breathing. So he was confused. He didn't really know what was going on. So of course, he said yes. 'If that's the help I need, then, *sure*.'"

"So how did that dialysis recruiter get inside of this ICU room, somewhere that his wife couldn't be?" Sherry Thompson asks rhetorically. "To me this shows the strong connection between the hospitals and the dialysis centers."

Rosansky's greatest concern about US dialysis seems to be its growing prevalence among older adults. One of his main reasons for writing his book *Learn the Facts About Kidney Disease,* he says, was to spare older people "unnecessary and horrible end-of-life experiences." He scrolls through slides that document the steep growth in early starts among elderly patients, and the high incidences of hospitalization and death that result. "So this is a study by Kurella, on nursing-home patients," he tells me, pointing to another slide. "She was trying to figure out why they put people on dialysis, and she was checking them every three months, signs and symptoms, one year prior. Eighteen percent of these people started at an eGFR of over 15. And less than a third of them had any goddamn reason to start dialysis. People were being pushed into dialysis, because we had guidelines that said over 15 eGFR, you should start thinking about it. Totally misguided."

I ask the obvious question: Are nephrologists railroading their patients into dialysis purely for profit, even when it may harm them? Rosansky demurs. "There are other reasons besides money into your own pocket. There's money into your department. And then there's a whole list of factors relating to management of people on dialysis three times a week, versus managing them in your office, which means their health is a lot less secure. It's a no-brainer. If you can put them on dialysis, nobody's going to question you. Especially when you've got the various guidelines which say you can. Guidelines which the nephrologists themselves have written."

Another example of how dialysis metrics are written by people who may be more intent on funding than on patient health comes from the formulation of CMS's ESRD Quality Incentive Program, or QIP. This program is designed to induce dialysis units to provide high-quality care, by measuring key indices of patient health at each clinic—Kt/V, type of vascular access, number of transfusions and so forth—and penalizing low-scoring clinics up to 2 percent of their Medicare reimbursement. (CMS's parallel "5-Star Quality Rating System" assesses all clinics according to their performance in similar indices, and assigns a number of stars—5 for top-scoring clinics, 1 for the poorest performers—ostensibly to help patients choose the best clinic in their area.) Such metrics should capture the main elements of good dialysis care, yet historically they have omitted two crucial measures of dialysis safety and success: treatment duration and ultrafiltration rate (UFR). For the past two decades, scores of peer-reviewed studies have concluded that short treatments and high UFRs increase the incidence of patient harm and death. In fact, this is one of the most unambiguous findings in nephrology research. Yet on average, treatment times remain shorter and UFR higher in the United States than in other industrialized nations.

Gradually, however, CMS has begun to acknowledge what doctors in many other countries have long accepted. For at least a decade, CMS has debated internally whether to implement a minimum treatment time of 4 hours, and UFRs no higher than 10 ml/kg/hr, as quality measures in hemodialysis. In other words, CMS has considered penalizing units that practice "bazooka dialysis." Decisions about whether to add new metrics to the QIP are made on the recommendation of technical expert panels, teams of experienced academic and industry nephrologists enlisted by CMS. In 2010 and again in 2013, a technical expert panel of authorities in fluid management agreed on the importance of establishing a minimum treatment time of 4 hours, and a maximum UFR of 10 ml/kg/hr, as quality metrics. In fact, the 2013 panel voted unanimously to institute both metrics as official quality measures.

However, one panelist who had been absent from the 2013 deliberations objected strenuously. John Daugirdas, a noted nephrology researcher at the University of Illinois College of Medicine and a leading theoretician and advocate of Kt/V as a central measure of dialysis adequacy, criticized the vote, organized colleagues to object to the proposed new standards and to write public comments in opposition, and called for a re-vote by the technical expert panel. Emails obtained under the Freedom of Information Act suggest that Daugirdas's objection to the revised standards may have had less to do with patient welfare than with a threat to his own research. At the time, Daugirdas and other scholars were seeking federal funding for a clinical trial on treatment times and patient life span, known as the Time to Reduce Mortality in ESRD (TiME) trial. In emails to colleagues, Daugirdas criticized the idea of a new, four-hour treatment threshold because it endangered his trial. After citing research that called into question the association between treatment times and mortality, he wrote, "The TiMe [*sic*] trial is designed to answer this question, and I think coming out with a quality standard > 4 hours based on very equivocal data ... will not be a service to dialysis. Most important, it may actually kill the TiMe [*sic*] trial, blocking successful recruitment for this trial." In a subsequent email, he wrote, "If we come up with a TEP rec [Technical Expert Panel recommendation] saying that the > 4 hr question has already been answered, the trial will either have to be aborted, or it will be unlikely to succeed due to various PC pressures."

Daugirdas called for another vote on the proposed new treatment duration and UFR thresholds; this time both were rejected. The TiME trial ultimately received $6.7 million from the NIH, but was discontinued early, and is widely considered a failure. "It was poorly designed and executed, and they failed miserably," says Brent Miller. "The TiME trial was supposed to answer the question whether more dialysis time impacted outcome. But the trial only increased dialysis time between control and intervention groups by nine minutes—a trivial amount. It was a TiME trial that didn't actually increase *time*. I think the people who led it should not be allowed to do another trial, *ever*."

❏

FEW THINGS excite an economist more than large, granular data sets. So in 2010, just after earning his PhD in economics, Ryan McDevitt was thrilled to learn that, because the government funds dialysis and wants to know where its money goes, every dialysis facility in the United States is required to compile a detailed yearly report card, creating a body of information that goes back decades. "As an academic, dialysis is a goldmine," he says, his good-natured blue eyes shining as much with irony, it seems to me, as with satisfaction. "Having high frequency, detailed data on an industry like that was really exciting. Not from a healthcare standpoint, but as an economist: at that time I wasn't really interested in dialysis per se, but I *was* interested in questions of firm reputation and firm quality, why consumers pick one brand over another. This is an excellent case study to test some economic theories with high-quality data that most economists just don't have. Once we got our hands on the full United States Renal Data System (USRDS) data set, every claim for every patient going back thirty years, we were all in."

When he started researching the industry, McDevitt says, he and fellow economist and collaborator Paul L. E. Grieco at Penn State University—and later Paul Eliason at Brigham Young University, Benjamin Heebsh at the Federal Trade Commission and Jimmy Roberts at Duke University—expected the data to confirm certain elementary laws about efficiencies and economies of scale. The fast food model of medicine made intuitive sense to them: for better or worse, fast food chains do a very good job of getting a consistent product out the door every day, at low production costs and low sales price. So McDevitt and his colleagues were predisposed to believe what Edmund Lowrie and Constantine Hampers had assured Congress and America back in the 1970s. "We thought we were going to find, quite frankly, that the big dialysis chains offered better care at a lower cost."

McDevitt crimps his lips and nods once, like someone who knows he's been fooled, but won't be falling for the same trick again. "Actually, we found the opposite. The big chains chase the dollar no matter what—they favor quantity *over* quality. That's part of their business model. It's a pretty fixed-cost-intensive business. Every extra patient they get goes right to the bottom line. So they want to get as many patients as possible through their system each day. The trouble is, in healthcare, the patient outcomes depend so much on the quality of care you get. That seems obvious to me now, but it wasn't before I looked carefully into dialysis. For example, outcomes for renal failure patients are directly tied to how long they're on that machine. You can't rush someone through a session. Trying to get more turnover, like you would in a fast food restaurant, leads to a direct sacrifice in patient care, and to bad outcomes."

For his next paper, Ryan McDevitt and his colleagues studied the roll-up, analyzing the effects of industry consolidation on the quality of care. Once again, they found that the roll-up had been good news for the executives and shareholders of the Big Two dialysis companies, but bad news for patients. "When DaVita and Fresenius acquire independent facilities, they start implementing their best practices, at least from their viewpoint, which means maximizing profits. So they're pumping patients full of drugs. They're cutting back staffing ratios. All the things that make a business really profitable and productive, they're doing. Unfortunately, we find this has severe consequences for patients. Death rates go up, hospitalization rates go up, transplant rates fall, and so on. Any measure that could get worse pretty much got worse, after the big chains acquired independent facilities."

During consolidations in most industries, he explains, it's difficult to identify the specific causes behind a given change. But because of the unique wealth of data being gathered on dialysis by the federal government, McDevitt had a clear view of what happened during the roll-up of the industry. "You can get inside that black box like researchers can't typically do. You get to see the clear before/after, the cause and effect. Because when the big chains acquire an independent facility, you're looking at the same patient, the same location, the same everything, before and after the acquisition. And the year after the acquisition, the quality of care gets worse. The only way you can explain that is, that now it's DaVita or Fresenius running the shop."

Another conclusion to emerge from McDevitt's research was that, for all the neoliberal rhetoric routinely spouted by dialysis executives, American dialysis is anything but a free market. Patients have high travel costs, meaning they need a clinic near their homes. They are "sticky," just as Kent Thiry says: they often rely heavily on the recommendations of their nephrologists, and are emotionally dependent on the staffs at their facilities. And because nephrologists enjoy certain exemptions from the Stark laws against medical conflicts of interest, they can steer patients to facilities where they have ownership stakes, even when those facilities are farther away from the patients' homes than alternative units. All this is in addition to the largely anticompetitive structure of the US dialysis industry, where two large corporations run more than three-quarters of all freestanding dialysis units. "There's really no hope for patients to shop around and switch to a better quality provider," says McDevitt. "On top of that, of course, we're talking about marginalized populations, who can't advocate for themselves like a rich white person could. It's just a recipe for disaster."

McDevitt has also noticed how for-profit dialysis has affected medical ethics. He points out that most patients can't know what the optimal EPO dose is for them, how long they should be on the machine, or other details of their treatment. They rightly rely on their doctors to make such decisions. "But the Hippocratic Oath is falling short in many cases," McDevitt says. "Some nephrologists who have a for-profit stake in facilities with joint ownership are either looking the other way at high drug doses, less time on the machine, and other things that are bad for patient health, or they're actually advocating for these things—they're complicit in the bad health."

Dialysis has taught McDevitt some of the limits of his discipline. "As economists, we value free markets because they do a really good job of allocating scarce resources. The textbook view of perfect competition is to just let the markets do their thing. But we've seen that when you have as many frictions and market imperfections as exist in dialysis—and in most of healthcare, for that matter—the markets can't do their thing. By now we have two firms that dominate this industry. They're not really competing for patients, as far as we can tell: they just carve up these markets and live a happy life. For many patients, life is less happy."

McDevitt looks at me unblinking, all traces of irony or satisfaction gone. "We started off being interested in this industry as economists. But as we did more research and peeled back the layers, we're outraged now as citizens and as human beings, at what's going on in dialysis."

❑

SINCE WORLD WAR II, researchers in a range of disciplines have revealed the psychological tools that certain organizations—the Nazi Party, the Nixon White House, Enron and Purdue Pharma—use to compel basically good people within their sphere to do bad things. Many such strategies draw on deep human susceptibilities to authority and peer pressure, and operate at the subconscious level. Social and evolutionary psychologists have established that most people take their cues on what to consider morally acceptable from members of their in-group, rather than from their own conscience. When an organization creates an intense us versus them culture, often expressed in metaphors of sports and war, many of its members experience a fading of conscience, together with a heightened self-identification with that organization, and a sense that it can do no wrong.

Another recurrent feature of malignant corporate cultures has been called "Tone at the Top": it is signals sent by leaders, rather than anodyne assertions set forth in press releases and mission statements, which determine how members of that organization will behave. "When the CEO of a large American for-profit dialysis company says, 'It's not about the patients,' or 'My primary goal is to enhance shareholder value,' some employees act accordingly," says Robert Bear, the Canadian nephrologist. Such messages, says Bear, determine the everyday details of how a for-profit company is run—hiring and promotion, infection control procedures, the unit's ability to customize dialysis run times to patients' needs, quality control, what's permissible and what isn't. "The rah rah sessions that the CEO holds with employees and physicians? Unfortunately, they just help desensitize employees to what is right and not right."

Many kinds of morally questionable conduct are facilitated by graying them out, turning them into repetitive, highly circumscribed tasks in a bureaucratic environment. Activities such as selling opioids, performing unnecessary surgeries or releasing poisonous waste into a local river can be ritualized, professionalized and euphemized as routine business tasks, thus distancing most employees from the human harm they cause. Reducing such actions to statistics—numbers on an Excel spreadsheet or sums of money on a profit and loss statement—further masks the faces and the pain of the victims who generate the company's income. Employees in such environments are also susceptible to the "slippery slope" phenomenon: when tasks gradually become more harmful over time, most employees who perform them fail to perceive this growing malignancy.

Incentives are another effective mechanism for inducing good people to commit harmful acts. In a perverse feedback loop that business psychologists Lisa Ordóñez and Max Bazerman have called "goals gone wild," organizations that drive their employees to meet specific goals, such as sales quotas, profit margins or earnings per share, often crowd out the ethical and legal dimensions of the activities involved. Incentive structures can reveal a corporation's true mission. Consider, for example, DaVita's pay schemes. The company's recent financial statements explain that short-term incentive compensation for its top executives is determined by performance in three areas: 70 percent of their pay depends on increasing operating income and cash flow, 15 percent on "strategic objectives" like "teammate engagement" and "energy efficiency projects," and 15 percent on increasing the "penetration" of home dialysis. Here, in dollars and cents, are DaVita's priorities, 85 percent of which concern the well-being of the firm, while only 15 percent have any link, albeit tenuous, with the health of its patients.

Goals with threats work even better: hit your numbers and you'll bank a fat bonus, but miss them and you're fired. Bully CEOs exist in many industries, but the high-tension corporate cultures at healthcare fraud empires run by Richard Eamer at NME, Rick Scott at Columbia/ HCA, Richard Scrushy at HealthSouth and Elizabeth Holmes at Theranos are legendary.

Ultimately, such tactics for graying out human harm represent forms of what behavioral psychologists call the "framing effect": restating a moral choice that affects human well-being as a straightforward business decision. Extensive research has demonstrated that most of us stop recognizing the harm inherent in our work when we're taught to see it in terms of profit and loss, risk and reward. "In America, there continue to be dialysis practices that health professionals in other countries find profoundly shocking," says Robert Bear. "In too many instances, the unthinkable has become completely acceptable."

Many of the bad things that happen to dialysis patients in America since the roll-up are not acts of malice aforethought, but byproducts of a specific philosophy of medicine that treats healthcare as a business like any other. Fraud and patient harm often arise as emergent phenomena from the initial conditions of the fast food model, and from its baked-in incentives. For instance, how are people placed—or not placed—on transplant waitlists? Renal failure patients can only leave dialysis by dying, or by getting a new kidney. Transplantation isn't always easy or risk-free: donor kidneys can fail, and some patients suffer chemotherapy-like side effects from the immunosuppressant drugs that they must take to minimize the odds of organ rejection. Still, a transplant frees patients from the often debilitating and dangerous experience of dialysis, and allows them to return to a comparatively normal existence. Cornelius Robbins, who received a kidney transplant in November 2021, has resumed his work as a cook at a barbecue pit, and says he feels completely normal most days, though he still has to remind himself to drink water regularly, after living with stringent limits on fluid intake for the seven years he was on dialysis. "Seven years," he says, as if he's still amazed to be talking about dialysis in the past tense. "I don't miss that world at all. I only wish I'd gotten a transplant sooner, and lost less of my life."

Trouble is, he says, the dialysis clinic in Evans, Georgia, where he began to dialyze never placed him on the transplant list, and the clinic in Augusta to which he later transferred actually removed him from the list. "I got kicked off the waitlist there in Augusta because one of the doctors decided she didn't like my attitude, which I didn't think I had an attitude, it was more so I just didn't agree with what she was saying." So Robbins entered himself on the transplant list in Charleston, South Carolina, and two years later, received a new kidney. "If I hadn't signed myself up, I'd still be sitting there on that machine," he says.

Here financial interests collide head-on with human welfare. Workers at dialysis clinics are responsible for informing patients of their transplant options, but consciously or subconsciously, they know that every transplant deprives their clinic of a portion of its revenues. Some clinic workers actively discourage patients from obtaining transplants, by stressing the negative aspects of transplantation; others, as Cornelius Robbins experienced, bump patients off the list as a form of reprisal. Medical researchers and economists alike have demonstrated a strong correlation between the dialysis industry's poor transplantation record and the profit motive: patients at for-profit clinics are consistently less likely to be placed on a transplant list, and therefore to receive a new kidney, than those at nonprofit clinics.

Several patients I've interviewed say they were denied a place on the waitlist after having been classified by their clinic staff as "noncompliant." Technically this means that a patient isn't following her treatment plan and is therefore ineligible for a transplant, but the term is highly subjective and, in my experience, is often used to stigmatize and punish patients who are unpopular with clinic employees. Other motives for excluding patients from a transplant waitlist appear equally arbitrary. Carrie Brito was passed over, she says, because a social worker at her clinic declared that her husband William did not provide a sufficiently supportive home environment—presumably implying that, were she to receive a transplant, she wouldn't get adequate help from her spouse while she recuperated from the transplant operation.

Another adverse effect created by the profit motive in dialysis, and in many other areas of medicine, is the laser focus on high-margin private payor patients—the HIPPERs we've already heard about. This not only diminishes Medicare and Medicaid patients in the eyes of some health workers, but can compromise their care in various ways. Patients and dialysis workers alike have explained to me how new dialysis patients are routinely steered by clinic staff—typically social workers or "enrollment counselors"—away from government insurance programs like Medicare, into private insurance programs, sometimes involving financial assistance from the American Kidney Fund (AKF), a charitable foundation that helps dialysis patients pay their insurance bills. Since, as we've seen, privately insured patients are far more remunerative than patients covered by government programs, it's hardly surprising that dialysis companies prefer privately insured patients. Private payors are so lucrative, in fact, that companies themselves would gladly pay their premiums, were this not a criminal offense under the federal Anti-Kickback Statute.

So the dialysis companies, it seems, found a work-around. A 2018 letter sent by major insurance organizations, including America's Health Insurance Plans and the Blue Cross Blue Shield Association, to Alex

Azar, then Secretary of HHS, asserted that "dialysis providers are paying premiums through a financially interested third party—the American Kidney Fund—for ESRD patients in order to steer them away from Medicaid and Medicare and into commercial Exchange plans so that they can profit from the higher reimbursement rates paid by these issuers." An equity research report issued by J.P. Morgan on October 9th, 2017, estimated that the return on charitable donations by dialysis providers to the American Kidney Fund likely exceeded 500 percent.

In a statement to me, AKF chief executive LaVarne Burton wrote: "Let us be clear: We do **not** refer patients to dialysis providers. We do **not** refer patients to insurance plans or advise them in any way on their choice of insurance. We help **any** patient who qualifies financially for our assistance, regardless of whether their dialysis provider contributes to AKF." (Emphasis in the original text.) A subsequent letter from an attorney representing the AKF emphasized that "AKF does not steer patients to insurance plans; it does not advise patients on selection of insurance plans; it does not offer or endorse health insurance policies; it does not base its grant approval on a patient's choice of insurance carrier or plan." In her statement, Burton explained that "a firewall established in Advisory Opinion 97-1 ensures that dialysis providers have no say in whether AKF will provide assistance to their patients; they may not condition or restrict their donations."

The advisory opinion mentioned by Burton was issued in 1997 by the HHS Office of the Inspector General, and marked a major shift in the evolution of the AKF. The opinion was issued at the request of the AKF and six companies, whose names are redacted in the published opinion. The seven organizations asked the HHS a straightforward question: was it legal for dialysis companies to donate to an independent 501(c)(3) charitable organization (e.g., the AKF), in order to fund a premium assistance program for dialysis patients? In response, the HHS OIG stated that it would consider such donations to be legitimate, provided that the AKF and its donors followed certain rules. In particular, the AKF could not "take the identity of the referring facility or the amount of any provider's donation into consideration when assessing patient applications or making grant determinations." In other words, the AKF had to distribute its aid in an arm's length manner, helping patients without considering whether their dialysis provider had contributed to the Fund, and showing no favoritism to firms that had made particularly generous donations. This is the firewall that Ms. Burton referenced.

The OIG advisory opinion opened the floodgates to donations to the AKF. Until 1997, the Fund had been a relatively small organization, primarily supported by individual donors—in 1996, for example, the AKF revenues were about $5 million, about 70 percent of which came from individual donors. But by 1998, the year after the opinion was issued, revenues had already risen to $14 million, and continued growing thereafter: to $68 million in 2004, and to $350 million in 2021. The Fund is now 54th on the Forbes list of large US non-profits, ranking above the Rotary Foundation and the Wounded Warrior Project. "Switching our emphasis to corporate partners in '97 was the real turning point in our organization," observed Don Roy, then the AKF's Managing Director of Finance and Operation, in a 2007 report. Indeed, after the OIG ruling, corporations swiftly replaced individual donors as the primary source of the Fund's revenues. In 2021, according to the Fund's audited financial statements, 86 percent of its total support and revenues—$302 million dollars—came from just two corporations. While the auditors do not name these corporations, there are two logical candidates: Fresenius and DaVita.

Assertions by the AKF and its attorneys notwithstanding, between 2016 and 2019 a series of lawsuits; investigations carried out by CMS, insurance companies and law firms; journalistic accounts; and testimonials by industry insiders have suggested that the AKF's work may be less impartial and charitable than the Fund claims. For example, a shareholder class action lawsuit filed against DaVita, Kent Thiry and other senior DaVita executives, which DaVita settled in 2021 by paying $135 million, alleged the following:

> As set forth in detail below—and as confirmed by internal Company documents and numerous high-ranking former DaVita employees—during the Class Period, Defendants implemented a Company-wide

*scheme whose entire purpose was to "steer" every single one of DaVi-
ta's Medicare and Medicaid patients to commercial insurance, thereby
inflating the Company's profits by hundreds of millions of dollars.*

*Moreover, because ESRD patients typically could not afford the
premiums for commercial insurance, and anti-kickback statutes prevented DaVita from directly paying its patients' premiums, DaVita
developed a fraudulent scheme designed to evade those regulations.
Specifically, DaVita engaged in a "quid pro quo" relationship with the
American Kidney Fund ("AKF"), a purportedly independent 501(c)(3)
non-profit. Pursuant to this relationship, DaVita ostensibly "donated"
hundreds of millions of dollars to the AKF, and in turn, the AKF used
those proceeds to pay the commercial insurance premiums for DaVita's
patients. DaVita then billed commercial insurers multiples of what it
donated. This scheme proved highly lucrative to DaVita.*

(AKF was not named as a defendant in this lawsuit, and denies
all allegations relating to it made in the suit. As part of the settlement
agreement, DaVita denied all wrongdoing.)

Another lawsuit, filed in 2019 by Blue Cross and Blue Shield of Florida against DaVita, alleged that "AKF and a handful of large dialysis
providers (including DaVita) have turned AKF's HIPP [Health Insurance Premium Payment] program into a lucrative investment vehicle,
wherein the dialysis providers use AKF as a conduit to pay (and con-
ceal the fact that they are paying) the commercial insurance premiums
of patients dialyzing at their facilities, to induce them to enroll in or
stay enrolled in the insurance plans that in turn pay lucrative reimbursement rates to the dialysis providers." (AKF was not named as a
defendant in this suit. On June 7, 2022, parties in the lawsuit issued a
joint notice of settlement, although details of the settlement agreement
have not been made public.)

The AKF strenuously rejects all of these charges, and has consistently denied that it has ever conditioned its premium assistance
payments on the level of donations of its corporate donors, or encouraged patients to seek treatment with firms that had made donations
to the Fund. However, several sources have suggested otherwise. In a

December 2016 article in the *New York Times*, authors Katie Thomas and Reed Abelson, citing public documents as well as interviews with social workers, dialysis employees, insurance officials, regulators and a former AKF executive, observed: "In multiple cases, the charity [i.e., the AKF] pushed back on workers at clinics that had not donated money, discouraging them from signing up their patients for assistance. Until recently, the Kidney Fund's guidelines even said clinics should not apply for patient aid if the company had not donated to the charity."

Similarly, a lawsuit filed in 2016 in Florida and Massachusetts by UnitedHealthcare against a smaller dialysis company, American Renal Associates (ARA), alleged that "AKF and dialysis providers have turned AKF's HIPP program into a pay-to-play scheme, whereby AKF instructs and requires providers to calculate and contribute 'donations' to AKF proportional to the amount of 'funding' those providers expect their patients to draw from AKF's HIPP program." (AKF was not named as a defendant in this lawsuit, and denies all allegations relating to it made in the suit. ARA settled this lawsuit in 2018 by paying $32 million, and admitted no wrongdoing.) And a whistleblower lawsuit unsealed in 2019, which was brought against the AKF, DaVita and Fresenius by David Gonzalez, a twelve-year veteran of the AKF, alleged that "Contrary to the conditions set forth on page 5 of the Advisory Opinion 97-1, the AKF has been taking into account the identity of the contributors by tracking, which provider was paying them and how much, for several years." Gonzalez further alleged that the AKF instituted a "blocked" list, "which meant that any application from a patient using that provider would not receive funds until such time as the provider contributed to the program"; and that he had heard his superiors at the AKF "directing social workers and patients to use Fresenius and DaVita if the provider had not contributed to the AKF." (The AKF denies all allegations relating to it made in the lawsuit. Gonzalez and his attorneys voluntarily withdrew the suit in 2019, after the Department of Justice elected not to join the case.)

On July 23, 2019, Representative Katie Porter wrote a letter to the HHS OIG, in which she noted what she called "disturbing revelations regarding the American Kidney Fund's practices." "Based on recent investigative reporting and legal challenges, AKF and its donors' practices appear to be clear violations of OIG's 1997 Advisory Opinion and may be putting patients' lives at risk. In short, the dialysis providers providing the biggest donations seem to exert significant influence on how AKF distributes its financial assistance to patients and clinics." Porter asked the HHS OIG to open an investigation into the matter, and in the meantime, to "suspend its agreement with the AKF and all relevant companies in order to reevaluate the legality of this agreement and the effects that it has on patients' ability to access affordable, quality ESRD care."

One of Porter's main points was that, regardless of the AKF's activities or intentions, the fixation of for-profit dialysis companies with their patients' insurance status can cause human as well as financial harm. According to a fact sheet and an interim final rule both published by CMS in 2016, patients who are eligible for Medicare or Medicaid, but who instead are enticed into private coverage funded by third-party premium assistance, may encounter difficulty obtaining transplants; face drastically increased out-of-pocket expenses; and suffer shortfalls in their insurance when they try to switch to public coverage.

This emphasis on insurance status creates a caste system among patients. "Our managers tell us to roll out the red carpet for corporate [privately insured] patients, make sure they get the dialysis schedules they want, any special requests," one dialysis worker in California told me. "But Medicare and Medi-Cal [California's implementation of Medicaid] patients are treated like second-class citizens." Another worker mentioned that privately insured patients were routinely offered the "Golden Shift," on Mondays, Wednesdays and Fridays at eight o'clock in the morning, which most patients prefer.

The Golden Shifts and kid-glove care often end when private payors transition to government insurance, which in most cases happens by law after thirty months. "So long as I had a great insurance through my wife's job, I got good care, even though I spoke out about what was wrong at the clinic," Cornelius Robbins remembers of his facility in Evans, Georgia. "But when my wife's company downsized and she lost her job, people started treating me differently, started making complaints about me." Before long, Robbins was discharged.

Even well-meaning incentives can go awry in the presence of a pervasively for-profit mentality. The CMS's QIP and 5-Star rating system are both designed to improve dialysis care by measuring each facility's performance on major health indices, and penalizing underperformers. In principle this seems a good idea, and no doubt has improved the quality of care in many units. In others, however, it seems to have engendered a culture of systemic fraud. In 2015, Canadian nephrologist Joanne Bargman gave the keynote address at the Annual Dialysis Conference in New Orleans, a presentation she called "Buffing the Numbers: The Decline and Fall of Dialysis Medicine." In it she listed a litany of fifteen fraudulent laboratory practices that she had witnessed in American dialysis centers, performed in order to make patients appear more healthy, and thereby to avoid financial penalties by CMS. These included:

> Keep doing the Kt/V until you get the number you want
> Draw bloods mid-week so P [phosphorus] is lower:
>   "Strategic Lab Drawing"
> Use a larger HD [hemodialysis] kidney on lab day
> Dump blood circuits if the hemoglobin level is too high

Bargman's list also included the useful tactic, explained to her by an eminent nephrologist, of provoking low-scoring patients into angry outbursts, in order to discharge them. At the end of the talk, she received a standing ovation from the audience of dialysis practitioners, who evidently knew all too well the problems she had described, and were glad that someone had finally dared to denounce them.

Such practices continue. I've interviewed dialysis workers who report they've worked in units that routinely tamper with laboratory tests, drawing blood post-dialysis instead of pre-dialysis as regulation requires (post-treatment blood is "cleaner"), forging test dates, and committing other irregularities. All the same, "buffing the numbers" is dangerous as well as dishonest. After all, how can a nephrologist prescribe appropriate treatment for her patients when their lab work has been doctored? Cornelius Robbins remembers how the nurses at his clinic in Evans, Georgia, complained about having to perform the same laboratory tests repeatedly, until the results were acceptable. When he began dialyzing at another unit in Claxton, Georgia, he says the staff there found that his bloodwork, which had always seemed normal at his old clinic, was badly out of range. "I used to look at it like it was a curse, getting kicked out of that clinic [in Evans], but it turned out to be the best thing that ever could happen to me. If I hadn't gotten kicked out, I probably wouldn't have made it." He describes a close friend who died from low potassium, a condition that can cause cardiac arrest. "He went to sleep and never woke up. But that's something I feel like they should have caught at dialysis, if you're doing all these tests, and you're not fudging the numbers."

Quality incentives also appear to drive patient terminations. "I always get a flood of calls from patients toward the end of the year, when clinics prepare for their quality ratings, and start terminating unhealthy patients who would lower their overall score," says Arlene Mullin. "I call December and January 'the Five Star Season.'" Preliminary analysis by economist Ryan McDevitt and colleagues, which is awaiting peer review, seems to confirm this. "Facilities appear to strategically drop patients with low QIP scores, who are likely to induce penalties," McDevitt says. In one example they considered, until 2013, patients received a quality measure on the basis of their urea reduction ratio (URR), which each unit had to report to CMS. After 2013, this URR metric was replaced with Kt/V. Until 2013, patients with poor URR but good Kt/V were much more likely to leave a facility; after 2013, when Kt/V became the official quality measure, this relationship was inverted: suddenly patients with poor Kt/V but good URR were being nudged out more often.

❑

RUNNING DIALYSIS clinics, nursing homes, hospices, urgent care units and other medical facilities as zealously for-profit concerns tends to emphasize the identity of patients as profit centers, and to obscure their condition as suffering humans. "Patient harm in a for-profit healthcare setting is highly predictable," says Steffie Woolhandler, an internist, researcher and teacher at the City University of New York at Hunter College, and a lecturer at Harvard Medical School. "There's not one indicator that does not suggest that we are harming patients by allowing for-profit dialysis, nursing homes, and other care. Every time that we can identify some way in which the profits of the providers could possibly get in the way of the well-being of the patients, the for-profit companies have done that."

If McDevitt is an economist who has CT-scanned healthcare with the analytical tools of his trade, Woolhandler is a practicing MD who has probed, and suffered, the distortions caused by for-profit medicine from within the medical-industrial complex. She has full, long, gray-brown hair and a kindly but slightly skeptical expression, at least until she sizes me up. She speaks in the fluid, weighty periods of the prominent public intellectual she is, with occasional flashes of the fire of social activism which she has practiced since her undergraduate days at Stanford in the 1970s, when she marched against the Vietnam War. Despite having worked most of her career in distinguished universities and hospitals on the East and West Coasts, the accent of her native Shreveport, Louisiana, remains strong: *For-profit dah-alisis companies are much less lahkly to refer a patient for trans-playnt.* Woolhandler is sharply critical of for-profit care, status-quo doctors, and the current state of American medicine.

"You could think of the for-profit dialysis companies as neoliberal rent-takers," she says. "A dialysis patient needs the machine, they need the supplies, they need a nurse who runs the dialysis machine, they need a doctor to supervise the process, all of which has to be paid for. But you don't actually need a for-profit company standing between you and those resources."

Neoliberalism has created a system in which the government collects money with taxes, but instead of using that money to provide healthcare directly to patients, the government hands the money over to private corporations, which have insinuated themselves between the population and the Treasury. These corporations become toll booths that collect economic "rents"—unnecessary profits that provide no additional services—from the practice of medicine. "Today many people say, 'Oh, isn't it just normal that a for-profit company has to stand between me and a dialysis machine where I actually need one, or a for-profit company has to stand between me and my doctor?'" Woolhandler continues. "But for-profit medicine was not considered normal until the neoliberal era. It was not considered normal in the New Deal era, it was not considered normal in the civil rights era. And it's really a triumph of ideology, turning into political power, that these neoliberal ideas have entered into healthcare. Neoliberalism created this process where corporate forces were able to garner a larger and larger share of total resources in the society, and continually use their financial and political power to tilt the playing field in their direction."

In 1980, the year Reagan was first elected president, America spent around 9 percent of its GDP on healthcare, roughly the same as other member nations of the Organization for Economic Co-operation and Development (OECD), and enjoyed strong medical outcomes compared to its OECD peers. Since then, as the share of US medicine provided by profit-driven companies has increased, healthcare prices have surged and quality has slumped. The transformation of US dialysis mirrors the broader evolution of the healthcare landscape in America, where roll-ups have created for-profit cartels in many medical fields, and a handful of large corporations use their economic muscle to drive up prices, suppress competition, blunt regulation and head off new laws that might curtail their profits. In 2019, after decades of neoliberalism, the United States spent 17.6 percent of its GDP on healthcare; CMS projects that medical expenditures will grow annually by 5.4 percent through 2028. And America's medical outcomes have dropped to the bottom of the OECD list by nearly all measures: the United States currently ranks twenty-ninth in life expectancy, and thirty-third in infant mortality.

Fast food medicine both illustrates and helps to explain these trends. Under the fast food model, high-risk medical procedures are routinely shifted from hospitals to outpatient facilities in strip malls, business parks and the like, where patients who experience health crises are in danger without the emergency medical facilities and expertise that hospitals provide. Consider the more than 5,800 freestanding surgery centers that currently operate across America, and receive $5.2 billion from Medicare. Chronic flaws at these facilities are putting more and more lives at risk: a 2018 investigation by Kaiser Health News revealed inexperienced staff, working without lifesaving equipment such as defibrillators, having to call 9-1-1 for advice in health emergencies; and hundreds of patients dying because they'd been sent home before being properly stabilized, or because their surgeon wasn't available. Nevertheless, federal officials, evidently eager to reduce runaway healthcare costs, continue to certify such clinics, just as they approve urgent care and cardiovascular units, sports medicine centers, and other outpatient facilities, which likewise have been the scene of extensive patient harm, and the target of numerous fraud investigations.

Woolhandler points out that private equity (PE) firms are driving a new wave of financialization and managerial control in American medicine. PE firms have invested almost $750 billion in healthcare acquisitions over the past decade, and more than $150 billion in 2021 alone. PE giants like Bain Capital, Carlyle and KKR wield increasing power in many medical settings, including hospices, acute care hospitals, substance abuse treatment centers, nursing homes, dentistry, ophthalmology, autism services, emergency medical transport and physician staffing. "Private equity" is a rebranding of the infamous leveraged buyout formula that emerged in the late 1970s, and PE firms today follow the same script: buy a firm, in large part with debt you've forced that firm to assume; extract as much cash as possible from it with techniques like selling the firm's own real estate out from under it, slashing its skilled staff and charging massive management fees; then sell off what remains of the firm, typically within four to seven years. Most PE transactions aren't required by law to be reported to antitrust or financial regulators, and though the Securities and Exchange Commission (SEC) is attempting to gain more control over the industry—senior SEC officials have denounced pervasive wrongdoing in PE—the commission currently has limited oversight. The freedom from scrutiny, short time horizons and extreme emphasis on financial returns displayed by PE firms have led to cost cutting and asset stripping on a whole new scale in healthcare: Fast Food Medicine 2.0. Poor care at PE-owned nursing homes and huge surprise bills for routine medical services at PE-controlled hospitals have recently been debated by Congress. A 2021 white paper on private equity in US medicine, written by scholars at the American Antitrust Institute and the University of California, Berkeley, School of Public Health, concluded trenchantly, "The private equity business model is fundamentally incompatible with sound healthcare that serves patients."

Trends at hospices and nursing homes recall those in the dialysis industry. In the increasingly for-profit hospice space, providers cherry-pick patients who have lower day-to-day needs and are expected to live longer, and decline to admit less lucrative patients. Hospice companies receive a per diem fee for every patient they admit, and earn more on lower-risk patients who live longer than on high-needs patients who only survive for weeks or days. Hence they prefer heart failure patients, for example, who tend to stay in hospice six months or longer, to cancer sufferers, who often enter in the last weeks of life, and have high needs that escalate as they approach the end.

In many for-profit nursing homes, high patient-to-caregiver ratios lower the quality of care, and patient terminations are on the rise. "I have heard of and found a lot of involuntary discharges from nursing homes," says Steffie Woolhandler, who has researched the industry extensively. "A very common theme is to send patients to the hospital, and then refuse to take them back." As it happens, her great aunt, who suffers from dementia, was terminated from a nursing home via this procedure. "She poked someone with a plastic fork and got discharged. They just didn't want to deal with her anymore. That happens all the time. What they're worried about most is that the patient is going to take a lot of the staff time, and not bring in enough money."

Woolhandler's tone doesn't change as she says this, but something in her demeanor hardens. "There's no constitutional right to run a for-profit nursing home or dialysis center," she continues. "There's no constitutional right to discharge a patient because she lost her temper and started yelling at your staff. That's not a right. And if you're taking public money, then you ought to have some obligation to do your job."

The collective result of America's prioritization of profits over patients is the nation's current $4.1 trillion annual medical bill, which is as unsustainable for patients as it is for taxpayers. Bankruptcy from health services is the leading cause of personal insolvency. Many Americans, to make ends meet, are forced to skip treatments and to leave prescriptions unfilled. All of which helps to explain why America is undergoing a period of rising mortality that has no modern precedent. And why life spans, infections, heart problems and hospitalizations for patients on dialysis in the United States, already worse than elsewhere, aren't improving.

Woolhandler stresses that this situation is not inevitable, but the result of specific political decisions, which can be reversed. "Medicare absolutely has the power to say, 'We are not using for-profit dialysis, we're demanding that for-profit centers convert to nonprofit status. Prior to 1980, Medicare had a prohibition against for-profit healthcare, and it was never challenged. That was just the rule. So this is a policy decision that has been made at the federal level, to allow for-profit healthcare companies, and then to ignore these pieces of evidence that tell you the for-profit companies have done exactly what you expect them to do: maximize their profits by every legal means. Even when we know, and they know, that it harms patients."

Ryan McDevitt, the economist, has reached similar conclusions, which might have sounded radical to him back in 2010, when he began exploring the dialysis industry. "As a healthcare system, maybe we shouldn't have so much of a for-profit mindset. Free markets don't work as well here as they would in some other settings."

To correct the distortions of the dialysis industry, his solution is simple. "I think we need to break up the big chains. That's where we're headed."

· 8 ·

Musketeers

A VILLAIN CLAD all in black, from her black mask and broad-brimmed hat to her swirling cape and jet-black boots, menaces the crowd with a sword. She says she's found evidence that DaVita, the company they work for, has been breaking the law.

"Somebody is going to *pay!*" she gloats.

"Oh nooooo!" exclaims an angel with droopy white wings and a furry halo, standing stage left. "What are we gonna do *now?*"

Abruptly the camera swings to one of the firm's senior executives, Dennis Kogod, dressed in the colorful silks, plumed hat and tall riding boots of a musketeer. "I am DaVita Director D'Artagnan," he shouts, waving a sword of his own, "and I'm going to save the Village!" Kogod charges the black-masked villain, fences briefly with her, then lunges forward and stabs her through the body. She falls lifeless to the ground, and the crowd roars its approval.

During the same skit, two more black-swathed enemies question the propriety of certain DaVita practices, and threaten to reduce the firm's profits. They too are confronted and killed by senior DaVita executives dressed as musketeers, who likewise claim to be defending their "Village" from the faceless forces of bureaucratic evil. In the end, after the last play-murder, the three triumphant musketeer-executives raise their swords and address the crowd.

"Once again the medical musketeers have persevered," Kogod shouts. "Justice has prevailed and dialysis spreads throughout the community. Please stand!"

Then he and his fellow musketeer-executives lead the rapt, standing viewers in a crescendoing call-and-response chant.

"All for one . . . ," the executives call out.

"And one for all!" the employees echo back.

"All for one . . ."

"And one for all!" they shout.

"All for one . . ."

"And one for allllllll!" they howl.

But who are the black-masked villains that DaVita's heroic leaders have dispatched? The female bandit killed by Dennis Kogod identifies herself as a federal prosecutor, to boos and jeers from the crowd. The other two thugs are a government healthcare regulator, presumably working for the Centers for Medicare & Medicaid Services (CMS), and an insurance executive.

When Eric Havian, a former federal prosecutor turned whistleblower attorney who has confronted DaVita in complex litigation, saw this skit, he says he had two strong reactions. "I wondered who possibly could have thought this was a good idea—to pretend to murder a career prosecutor just for doing their job? But then I thought, 'Couldn't they do better?' It struck me how thoroughly brainwashed the DaVita 'Village' must be, to think this kind of lowbrow frat humor is funny."

What, in fact, is life in the Village really like?

❑

"THE MUSKETEERS skit shows DaVita's two-faced nature," says David Barbetta, a former financial analyst with DaVita, who won a major whistleblower suit against the company in 2014, with the help of whistleblower attorneys Eric Havian and Jessica Moore. "The company wants to have a good relationship with CMS. Ultimately it wants to convince the government that it should pay more money for dialysis. But then, behind closed doors, they're sword fighting, stabbing, murdering a government adjuster, a person at CMS that is deciding the rate to pay."

Barbetta joined DaVita in April of 2007, after six years on Wall Street, where he'd most recently worked in the equity research department at Goldman Sachs. When he became a financial analyst in the DaVita "Deal Depot," the firm's mergers and acquisitions department, he entered a culture that, at least on the surface, couldn't have been more different from the culture of a Wall Street bank. "One of the company's core values was 'fun,'" Barbetta remembers. "Everyone would sing at company meetings. People dressed up in costumes, there were skits and dancing. It was very . . . *different*. I thought it was better than a boring, dry office, but it still seemed a little strange. You felt obligated to participate even if you weren't into singing and dancing." He said that many employees recognized that the atmosphere resembled a cult. "To see how committed you were, people inside the company would literally ask, 'Have you drunk the Kool-Aid?' People talked about it all the time. Even the ones who were fully, both feet in, people who loved this culture and everything about it, even *they* were aware it was unique, and that some other people thought it was cult-like."

Early in his training, Barbetta attended a large corporate gathering where he and the other employees were told to stand and clasp the hands of nearby "teammates," much as Catholics exchange the sign of peace during the Mass, and to tell each other, "I save lives." Barbetta heard frequent references to DaVita's commitment to make the world a better place: "'Caring for our world' was a common refrain." Later, however, he came to question the sincerity of these goals. He remembers a senior executive calling an impromptu meeting in a conference room, to announce that DaVita had successfully lobbied a state legislature to pass a law making it more difficult for insurance companies to negotiate lower dialysis fees.

"He told us, 'We passed a law!' and everyone cheered," Barbetta remembers. "But I didn't cheer."

He hesitates, as if scouring his memory for the reason he didn't applaud—for his exact thoughts at that moment. Barbetta is a clean-cut man in his mid-thirties with close-cropped black hair and dark, thoughtful, slightly amused eyes. He speaks carefully, and has a habit of precision; he is obviously concerned not only to convey the details of his work accurately, but also to grasp their deeper meaning for himself. "This new law was good for DaVita, clearly," he continues, "because insurance companies would be less able to negotiate lower prices, so the company's profits would be higher. But how was this about saving lives or helping patients? How was this good for society? If insurance companies had to pay higher prices, then Americans would have to pay higher health insurance premiums. For a company that claimed to be 'Caring for our world,' it seemed a strange thing to celebrate."

In the Deal Depot, Barbetta and his workmates bought, sold and formed joint ventures with independent dialysis centers owned by nephrologists. Joint ventures were an essential way for DaVita to increase its revenues, because the nephrologists with whom the company struck bargains would likely refer their patients to DaVita clinics. In view of the sensitivity of the doctor-patient relationship, however, and the risk that a nephrologist could prioritize profits over patient well-being, the federal Anti-Kickback Statute (AKS) specifically prohibits paying doctors to induce them to refer patients to clinics that would then collect insurance payments from those patients. The AKS also requires that all payments to doctors, including the cost of buying or selling their practices, be made at fair market value. When companies buy practices from doctors at above-market value, or sell them to doctors at artificially low rates, the doctors' profits could represent payments for their future referrals of patients: in plain words, kickbacks.

In Barbetta's first deals at the company, he was assigned to work on only one-half of the transaction—the valuation that DaVita applied to the shares of a dialysis practice it was buying, or one it was selling. After about a year, his bosses, evidently satisfied with his performance and trustworthiness, started assigning him to deals where he saw both sides. Right away, he noticed puzzling mismatches. "You'd sell a doctor a piece of paper worth $1 million," he remembers, "and then you'd buy it back from the same doctor shortly after, for $3 million. The contrast was striking. It just looked off. There was clearly something not right about it."

As his transaction experience grew, Barbetta began to recognize mechanisms that were being used to manipulate the valuations. He learned about HIPPERs, the DaVita shorthand for privately insured, high-worth patients, whose red-carpet treatment Brent Miller and others have objected to. Barbetta also learned of a financial trick called "HIPPER compression," which worked like this: by assuming that, within three years of starting dialysis, the insurance companies of all HIPPERs receiving treatment at a given dialysis business would be able to negotiate a 40 percent lower payment rate, DaVita could arrive at an artificially low valuation for the business, thus making it more attractive for nephrologists to whom DaVita wished to sell. Conversely, when buying joint venture shares from nephrologists, DaVita analysists would employ another financial gimmick, the "HIPPER bus," to inflate the value of those shares. The deal team simply assumed that a bus full of high-value, commercially insured patients was one day going to appear magically at the center, and *voilà*, DaVita could justify paying millions of extra dollars to the doctors who owned that center.

Just how routine such manipulations had become was spelled out by Bryan Parker, a DaVita vice president in special projects, in an email exchange with other members of the Deal Depot on July 24, 2009, not long after Barbetta had announced his resignation. "Sorry to hear you are leaving us, but do wish you the best," Parker wrote to Barbetta. "I was hopeful before you leave you . . . can give us a list of the most common things one could do within the model to make sure it passes the COC [cash-on-cash] and IRR [internal rate of return] hurdles."

Chet Mehta, a vice president in finance who had been copied on the email, fired back, "Bryan—you mean 'gaming' the model, right?"

"I do," Parker replied. "Thanks Chet."

The company's compliance department struck Barbetta as a façade, more concerned with concealing problems than with preventing them. The compliance policy, Barbetta says, contained a series of "What's Wrong to Write Commandments," a list of activities that employees should never, *ever* put in writing. "Not that you shouldn't actually *do* anything wrong," Barbetta explains, "just that you shouldn't write it down." (He remembers that Edwin Winstead and Jaime Peña, federal prosecutors with whom he worked on the government's lawsuit against DaVita, took particular note of these Commandments.) Managers in the Deal Depot employed similar practices. Barbetta remembers, during a conference call on February 16, 2009, a Deal Depot vice president telling members of the team to "Stop putting stuff in emails." If there was any sensitivity in a model that would result in a value going up or down depending on assumptions made by the financial analyst, the vice president said, they were not to write this fact down, but simply to email the Excel file that contained the financial model, then phone the recipient, and explain the problem verbally. "He was telling us not to leave a paper trail," Barbetta says, shaking his head. "I could not *believe* this was happening. None of it seemed real."

"There was a sort of fatalism," Barbetta remembers. "Everyone who saw both sides of the deals knew there was something wrong, but I guess they didn't feel they had the power to change it. So they just kind of joked about it. I think humor was a coping mechanism—the cognitive dissonance came out in the form of jokes."

Despite the merriment, everyone who took part was participating, more or less knowingly, in this scheme. "You could tell yourself that any one of these things by itself isn't such a big deal," he remembers. "One financial projection that perhaps is not accurate is not the end of the world. But as soon as you take that first step, you're going to be asked to take another, and another. So as soon as you take that first step into a light gray area, you start walking, and the next thing you know, you look around and you can't tell, 'Is it dark gray right now, or is it black? And how did this happen?' The last thing I knew I was trying to make good decisions in life, and all of a sudden I took a couple of steps in this one direction, and I'm looking around now and thinking, 'Oh my goodness, where did I end up?'"

The deal that shocked him into action took place in the summer of 2008, in Denver, one of the Deal Depot's "competitive hotspots"— regions where DaVita was at risk of losing business to competing dialysis firms. Deal Depot members carefully tracked hotspots on a computer database, and executives strove to close joint venture agreements with nephrologists in these regions. When they succeeded, they quantified the number of patients and revenue DaVita had "saved" by preventing patients from being referred to competitors. To maintain its market share in the strategic Denver area, DaVita approached Denver Nephrology, a group of doctors that was already referring a substantial number of patients to DaVita dialysis centers on the east side of Denver, with the aim of forming a joint venture on the west side of the city. The transaction involved DaVita selling shares in eight dialysis centers in west Denver to the Denver Nephrology doctors, and simultaneously buying shares from the same doctors in three centers just across town.

In accord with the Deal Depot valuation, DaVita bought the three centers in east Denver for about $13 million each, and sold the eight centers in west Denver at only $635,000 each—DaVita valued the centers it bought at *twenty times* the price of those it sold. "One day the doctors have 50 percent ownership of three clinics," Barbetta explains, "and on the next day, after transaction closes, they have 50 percent of eight centers, and more than $15 million in cash in a wire because of the valuation discrepancy." Barbetta heard that a DaVita vice president had described the transaction as handing the doctors "a bag of money."

After that deal, Barbetta started looking for another job. He also began trying to decide what, if anything, he could do to stop the practices he'd seen at work, which he was convinced were illegal. Working together with his attorneys Havian and Moore, and later with federal prosecutors, Barbetta pieced together what he believed to be DaVita's business model in forming joint ventures. (Barbetta spent about 5,000 hours analyzing internal DaVita documents, and explaining them to prosecutors and his attorneys.)

According to federal prosecutors, the company was systematically targeting specific physicians and physician groups with whom to form partnerships. They referred to promising nephrologists as "winning practices"—not because of their superior expertise or quality of care, but for the number of patients they could refer to DaVita, and for certain factors that made them appear more likely to enter a joint venture agreement with the company. (One physician group was identified as a "winning practice" because its doctors were "young and in debt," and therefore presumably more apt to sign an agreement.) The company then created an enticing financial opportunity for these physicians, allegedly by manipulating the valuation of the centers it was buying or selling. On signing the joint venture deal, DaVita would lock in the nephrologists with a series of mandatory noncompetition, nonsolicitation and nondisparagement clauses, which prohibited them from competing with DaVita or advising patients to seek treatment outside the company. Prosecutors alleged that many such agreements violated the Anti-Kickback Statute, because they once again placed profit motive before patient care.

Most patients don't stop to think why their nephrologist refers them to one clinic rather than another. They assume this choice is made to benefit their health and convenience—by sending them to a unit with a record of high-quality care, for example, or to one that is located near their home. But when a doctor owns a financial interest in a center, or has signed an agreement not to refer patients elsewhere, financial incentives can easily muddy her medical ethics.

This business model, as Barbetta and his lawyers understood it from their extensive review of internal company documents during litigation, wasn't created by a few rogue employees or clinics, but was a top-down business plan run from DaVita headquarters, and championed by its highest executives, including its CEO. "We saw Kent Thiry's fingerprints and name on lots of stuff," says Eric Havian. "Thiry micromanaged that company, and was very focused on the details of the operation. He knew how they did their valuations, and there was a very low dollar threshold on deals that required his sign-off. And he didn't just rubber-stamp the deals—he really got into the details, and asked a lot of questions. He was the driving force behind a lot of bad practices. In my opinion, he knew exactly what was going on." (Havian stresses that these observations summarize or repeat matters that he uncovered while preparing the case, and that he and his client alleged in their lawsuit.)

Havian says, for example, that from internal company documents it was clear that Thiry had championed the use of HIPPER compression in the valuation of dialysis clinics. "For years there were people who objected to HIPPER compression, but nobody could tell the CEO, 'We can't do this.' When you see that people right up through the CFO object to a practice, and yet that practice continues, there's little doubt about who is driving it. When you see a continuous revolving door of CFOs, as happened at the company, there's little doubt why." Barbetta observes that from 1999, when Total Renal Care became DaVita, to 2019 when Kent Thiry retired as DaVita's CEO, the firm went through seven full-time CFOs and six interim CFOs, some lasting only months in the position. "The only other Fortune 500 company I am aware of that had a similar track record in CFO turnover is HealthSouth under Richard Scrushy," he says, referring to the scandal-ridden hospital chain and its former CEO, who was jailed for bribery, conspiracy and mail fraud.

The Department of Justice joined Barbetta's case, and the United States Attorney in Colorado opened a grand jury investigation into the company's joint venture relationships with nephrologists. Prosecutors subpoenaed some executives and board members. Commenting on the criminal investigation, Kent Thiry said that his company would cooperate with government investigators. "We are eager to educate them," he said. "We are comfortable and confident with our business practices."

DaVita eventually paid $400 million to settle all civil and criminal charges. The company was required to sign a corporate integrity agreement, which included additional scrutiny by an outside corporate monitor for three years. DaVita admitted no wrongdoing and accepted no liability. The grand jury did not hand down any criminal indictments.

After resigning from DaVita, David Barbetta continued to meet with several of his friends who still worked at the company. Frequently the firm's unique culture came up in conversation. During lunch with one vice president, Barbetta mentioned that he'd recently re-read *Animal Farm*, and that it had reminded him of DaVita.

Barbetta was struck by the vice president's response. "He perked right up, and said, 'Oh yeah, it's *exactly* like that! The rules written on the barn door that are totally different from what's really going on behind the scenes.'" The two shared a few more similarities. Then his friend said something that rocked Barbetta back on his heels.

"At least it's nice, though, when you make it into the farmhouse, and you're sleeping in the beds with the pigs."

Years later, those words still seem to haunt Barbetta. "I couldn't believe he'd said that. I thought, 'Wow, you've basically just told me that you sold your soul.' It's sad to see good people taking the first step into that gray area, and soon finding themselves in really dark gray or black terrain, and now having to assimilate or justify why it was okay to be there."

Since blowing the whistle on DaVita, Barbetta has continued to reflect on his experiences at the company, and on the malevolent power of certain corporations over the human conscience. He has read extensively on the subject of hierarchies and bureaucracies, charismatic leadership, and the powerful gravitational pull of corporate culture. Repeatedly in our conversations, he points out how the structure and ethos of an organization can separate human beings from their ethical principles, and from their essential humanity. Barbetta has examined the mantra of shareholder value, and seen how it is used to reframe ethical questions as business decisions, sometimes even portraying morally aberrant choices as a manager's clear duty, ethically as well as legally.

He observes that many companies, particularly in healthcare, speak movingly of their compassion and public service, but behave like predators. "As a society, we've agreed that life isn't purely economic survival of the fittest. So we pass laws to say, 'Okay, we have these higher values.' But those values get in the way of the corporation, which is like a shark that can never be full, no matter how much it eats. You never have a boardroom conversation when you say, 'Hey, we made $330 million this year, and that's up from $320 million last year, and okay, that's enough: we're just going to make $330 million from now on.' Corporations always want more. Their appetite can never be satisfied."

❑

A CENTRAL feature of fast food medicine as practiced in America is that it produces massive, repeated fraud. Most major hospital chains, pharmaceutical giants, medical device, biotech and other large healthcare companies have records of recidivist wrongdoing, though their executives are almost never prosecuted, nor are the firms barred from working with Medicare and other government programs. All manner of flagrant misconduct, including serious criminal charges, is routinely resolved by the payment of a legal settlement, which often represents a fraction of the money that the firm made during the period of alleged fraud. Worse, prosecutors routinely allow defendants to buy, through the payment of the settlement, the right to claim that they are innocent, to deny all liability for their actions, and to seal compromising documents that may have surfaced during litigation.

The result is an abiding sense of impunity among large healthcare organizations, which leads to more fraud. "Certain very large healthcare companies, who feel confident the government will never invoke a 'death sentence' exclusion from Medicare against them, can perceive lawbreaking, and paying settlements when they're caught, as a cost of doing business," says Jacob Elberg, a former prosecutor specializing in healthcare fraud who now teaches at Seton Hall University Law School. "When sentencing individuals convicted of crimes, we speak a lot about the overall conduct of their lives. But corporations almost never receive sentencing. There's never a public accounting of their conduct."

The history of Big Dialysis bears this out. Each of the large companies that participated in the roll-up of the dialysis industry in the 1990s and 2000s faced charges of and paid large settlements for Medicare fraud, kickbacks and other alleged misconduct. Already in the early 1980s, NMC, the original dialysis giant, was receiving subpoenas and fending off lawsuits for various frauds. In 1996, incapacitated by massive criminal and civil investigations, the company was acquired by Fresenius—which four years later had to cough up $486 million to settle NMC's previous alleged misdeeds. Vivra, Kent Thiry's old firm and America's second-largest dialysis company in the early- to mid-1990s, underwent fraud investigations before being bought up by Gambro. Steven Bander says that, although senior Gambro management felt that certain practices Vivra used to boost profits were highly questionable, several top Vivra executives who had employed those practices were nevertheless retained and promoted at Gambro. Soon enough, Gambro itself was accused of fraud. After repeatedly warning senior managers that they were breaking the law, Bander filed a whistleblower lawsuit against Gambro, settled for $350 million, which detailed how the company was submitting inflated bills to Medicare, paying kickbacks to doctors for referrals, and charging for unnecessary tests and services. The faltering Gambro was bought up by DaVita.

Since becoming the de facto duopoly of American dialysis, DaVita and Fresenius have maintained a brisk pace of business with the Department of Justice, paying multiple major settlements for a variety of alleged wrongful, and sometimes harmful, behavior. Between 2014 and 2018 alone, DaVita and its subsidiaries paid out more than $1.5 billion in legal settlements and damages. Its founder and former CEO, Kent Thiry, stepped down as chief executive in 2019 after a twenty-year tenure, and was indicted two years later by a federal grand jury in Denver on two counts of conspiracy to violate antitrust laws, a felony offense. (In April 2022, a jury acquitted Thiry and DaVita on all charges.)

Though less theatrical, Fresenius, the world's biggest dialysis company, has likewise paid numerous large legal settlements and fines for a variety of alleged civil and criminal misconduct, most recently a $231 million charge for bribery under the Foreign Corrupt Practices Act. On July 12, 2022, the Department of Justice announced its latest whistleblower suit against Fresenius, claiming that the firm has subjected dialysis patients, including elderly, disadvantaged minority, and low-income individuals, to unnecessary fistulagrams, angioplasties and other procedures, to increase its revenues. "The conduct alleged in this case is egregious," said Breon Peace, the United States Attorney for the Eastern District of New York, "as Fresenius not only defrauded federal health care programs but also subjected particularly vulnerable people to medically unnecessary procedures." (Fresenius rejects these allegations and "intends to vigorously defend the litigation.")

More legal battles may be on the way. The 2021 annual report of Fresenius SE & Co. KGaA, the parent company of the Fresenius dialysis subsidiary, mentions fourteen instances of ongoing litigation, subpoenas served by prosecutors, and other legal "contingencies." Another subsidiary, the pharmaceutical manufacturer Fresenius Kabi, also

produces drugs used for executions by lethal injection in some US penitentiaries, so although Fresenius Kabi has publicly objected to this use
of its products, the parent company's overall commitment to "First,
do no harm" may be less than absolute. In 2011, Fresenius (the dialysis company) sent an internal memorandum to its clinics warning that
improper use of a dialysate component manufactured by the company,
called GranuFlo, appeared to be causing higher serum bicarbonate levels in their patients' blood, and a resulting 600 to 800 percent increase
in the likelihood of cardiac arrest and sudden death. Fresenius did
not share this information with other firms that used GranuFlo until
March 2012, after the memo had been leaked to the FDA. (Fresenius
claimed that the data contained in the 2011 memo were erroneous and
has consistently denied all liability, but ended up paying $250 million
to settle more than 10,000 lawsuits alleging patient harm and death.)

Rap sheets like these are the natural outgrowth of business cultures, ethical norms and legal practices endemic to American healthcare as a whole, and appear in many other medical fields. The American
hospital industry illustrates with particular clarity how financial fraud,
unconstrained by weak regulation and rubber-stamp legal settlements,
has degraded patient care. Several prominent for-profit hospital chains
were founded and run by micromanaging, high-pressure, abusive
CEOs willing to flaunt the law. Richard Scrushy, the flamboyant CEO
of HealthSouth, was indicted for securities fraud, money laundering
and other crimes; though these charges were dismissed at trial, Scrushy
was later jailed for bribery, conspiracy and mail fraud, and ordered to
pay $2.9 billion to HealthSouth shareholders because of the leading
role he had played in accounting fraud at the firm. In December 2002,
Columbia/HCA, led by attorney and sometime food entrepreneur Rick
Scott, paid the largest healthcare settlement in history at the time, $1.7
billion, for serious and pervasive wrongdoing. (Scott, now a US senator,
has always maintained that he was unaware of the fraud taking place in
his business, but as HCA accountant-turned-whistleblower John Schilling has pointed out, this seems implausible, given Scott's well-known
attention to the minutiae of managing Columbia/HCA.)

One of the most graphic cases of the fast food business model pushing a hospital enterprise into fraud, with serious ramifications for patients, is National Medical Enterprises (NME). NME was founded in 1969, one year after the dialysis company NMC, by three attorneys, Richard Eamer, Leonard Cohen and John Bedrosian. NME rapidly rolled up 143 general-care hospitals into a $4 billion colossus that also ran nursing homes, pharmacies, substance abuse treatment centers and a medical equipment firm, as well as a dialysis subsidiary called Medical Ambulatory Care. After posting double-digit earnings growth for more than a decade, in the mid-1980s Medicare cut reimbursements to conventional hospitals. So NME followed the money, selling off many of its conventional hospitals and refocusing on "specialty" hospitals that provided psychiatric care and substance abuse treatment. Here government funding was more generous, making higher profit margins possible, for those with the stomach to take them.

NME managers instituted sweeping cost-cutting programs at facilities they acquired, during which, according to court documents, certified mental health professionals were routinely laid off and replaced by unlicensed counselors and student interns. Intake became controlled by salespeople, and employees were tasked with increasing the length of patient stays, regardless of whether a patient's mental health required a longer stay. Nurse managers sometimes countermanded discharge orders issued by psychiatrists and psychologists. Later investigations and court testimony revealed that NME management had followed a stringent policy of maximizing admissions and durations of stay—"put heads on beds at any cost" was the corporate mantra, according to one former employee. NME employees were told to target patients with lucrative private insurance coverage; members of a network of bounty hunters were paid a fee for every insured patient they produced. To admit patients, NME needed the signature of compliant psychiatrists, whom the company paid generous (and illegal) bribes on the basis of the number of patients they referred. Such bribes were often concealed behind impressive-sounding job titles—medical directorships and chiefs of treatment units—which required no actual work.

"In many ways," Richard Eamer told Forbes magazine, "running a hospital chain is like operating a hotel or retail chain." A favorite among

Wall Street stock analysts, Eamer was fêted by the business community for his entrepreneurial brilliance. In 1991, he was paid $17.5 million, which earned him fifth place on the *Forbes* list of top executive pay packages in America.

"The corporate culture at NME was about making money at any cost, the rules be damned," says Jim Moriarty, who represented more than 600 former NME patients in lawsuits against the company. Moriarty is a quick-thinking, fast-talking Texas lawyer who served three tours of duty in Vietnam. "I was trained as an aviation electronics technician, but as I explained to my superiors, I dropped out of high school and joined the Marines to have the opportunity to shoot at indigenous personnel." Moriarty got his wish, serving as a door gunner and then a crew chief on Huey gunships in Chu Lai and Marble Mountain.

Moriarty mentions a corporate video made by NME, set to the tune of the Johnny Lee song "Lookin' for Love," which parodied the firm's tireless search for heads to put on its beds—preferably small heads, because children were easier to manipulate, and often had six months of insurance coverage, while adult coverage typically ended after twenty-eight days. Moriarty sings the first lines of the video's theme song from memory:

> *No more looking for patients in all the wrong places,*
> *Slumming for admissions in non-insured spaces,*
> *Spanning the globe, covering my bases, for a six-month*
> *   length of stay . . .*

But behind NME's sleek business façade and the camp humor of its corporate theatrics lay a little house of horrors. "They bribed counselors, probation officers and religious therapists to recruit children," says Moriarty. "We saw cases of private security guards literally abducting kids off the streets, removing them from their parents against their will, and locking them up in NME psychiatric wards." Here, Moriarty says, they routinely received inappropriate and sometimes harmful treatments, which were billed to Medicare and private insurance companies at inflated prices. "My favorite was the eight-year-old who was billed for ten hours of therapy in a day, including alcohol and drug therapy and how to hold a job." When the patients' insurance ran out, however, they were promptly discharged . . . or "terminated," in the dialysis parlance. (Though unlike dialysis patients who are dropped by their clinics, many NME internees must have been grateful for their freedom.)

In March 1992, Christy Scheck, a thirteen-year-old Californian honor student with a history of mental health problems, hung herself with the belt of her shower robe, after four months of confinement in an NME psychiatric facility in San Diego. Shortly before Scheck's arrival, the facility had undergone the signature NME cost-cutting exercise, leaving her in the hands of low-skilled aides and interns, or entirely unsupervised. Scheck's death helped trigger a series of investigations, culminating in an August 1993 raid by 600 FBI and other federal agents on NME's Santa Monica headquarters and nine of its hospitals. The Department of Justice charged NME with overbilling, bribery, kickbacks and other misconduct; the firm eventually paid $379 million in fines, penalties and civil damages, and pled guilty on several criminal charges. A dozen insurance companies also sued NME for similar conduct, and won a settlement of $300 million. Moriarty's accusations were even more serious. On behalf of his clients, he alleged that the company and certain of its doctors had imprisoned patients, particularly minors, against their will, and caused physical and mental harm to many. In July of 1997, just before the civil trial on these charges was set to begin, the defendants paid Moriarty and his clients a $101 million settlement.

In all, the company paid about $780 million in settlements and fines, yet no senior managers were prosecuted. CEO Richard Eamer, recognized as the architect of the company culture, retired with more than $2.6 million in severance pay and generous retirement benefits. The new chief executive officer, Jeffrey Barbakow, vowed to transform NME, and renamed the company "Tenet" as a sign of its new commitment to integrity. "Tenet is a very different company," executive vice president W. Randolph Smith said. "It has a brand new management team, and is a company that is intensely steeped in an environment of high ethical standards."

In reality, eight of NME's original twelve senior managers continued working at Tenet. Barbakow himself was no newcomer, having served on the NME board since 1990, and before then, handled the company's account as an investment banker at Merrill Lynch, the Wall Street firm. Barbakow adored NME for its financial performance, so he left NME's original corporate culture in place: growth, profitability, cost-cutting and privately insured patients remained the watchwords. Before long, Tenet was embroiled in new scandals with familiar names—kickbacks to doctors in return for referrals, wildly inflated Medicare bills, patient harm and death (this time from high-margin businesses like unnecessary heart surgeries). Tenet signed more big settlements, and admitted no wrongdoing. No senior managers went to jail. Barbakow stepped down, and Trevor Fetter, the firm's former CFO, became the new CEO.

"Tenet appears to be a corporation that is ethically and morally bankrupt," Senator Chuck Grassley, then chair of the Senate Finance Committee, told Fetter in a letter of September 5, 2003. "Tenet's failure to acknowledge any liability or wrongdoing, is further evidence, in my opinion, that Tenet views health care fraud settlements as the cost of doing business with the federal government, while profiting at the expense of innocent victims and America's taxpayers." Jacob Elberg, the former prosecutor, is also concerned by this kind of behavior. "Failure to remove or discipline executives responsible for misconduct is a red flag for the DOJ, that a company may not have reformed."

Some NME subsidiaries that spun off after their parent company hit the rocks appear to have inherited the same defective moral compass. After becoming independent, NME's former addiction recovery and nursing-home divisions faced accusations of frauds of their own. As did Medical Ambulatory Care, the firm's dialysis subsidiary, which left NME in a 1994 leveraged buyout and went public the following year: despite changing its name to Total Renal Care, the apple seems not to have fallen far from the NME tree. By 1999, having expanded too fast and come under scrutiny for alleged securities violations, the firm was on the verge of collapse.

Total Renal Care was the company that Kent Thiry took over in 1999 and rebranded "DaVita." Behind the jazzy new name and corporate culture, however, the fixation with growth, profits, cost-cutting and privately insured patients remained. As did the habit of pushing up to or beyond the limits of the law, at least to judge by the lawsuits that the company has settled over the past decade. All of which, as in the firm's past incarnations, was presided over by an outsized, charismatic CEO who seemed to be able to make up his own rules for the health-care game. Jim Moriarty, the lawyer who took on NME, believes that DaVita inherited important strands of corporate DNA from its former parent company, NME. "DaVita first mimicked, then improved, all of the lessons of limitless greed it learned suckling at its parent's breast," Moriarty says. "Heads on beds, bribing doctors to refer patients, grossly overtreating patients, homing in on privately insured patients—these practices naturally flow from parent companies to their subsidiaries, because they're so profitable. So long as harming people in America is more profitable than healing them, and we Americans fail to punish serious medical crimes, we'll get the kind of healthcare we deserve." (DaVita rejects these assertions as "entirely inconsistent with our com-mitment to patient care, quality and clinical leadership.")

❑

FOR MANY patients, chronic dialysis is a life of emotional and physical strain. The phrase "crashing into dialysis" is often used to describe the impact of abrupt, utter dependence on a machine. Many patients are going about their daily lives when they have a sudden health crisis, and are rushed to a local ER. There a nephrologist describes a deadly dis-ease they've never heard of, much less suspected they had. He says they have to run all their blood through a machine three times each week, or they will die. "They've lost control of their lives," says Betty Smith, the former dialysis nurse, executive and ESRD regulator. "That's what their disease does. Many times it takes their employment from them, it takes life as they've known it from them." The patient must deal not only with the debilitating symptoms of disease and of the treatment itself, but also with the myriad complications that dialysis creates in life outside the unit, particularly for people with fragile finances. "We've some-times had to choose whether to buy a meal or fill the car with enough gas to get to the clinic," says Sheldon Winters, whose wife, Vanessa, has dialyzed in the Baltimore area for more than a decade. "When you realize you cannot do both, that is a very low moment."

Dialysis forces family members to serve as unpaid nurses, drivers and psychologists. The anxiety of dealing with a loved one's terminal disease can be overwhelming. "I'm six foot seven and 300 pounds, but I'm powerless to help my wife when she goes into that clinic, and that haunts me," says William Sarsfield. Another dialysis spouse, the 9-1-1 dispatcher Sherry Thompson, concurs. "On any given day, I'm saving lives. I'm coaching people how to revive their loved ones until emergency health can come. I'm delivering babies. I'm reviving people who have drowned. But when I'm at home, I can't help my husband."

As I speak with the Thompsons, Gerald weeps as he remembers the fear and bewilderment that his battle with dialysis has brought, and the strain it has put on their marriage.

"I took all that hurt, and I put it right back on my wife." He touches Sherry's face hesitantly, and moans from the memories.

"It's okay, Honey," Sherry says.

The atmosphere in many dialysis units compounds this stress. A group of very sick people, most of whom will never recover, undergo painful, potentially dangerous treatments together three times each week. Clinics are typically on an open plan; private conversations between patients and caregivers can be heard by all, and medical procedures are performed in plain sight. Patients watch the long needles disappear into their arms and their neighbors' arms, see their blood pump into the plastic tubing, beyond which other scarlet tubes pulse to the rhythm of many hearts. They also watch each other. "You sit next to someone for three hours, three times a week, every week of your life, and sometimes you become close," says Gregg Hansen, the patient in San Rafael, California. "You share jokes, celebrate holidays, talk about your fears. You look forward to seeing them again. And then one day, their chair is empty. None of the staff will tell you what happened. All you know is, they're not coming back. And someday, your chair will be empty, too." On average, nearly one in four dialysis patients in America die each year.

"Death is a constant presence," says William Sarsfield forthrightly, and Carrie Brito nods. "We meet a lot of people who are surprised to hear Carrie's still on dialysis. 'Oh, is she still doing that?' They don't get it. This isn't like chemo. Unless you get a transplant, dialysis ends in death. They don't call it 'end-stage renal disease' for nothing.'"

Some dialysis workers find these realities demoralizing. "Nephrology is a terribly tough job," says Steven Rosansky, the retired VA nephrologist. "We get the sickest people, with very high comorbidity. We're having a hard time getting people to work in the field." Add to this the intense pressure to meet schedules and treatment quotas that many employees face, and confrontations between patients and staff become inevitable. Some trigger terminations.

Betty Smith began working as a dialysis nurse in 1971. "When I started in this business, and for many years after that, you didn't kick somebody out of a dialysis unit. You were there to save their life, right? I mean, that's why the unit exists: to get dialysis, which saves people's lives."

From the late 1990s, however, as the roll-up reached full swing, more and more patients were accused of disruptiveness, even violence, and involuntary discharges spiked. A spate of articles and studies scrutinized this sudden increase in terminations, discussed how to deal with "disruptive" patients, and assessed what ought to be classed as legitimate grounds for discharge. The ESRD Networks formed a national task force to analyze and respond to the rise in involuntary discharges. By then, Betty Smith was working in one of the regional ESRD Networks, and watched the trend with growing alarm. She tells the story of one elderly man's termination, which she says is characteristic of numerous grievances that she and her colleagues received at the Network. I've heard many termination stories that are more brutal and lethal than hers. Yet even years after it happened, something about this incident clearly still troubles her.

"Here's one story. This is a true story," she begins, as if telling a parable. "It's my story, about Mr. Popcorn Man. An older gentleman that had been dialyzing in a dialysis unit for a long time, several years. Never caused anybody any trouble—*never*. Not a single minute of trouble.

And one day they admitted a new patient and put the patient in the chair beside Mr. Popcorn Man. And that guy liked to bring popcorn all the time, to dialysis."

"Well that made Mr. Popcorn Man sick, literally made him nauseous. And he told them [his staff] about it. He asked them, 'Can we please move him? Does he have to bring that?'"

Betty Smith pauses. "Well, guess what happened?" she asks me. "What do you think happened?"

I know what's coming, but say nothing.

"This went on for awhile," she continues. "He became a 'difficult patient.' Then he jumped up one day, and said basically, 'By God I can't take this anymore!' And guess what happened? The man who had never caused anybody any trouble, until the guy next door started bringing popcorn which made him sick, got thrown out of the clinic."

Smith explains that, in time, her Network was able to place Mr. Popcorn Man in a new clinic. In many cases, however, she witnessed patients who were discharged as "difficult" or "disruptive" being blackballed by other clinics. "A lot of times these patients are unplaceable. They end up just like the undocumented patients. They have to go to the emergency room."

Betty Smith laces her fingers, and looks at me to see whether I've comprehended, from the faintly tragicomic fable of Mr. Popcorn Man, the seriousness of the situation. "*Lots* and *lots* of patients get discharged," she says, with slow emphasis. She speaks now not as the regulator or the dialysis executive she once was, but as the young nurse who began work in medicine back in 1971, who to this day feels a deep allegiance to her patients, and a weight on her heart because so many have suffered.

Involuntary discharges happen for many reasons. Extreme cases may involve dangerous patients or sadistic staff. Though I've never seen a proven instance of violence by a patient—most accounts sound to me more like urban legends or outright fabrications—no doubt a few patients represent a genuine threat to the safety of others. In June of 2020, the results of an ongoing survey of violence in US dialysis clinics from 2013 to 2020 were published online, revealing twenty instances of gun-related aggression (mostly threats), and five violence-related deaths. (In half of the incidents described, patients were the victims, not the perpetrators, of violence.) Conversely, certain workers appear to relish the power they wield over their defenseless patients. "Some dialysis techs and nurses are on a power trip," says another industry insider. "In a clinic you may only have one or two RNs, and everybody else is a [dialysis] tech. They came from McDonald's, they got their six weeks of training, and now they've got people's lives in their hands." In the early 1980s, Alonzo Plough had already noted the inherent authoritarianism of the patient-caregiver relationship in his New Haven dialysis clinic. In a few "caregivers," this power of life and death brings out what Leonard Stern calls "the prison camp guard" syndrome.

Yet many of the terminations I've examined resulted neither from patient aggression nor from worker cruelty, but were fueled and eventually ignited by the abiding tensions in many clinics. Workers under pressure to complete tasks quickly tend to dislike patients who require extra time; they prefer passive widgets to engaged, questioning partners in care. Autocratic behavior by techs, nurses and nephrologists, in turn, causes patient flare-ups. "A lot of times these patients get psychologically pushed into a corner, and they come out swinging, when they feel like they have no other options," Betty Smith says. "We march them into the dialysis unit. We say, 'You sit in that chair, you don't make any complaints, any noises. We'll tell you when to come in. We'll tell you when to sit down. We'll tell you when you can ask a question.' And then when they get mad, and they start blowing off steam verbally, we say, 'What's happened to *you*? What's *wrong* with you?'"

In the final analysis, involuntary discharges occur because they've become an option. The culture of corporate dialysis in America, as in no other nation I know of, has accepted the termination of lifesaving dialysis care as permissible, sometimes even necessary. "In my opinion," says Robert Bear, "involuntary discharges are the end product of the organizational cultures consistently promulgated by the for-profit dialysis companies that dominate the American chronic dialysis market."

Though I have been unable to obtain comprehensive statistics on the numbers or the causes of involuntary discharges from dialysis, most cases I've examined follow the same playbook we've already encountered. First, target patients who complain about bad care or question staff practices. Then begin compiling a written record of infractions in these patients' medical records, sometimes adding back-dated accusations to make them appear to have been troublemakers over a long period of time. Prod them into acting out, through bullying, demeaning treatment, petty insults, poor care. If they rise to the bait, terminate them on charges of violence or threat of violence. If they don't, find another reason. Charge them with failure to pay some part of their dialysis bills, which are so complex that few patients understand them. Or accuse them of "noncompliance"—refusal to follow their prescribed treatment—which though illegitimate as a motive for discharge, is rarely disputed by stunned patients and their families.

Patients are also terminated from home dialysis. Peter Laird, a retired doctor who practiced self-care dialysis at his home in Coeur d'Alene, Idaho, began to suffer nausea and headaches after every session, which he believed was caused by a new piece of dialysis equipment that his Fresenius clinic had recently supplied him. After Laird requested repairs and improvements to his machine, his clinic managers demanded that he stop dialyzing at home and start treating in-center. Having lost confidence in his medical team, Laird asked that his care be managed by a different clinic. Whereupon he was involuntarily discharged. (With Arlene Mullin's help, he was able to resume treatment at another Fresenius facility.) "If the dialysis companies can deal with a medical doctor like this, what must they do to the average patient?" Laird says.

Other home dialysis patients are deprived of care more gradually. After Gerald and Sherry Thompson challenged their clinic staff about the bills being sent to Cigna, their insurance company—the Thompsons believed the clinic was double-billing Cigna, and charging for medication that Gerald never received—the termination process began. First came the security guard, the forced psychological evaluation, and the surprise visit to the Thompson's home by a clinic worker. Next the local police burst into their house on a "welfare check" that had evidently been requested by the clinic. On January 4, 2020, the behavioral contract arrived, followed, in May, by the discharge letter accusing Gerald of "aggressive behavior and continued noncompliance." The Thompsons say that Satellite stopped delivering Gerald's dialysis supplies, and threatened to remove his machine. Every Fresenius clinic they contacted in Tennessee and Mississippi declined to treat him. "We're sure they did that because of something in Gerald's charts, but Satellite refused to give us those, so we don't know what it is," Sherry says.

"I still had some supplies at home, and was afraid of dialyzing in the hospital, because of the pandemic—I was afraid to die," Gerald remembers. "So I started washing needles with alcohol to reuse them, cutting back my treatments to conserve supplies." Soon he was dialyzing only once a week, when he should have been dialyzing at least three times. His foot became gangrenous, making a hospital stay unavoidable. Several toes had to be amputated. "They wouldn't prescribe painkillers, because something in his file said he was 'drug-seeking,'" Sherry says. "So he had these amputated toes, and the best we could do was ibuprofen."

Until this moment, the most emotion Sherry has shown is an occasional snort of anger or a cackle of gallows humor. Now she, like Gerald, begins to tear up. "My husband's health was declining quickly. I was so afraid. It was leading up to the holiday times. And I was praying to God—I'm getting a little emotional here—because I didn't think my husband was going to make it through the holidays. Is this the last holiday I'm going to be able to spend with my husband? How is this happening? How is this okay?"

She squares her shoulders and wipes her eyes. "I'm writing my senators," she remembers, "I'm calling the ESRD system, I'm calling CMS, I'm appealing to civil rights, the county, the city, every person that I could think of. No one would help. They just didn't understand. I did a lot of praying, I did a lot of crying. I'm watching my husband's health decline in the meantime. And they told us our option was to go to the emergency room for cleaning [dialysis]—in the middle of a pandemic."

Sherry's eyes narrow and she looks past me, as if surveying an unfamiliar land. "I served my country for seven years in the Air Force. *America*—this is the country that people are swimming to, risking their lives to get here. And yet right here at home, they're treating Gerald in this way, and who knows how many others? 'The Land of the Free and the Home of the Brave'? *Really*?"

Finally, with what Sherry describes as a blend of prayer and Google, she found Dialysis Advocates on the web, and called Arlene Mullin. Mullin managed to place Gerald in a nearby DaVita facility, where the Thompsons say the nephrologist and staff are superb. "Thank God for Arlene, and thank God for DaVita," Sherry says. "But we're still on pins and needles, because we don't want. . . ." She falters. "We're trying to do everything right. Because they're still in control."

Discharging and blackballing dialysis patients is not only harmful and wrong, it's also an enormous waste of money—not for the dialysis firms that turn nonpassive patients away, a tried and true form of cherry picking, but for the healthcare system which must somehow care for them, usually in a hospital emergency room. While I've found no statistics on the number of involuntarily discharged patients dialyzing in American ERs, data do exist for an analogous patient population: undocumented immigrants with kidney failure, who in most states must seek treatment in the ER because they have no insurance. A recent study of uninsured kidney failure patients, many of whom are undocumented, who dialyzed in eleven Texas emergency rooms in 2017, revealed that such patients received 10,390 treatments costing a total of $21.8 million—$2,100 per dialysis session in the ER, as compared with roughly $250 that Medicare would have paid for a scheduled outpatient treatment. "This is a ludicrous waste of resources, of many millions if not billions of dollars a year nationwide," says Henry Wang, a coauthor of the study. "I'm an ER doc, with an ethical duty to treat everyone who walks through my door. But ESRD is a chronic disease that should be treated in an outpatient setting. When uninsured patients don't have access to healthcare, and go so long between treatments that they end up as an emergency in an ER bed, that's a failure of the primary care system. We ultimately have to pay a lot more for that, as a society."

Robert Bear, the Canadian nephrologist, believes such social costs could be reduced relatively quickly by the large dialysis companies. "If the CEO models behavior that emphasizes putting the patient at the top of the care pyramid, not at the bottom, change will occur rapidly. Yes, there would be a cost, but ultimately, low-quality healthcare costs vastly more."

· 9 ·

The Fox in the Hen House

JUSTIN CHARLES EVANS is an atypical dialysis patient. He works as a stuntman in Hollywood films, and has been the body double for Kevin Hart. He's a ballet dancer, gymnast, martial artist and circus tumbler. He has been cast to dance the Trepak, the famously acrobatic "Russian dance," in a major production of *The Nutcracker*. He's young and strong, as his various professions require. He lost his kidneys in 2017 to an acute urinary infection, and the massive doses of antibiotics administered to treat it. But despite the physical and psychic drain of dialysis, Evans remains clear-headed, a strategic as well as a tactical fighter. And he has one trait that most great stuntwomen and stuntmen probably share: Justin Charles Evans feels no fear. Or at least, he's an expert at controlling his fear.

So in the spring of 2017, when the staff at his DaVita clinic in Atlanta, Georgia, began canceling treatments for Evans and other patients at the last minute, and advising them to dialyze in the local ER instead, Evans told the staff that their behavior was unacceptable. The scheduling uncertainty was interfering with his film work, because dialysis in the ER is a time-consuming process, typically involving many hours of waiting. Worse, sporadic treatment was endangering his health. After missing dialysis for five days, a blood test in a local hospital revealed a critical level of serum potassium, meaning that Evans was at risk of sudden cardiac arrest. Evans also noticed that a number of other patients at the clinic, who were less active and healthy than he, were suffering from the sporadic care.

So Justin Charles Evans organized. He convinced eleven of his fellow patients to cosign a letter he was drafting to Johnny Isakson, then a US senator from Georgia. "I just told Senator Isakson and his staff, 'Hey, taxpayers are paying for our care, but we aren't getting it. And people are going to die here.'"

"We are asking that you reach out to Medicare immediately to resolve this issue," read the letter that Evans and his fellow patients, whom we'll call the Atlanta Twelve, sent to Isakson on July 21, 2017. "While we understand that DaVita is a private company, we are also aware that they receive monthly payments from Medicare, and they are still being payed [sic] thousands of dollars per month, even when they fail to provide the contracted services." Sensing their clinic's likely response to this plea for help from Isakson, at the end of the letter they requested the senator's protection: "Finally, we ask your office and Medicare to make DaVita aware that they are not to harass, or blackball us for reaching out to you for help. That is our right as American citizens and Medicare recipients."

Isakson's staff apparently passed the Atlanta Twelve's complaint letter to CMS, which in turn sent it to ESRD Network 6, the contractor that CMS pays to oversee dialysis clinics in Georgia and the Carolinas. Inspectors from the Georgia state healthcare department visited the clinic, found irregularities, and wrote them up in a report to CMS.

Senator Isakson's intervention had so far been constructive. But then clinic managers learned of the letter, a copy of which they apparently received from ESRD Network 6—the same ESRD group that Kenneth Bays, during the 2000 Senate hearings, had warned Chuck Grassley was doing such a poor job. Clinic workers turned on several of the signatories, and threatened two of them—Debbie Johnson, a registered nurse who had already objected to poor infection control in the clinic; and Richard Mahone, a frail, elderly, impoverished patient—with involuntary discharge.

For Justin Charles Evans, whom the clinic staff had identified as the ringleader, worse was in store. He says the staff began harassing and demeaning him, evidently hoping to trigger an outburst. "They really tried to make me mad, and get me to be the angry black man," Evans remembers. "But I never acted out."

Evans *did* act, however. He began questioning patients and clinic staff, sometimes with a digital voice recorder in his pocket. He taped phone calls with local and regional managers at DaVita. He discovered Dialysis Advocates on the web, and struck up an alliance with Arlene Mullin, who drove to Atlanta from her home in southern Georgia to meet him. "You should have seen Justin's face when he realized I was white!" Mullin laughs. "He was shocked, and a little suspicious at first. It took him awhile to trust me. I don't blame him. With the racism that African Americans face in dialysis, many have stopped trusting white people."

On the morning of December 29, 2017, while Evans was getting ready to dialyze, a nurse said she needed to draw blood for testing. Evans objected that he had recently given blood, and because (like many dialysis patients) he was anemic, he didn't want to part with any more red blood cells. They argued, and Evans insisted that she not draw more blood against his will. He closed his eyes, settled into his chair, and began dialyzing. Some time later, he looked up. The nurse was taking a blood sample anyway.

Evans demanded that she stop, and they quarreled again. Someone called the police. Though Evans protested that interrupting his treatment might harm him—he knew he was fluid-overloaded after several days without dialyzing, and his blood pressure had shot up during his argument with the nurse—the responding officer said he had no choice: this was a private clinic, he explained, and its managers wanted Evans out. The policeman called emergency medical technicians to detach Evans from the machine. In his report, the officer noted the claim by the clinic manager that she feared Evans, because he had mentioned plans to buy a handgun.

Evans remembers the manager's smile, as the EMTs wheeled him out on a gurney. From this moment on, she told him, his nephrologist would no longer treat him: he was being terminated with immediate effect. The police officer confirmed that he would be arrested on sight if he returned.

Evans spoke with Arlene Mullin during the ambulance ride, and while dialyzing in the ER. With her guidance, Evans reported the abuse and terminations at his clinic to ESRD Network 6. This produced no results. "They seemed to be on the side of the company, never on my side—as if they were trying to document all the bad things the clinic was saying about me," Evans remembers. "They never asked for my version of what happened. They never sent anything to me in writing."

Mullin immediately contacted DaVita headquarters and challenged the termination as illegal. "They hadn't followed any of the procedures, hadn't given him the mandatory 30-day warning," she explains. "They used the claim that Justin had a gun—which was an outright lie—as an excuse to terminate him."

The situation gradually improved for Evans and the rest of the Atlanta Twelve. Ron Ceasar, a firebrand civil rights activist from Baton Rouge who had helped Mullin advocate for patients of color, joined a conference call with facility staff and demanded that they halt their retaliation. The nephrologist at Evans's clinic denied that he had ever refused to treat Evans. While speaking with staff members, Evans discovered that many were being mistreated and threatened with termination by clinic management, much like the patients. Evans even befriended the nurse who had taken his blood without his consent, and who had been one of his chief tormentors at the clinic. She confided that she'd inserted the reference to the gun in Evans's medical records, although she had known nothing about a weapon, on orders from the facility manager.

"I prayed that God make my enemy my footstool," Evans remembers, "because that nurse was the one who'd said I had a gun, who'd done bad things to me. But at the same time, I had to find forgiveness for her, because they were threatening her job and livelihood, her nursing license." Evans came to see her as another victim of the same poisonous environment at their facility that was putting his life at hazard.

Using the defamatory and dangerous lie about the gun as leverage, Mullin managed to get Evans readmitted to his clinic, and subsequently transferred to another DaVita facility, in Tucker, Georgia, just outside Atlanta. She also prevented or reversed the involuntary discharges of other members of the Atlanta Twelve, including Debbie Johnson and Richard Mahone. Evans trained to do home dialysis. For a time, he felt safe.

But when Evans encountered difficulties cannulating himself, and had to return to the clinic for treatment, his ordeal began all over again. He and Mullin say that staff at his Tucker, Georgia, clinic launched a new offensive against him. Certain clinic workers crowded around his chair, they say, threatening and provoking him while he dialyzed. On October 12, 2021, Evans received another termination letter, citing noncompliance with his treatment plan. When Mullin pointed out that noncompliance was not a legitimate motive for termination, she says, clinic managers changed their story, and claimed that Evans was actually being discharged for failure to pay his dialysis bills: he was enrolled in the wrong Medicare plan, they said.

Evans and Mullin attended an advocacy meeting with clinic staff, in an attempt to resolve the conflict. Evans's nephrologist and dietitian, who had been sympathetic, did not attend the meeting, though Mullin had requested their presence. But Evans and Mullin did see the DaVita regional manager who had been involved in Evans's termination years earlier. The original clash at that first clinic, the letter to Senator Johnny Isakson, the fictitious gun . . . all these traumatic memories came flooding back to Evans. "When I saw that guy at the meeting, right then I knew I was a marked man," he says.

After another intense exchange with clinic and regional managers at DaVita, which caused several risky interruptions in Evans's treatment, Mullin succeeded in getting him placed in a third DaVita clinic. Today, Evans says his new staff is kind and helpful, though he reports that his treatment time has been cut from four hours to three, and his ultrafiltration rate (UFR) has been increased. But by now Evans has no more illusions. "Sooner or later, I'm afraid I'll be terminated again. When you speak out, this company doesn't forgive or forget."

❑

JUSTIN CHARLES EVANS grew up in Lowndes County, Mississippi, in one of America's many dialysis deserts: a neighborhood that is predominantly Black, with high rates of diabetes, hypertension and obesity, and limited access to healthy food and regular medical treatment. All of which virtually guarantees widespread kidney disease. "Dialysis is just a fact of life for people of color, something that happens to a lot of folks you know, and might happen to you one day," Evans says. "In Atlanta where I dialyze, we're nearly all Black and brown."

Alonzo Plough, the health policy expert and chief science officer at the Robert Wood Johnson Foundation, has been aware of this kind of neighborhood for his entire career, since he embedded with the New Haven dialysis facility in the early 1980s. At that unit, as in most facilities today that are located in low-income neighborhoods, most patients were people of color. Plough watched white doctors and healthcare workers dialyze predominantly Black and brown patients, and sometimes denigrate or mistreat them, in ways he believed they would not have cared for a white person. Plough saw the truth of an observation by Richard Rettig, the meticulous historian of dialysis practice and public policy, that kidney disease "illustrates one of the most common burdens of inadequate health care in the United States, the deeply unpleasant overrepresentation of underserved and minority individuals who have chronic illness."

As freestanding dialysis clinics sprang up across the nation, Plough noticed that they often signaled the presence of a specific kind of community. "Wherever you found dialysis clinics, dollar stores, predatory loan places, and an over-concentration of fast food and cheap alcohol outlets, you were in a risky, marginal neighborhood. These were all businesses that functioned on the marginality of the residents. On their inability to have just and fair access to financial tools, their inability to have just and fair preventative access to primary care." (Marcel Reid, a civil rights activist and whistleblower, calls this situation "death by zip code": "You tell me where you live, and I can predict when you'll die.")

"Later in my career, when I was running large health departments in Boston and Seattle and Los Angeles," Plough continues, "if you could find the neighborhood that had a dialysis facility, you knew it was going to be the epicenter of health disparities of many types. And if you drive through urban America and Black America today, you will find that's where the freestanding dialysis centers are. So it becomes kind of a sentinel indicator for this whole problem of health inequity. And the real tragedy of this final common pathway: it's largely preventable."

We are speaking on Zoom in January 2021. From his room in Los Angeles, where he is under COVID-19 lockdown, Plough points a finger at me where I sit in northern Italy. "You don't see those neighborhoods in various parts of Europe, in Canada, or in most other industrialized countries. They have comprehensive, prevention-oriented national health policies. They work to give access to primary care treatment, and preventative medicine. They don't concentrate, as in America, on precisely the opposite: on charging for expensive treatments, for people at the precipice of death."

Plough goes silent. "I just shake my head with amazement and sadness," he continues after a while, "that those same problems I worked on when I was in Boston years ago, the Black infant mortality, the Black maternal mortality . . . the many other problems I thought we would have solved by now, are still with us. These race-based disparities, these inequalities, just continue and expand."

Plough is talking about Kaufman, Texas. About Washington Heights in Manhattan. About the Atlanta neighborhoods where Justin Charles Evans has dialyzed. About so many other places in America, where the path from fast food restaurants to dialysis at the mall is straight and sure.

America has many different dialysis neighborhoods, shaped by race, poverty and environment. "Neighborhoods with higher rates of kidney disease are typically food deserts and food swamps," says Milda Saunders, an internist and associate professor of medicine at the University of Chicago Medical Center, who has helped to expose the racism inherent in renal medicine in America. "They lack grocery stores with fresh, affordable produce, and have a lot of cheap, really tasty foods with high salt, high fat and concentrated sugars. We all love those things, but if they're a significant part of your diet, they make your diabetes or your hypertension virtually impossible to control. Which in turn harms your kidneys."

Rates of end-stage renal disease (ESRD) in America are higher in Black, brown and Native American populations than among whites, though the incidence of ESRD varies considerably within each of these groups, due both to the different environments in which they live and to certain genetic predispositions to kidney disease or to one of its main drivers, diabetes, that are often poorly understood. Hispanics as a group suffer kidney failure nearly twice as often as whites, yet the Hispanic population in the United States is genetically diverse, with different communities exhibiting highly variable proportions of African, Native American and European ancestry. For example, Dominicans like those Leonard Stern treated in Manhattan, together with Cubans and Puerto Ricans, have a higher prevalence of kidney disease and diabetes than do South or Central Americans. Incidence of renal disease among Asian Americans remains relatively low, particularly since 2017, when the United States Renal Data System (USRDS) began to split out the health data on Native Hawaiians and Pacific Islanders, who until then had been classed by the government as Asians. Native Hawaiians and Pacific Islanders, it emerged, have an extremely high incidence of kidney failure, some 2.7 times greater than that of whites.

Prevalence of kidney failure among Native Americans, who comprise more than 570 different tribes throughout the United States, is even harder to measure. USRDS reports that the average incidence of kidney failure among Native Americans is twice that among whites, yet the risk in certain tribes is *twenty* times that among whites. The Pima and the Zuni of the desert Southwest are particularly hard hit by both kidney disease and diabetes; the Pima have the highest known diabetes rate in the world, possibly because, after millennia of adaptation to a hunter-gatherer existence in a desert landscape, their heightened ability to survive periods of famine has left them vulnerable to the unending barrage of low-grade food they face today. Tribal leaders in these high-risk areas see some families entering dialysis generation after generation, and consider kidney failure a threat to their tribes' survival.

Kidney failure among Native Americans can also have environmental causes. For example, the high rate of kidney disease among the Navajo appears to derive, at least in part, from exposure to uranium, which from World War II through the 1980s was mined extensively on their tribal lands in New Mexico, Arizona and Utah. Carrie Brito's father, who lived for years on the Navajo reservation at Shiprock, New Mexico, died of a stroke that public health officials linked to uranium poisoning. Brito believes her kidneys were compromised by the uranium that killed her father, though no doctor has confirmed this.

The group hardest hit by dialysis is African Americans, who make up only 13.6 percent of the US population, yet constitute 35 percent of kidney failure patients. Prevalence of kidney failure among Blacks is due to structural factors that lead to poor diet and medical care, as well as to high rates of diabetes and hypertension, but also to genetic factors: having two copies of the APOL1 allele, a mutation more common in people of West African descent, doubles one's risk of kidney disease. (Much as the sickle cell gene protects against malaria, APOL1 helps prevent African trypanosomiasis, or "sleeping sickness.") About 13 percent of African Americans have this high-risk genotype. Genetics also helps to explain the higher ESRD incidence among Dominicans, Puerto Ricans and Cubans as compared with Hispanics of other origins, as these three groups have a higher prevalence of West African ancestry, and therefore more frequently carry the APOL1 allele.

Before medical school, Milda Saunders worked as a policy analyst in housing and community development, which made her acutely aware of how individual neighborhoods can influence their residents' access to resources. "And even before that," says Saunders, who is Black, "I grew up in Chicago, one of the most segregated cities in the US, so I know at an instinctive level how neighborhoods shape people's lives." Both medically and in public policy terms, Saunders says the poor kidney care in many African American communities illustrates the structural racism that shapes American health. Extensive research shows that in many pivotal categories—including access to a high-rated dialysis facility, frequency of hospitalization during dialysis, ability to dialyze at home, time required to be placed on a transplant waitlist and to obtain a transplant—African Americans receive worse kidney care than whites or, in many cases, than Hispanics and Asians. Even the estimated glomerular filtration rate (eGFR), the algorithm used to assess kidney function, is incorrectly adjusted for race in a way that many researchers say has harmed Blacks, by artificially increasing their eGFR, thereby reducing their perceived need for kidney care and their eligibility for a transplant. (In September 2021, the National Kidney Foundation announced that, after a lengthy scientific reassessment of the eGFR algorithm, it recommended the immediate removal of the race modifier from the algorithm in all laboratories in the United States.)

One of Milda Saunders's current areas of emphasis is improving access to transplants for kidney failure patients, particularly in African American neighborhoods. Part of this work involves convincing residents to become living organ donors. When I ask her whether people in Black neighborhoods are particularly averse to donating one of their kidneys, Saunders shakes her head a little sadly, maybe at the way things are in many Black neighborhoods, or at the naivete of my question, its implied assumptions. "Sometimes we say that culture is a community's response to injustices or disparities that have been passed down," she tells me gently. "So if you have grown up in a community where you have not been well served by the healthcare system, then you don't necessarily trust that someone could take your kidney, and have that work out well for you."

From his perspective as a nurse, Megallan Handford, the former Los Angeles policeman, sees American dialysis as the result of generations of systemic racism. "It starts with the Black diet, which is basically a slave diet—the chitlins, the crackling pork and such, what was left over when the master was done. Today in our neighborhoods there's a McDonald's on one corner, a Jack in the Box and a Burger King on the others. That's what people of color eat, so it's no wonder they end up on dialysis. This is a system, a cycle, a trap for many people of color." Handford's mother and father were both active in the civil rights movement in Mississippi, defending Black voting rights, which instilled in him a strong sense of duty to serve the public good. "We grew up with stories of the racism they experienced, and how they overcame it," he remembers. "They taught us, 'People are people, *period.*'" In dialysis, Handford feels, America is falling short. "The whole thing has Jim Crow written all over it."

None of the limited official statistics I have found on involuntary discharges are broken down by racial group. However, my interviews with hundreds of patients, caregivers, advocates and former ESRD Network regulators have left me with the clear impression that a disproportionate number of victims of involuntary discharge are Black and brown. "By far the majority of the patients who call me for help with terminations are people of color," Arlene Mullin says.

In financial terms, a racial bias in involuntary discharge makes sense. Proportionately more Black and brown dialysis patients are on a government insurance program, and thus offer lower profit margins to dialysis companies than those provided by privately insured patients. Statistically speaking, more Black and brown people live below the poverty line, where they become targets of the kinds of patronizing and denigrating comments that Alonzo Plough heard in his New Haven clinic back in the 1980s, and which several patients of color have told me they've heard from caregivers. Comments like: "You should be grateful you're getting any care at all, because it's being paid for by the government." Or: "You brought this on yourself with your bad diet and lifestyle."

Certain accusations used to justify involuntary discharge, such as "drug-seeking behavior," match a pattern of racial bias that has been identified in other areas of US medicine. "A Black patient shows up in the ED in great pain, gets typologized as a possible drug user," says Alonzo Plough. "And that's the first screen. A white patient comes with that same presentation, they aren't going to be characterized in the same way." Like false accusations of firearm possession by dialysis patients, the drug addict tag seems a reflexive charge against people of color that caregivers would rather not treat—a codeword for patients who have become expendable.

Of course, examples abound of Blacks suffering more illness and worse healthcare. They have a higher incidence of chronic conditions such as hypertension and diabetes; face grim disparities in mortality and the financial burden caused by cancer and heart disease; and experience higher infant mortality and lower life expectancy. COVID-19 honed the endemic racial bias of the medical system to a razor edge: Blacks, together with Hispanics and Native Americans, have had a disproportionately high number of COVID-19 infections, hospitalizations, ICU admissions and deaths compared to whites. "COVID-19 made clear, for anyone who wasn't looking before, the huge impact of disparities and lack of access on a race basis," says Alonzo Plough. "There's a new awareness of structural racism in parts of traditional medicine, like the National Academy of Medicine, where I hadn't seen it in years past."

Nor can these differences be explained solely by socioeconomic status; racial bias in medicine frequently operates at a psychological level as well. According to a 2016 study published in the *Proceedings of the National Academy of Sciences*, the prominent US journal, half of a sample of white medical students and residents endorsed at least one from a list of false statements containing racial biases—statements such as, "Black people's nerve endings are less sensitive than white people's" and "Black people's skin is thicker than white people's." (In the same study, 73 percent of white respondents without medical training accepted at least one such statement as true.) A 2019 article in *Frontiers in Pediatrics* revealed that ER doctors are less likely to order blood tests, CT scans or other imaging for Black, Hispanic, or Asian children than for white children; refer fewer Black and Hispanic children for emergency care; and admit them less frequently to the hospital after an ER visit. A 2022 paper in the *Journal of Internal Medicine* showed that the staff of the Brigham and Women's Hospital in Boston was 30 percent more likely to call security when treating Black patients than when treating whites or Hispanics. Unsurprisingly, therefore, recent research shows that involuntary discharges from for-profit, long-term care hospitals are not only on the rise, but also target African American patients disproportionately.

❏

SINCE JUNE 2000, when Kenneth Bays and Brent Smith told Chuck Grassley about the flawed regulation of the dialysis industry, neither Congress nor CMS, nor the Department of Justice nor the judiciary nor anyone else has improved industry oversight. Rather, several insiders say that regulation has grown even more lax and ineffectual in the intervening years.

Why has so little changed? One explanation is that the coziness, even complicity, between regulators and regulated, which Kenneth Bays noted in Georgia at his local ESRD Network 6, permeates the dialysis world. During the 2000 hearing, Senator Pete Stark sent his urgent demand to discipline centers who were killing and terminating dialysis patients to Nancy-Ann DeParle, who then headed the Health Care Financing Administration (HCFA). Less than a year later, however, DeParle left government service and joined the board of directors of DaVita, together with William Roper, another former HCFA chief. The same DaVita press release that announced the arrival of these two new board appointments also noted that Thomas Scully, former DaVita board member and for-profit hospital lobbyist, was resigning from DaVita to become the new head of HCFA. Kent Thiry remarked: "Nancy-Ann and Bill can help us, as Tom already has, to work toward achieving our objective of a more constructive partnership with the federal government."

In the involuntary discharge cases I have reviewed, the ESRD Networks, the contractors hired by CMS to regulate the dialysis industry, have almost never helped patients. Instead, Network employees often seem to have coached clinic managers on proper termination protocol, counseling them to keep a written record of alleged patient misbehavior, for example, and to compel the patient to sign a behavioral contract. When Cornelius Robbins called his local ESRD Network in Georgia to request help with his ongoing discharge, Robbins says the Network representative admitted having briefed his clinic on the steps it needed to follow in order to terminate him. When he asked why she'd done that, Robbins says the employee responded, "Well, the paperwork's gotta be filed properly, so I was just letting her [the clinic employee] know how to file the paperwork properly." To which Robbins replied, "No, what you did was let her know how to cut my throat."

Networks routinely share information about a patient's grievances with the staff of the clinic where these grievances occurred. This is ostensibly done to encourage patient and staff to work together to de-escalate conflicts, but all too frequently causes more bad blood instead. Networks also advise patients who have filed complaints against their facility, even for involuntary discharge, to take up their complaints with clinic staff—the very people who the patients say abused them. Sherry Thompson, who witnessed this pattern herself after her husband was discharged by Satellite Healthcare, calls it a "chain of fools." "The ESRD system told me, 'We wish we could help, but you need to go back to Satellite.' That's just like getting raped, and the police telling you, 'Yeah, we know you got raped, but go talk to the guy that raped you and see if you guys can work it out.'"

State agencies charged with surveying dialysis facilities remain chronically underfunded, and their investigations are often inadequate, much as witnesses at the 2000 Senate hearings reported. And as Arlene Mullin discovered in Oregon, so too in many areas of the country, dialysis units are frequently alerted about "surprise" investigations before they occur, in time to add extra staff and put on a good show for the investigators. California dialysis workers report how their workplace is transformed just before state inspectors arrive. "Suddenly our workers have got to do everything by the book and follow every procedure," says Cass Gualvez, who serves on the executive board of the SEIU-UHW union. "So even with the extra staff they always lay on for state inspections, they're still running far behind. That just tells you it's already built into the business model, that you are supposed to cut corners in order to get folks in and out of the clinics as fast as possible. Which is a problem."

At times, inspectors appear too close to clinic staff to be able to perform a meaningful investigation. Cornelius Robbins remembers a state inspector who visited his clinic after he lodged a complaint with the

Georgia Department of Health. "Turned out she was best friends with my clinic manager, the one who threw me out. They were talking and laughing and catching up on old times—'How's your husband doing?' 'And how's *yours* doing?' I was like, are you *serious?* When she finally came over and talked to me about the investigation, I said, 'Ma'am, this is a conflict of interest. I can't even talk to you now.'"

CMS, evidently recognizing that inspections by state health boards frequently fail to identify noncompliant or downright dangerous dialysis units, maintains what it euphemistically calls an "Outcomes List": the 5 percent worst dialysis clinics in the nation with the highest number of deaths, hospitalizations, and septicemia cases, which are required by statute to be investigated every year. (CMS has refused to disclose this list even under an FOIA request.) But as Kenneth Bays and others said in their 2000 testimony, while the data on which these ratings are based look bad, the reality is probably worse. Researchers have cross-checked the causes of death of dialysis patients as reported to the USRDS by individual centers against the death certificates of the same patients, and found that many deaths were apparently misreported by dialysis centers. This is hardly surprising, given that at dialysis facilities, such information is typically entered by administrative staff with little or no medical training ... and that facilities are incentivized by CMS quality metrics to downplay certain causes of death.

After publishing *Sorrow's Reward*, a novel based on his experiences in nephrology, in 2011, Robert Bear was invited by a regional ESRD Network to act as a consultant to the Network. By and large, the impressions he formed of the ESRD Networks system as a result of this collaboration match Kenneth Bays's assessment in 2000. "Abundant evidence from the work of dialysis patient advocacy groups suggests that while the CMS ESRD Networks have a strong mandate to defend patients, they too often fail to do so," Bear says. "Some people have observed that their boards are populated by industry and industry surrogates, meaning people being paid by the industry. Similar questions have been raised regarding the dialysis industry oversight responsibilities of the CMS. Why does the CMS not demand more of their ESRD Networks regarding quality of care and patient safety? Who advises the CMS on this matter? What are their interests? The whole notion of how dialysis units are reviewed may itself benefit from an in-depth review."

I've interviewed four former executives of the ESRD Networks system, all of whom spoke on condition of anonymity. While strongly denying that the ESRD Networks have always been compromised by industry—one called the Networks system, at least in the past, "a gloriously successful program and model of quality oversight/ improvement"—collectively they paint a grim and consistent picture of the ESRD Networks' decline in recent years. What follows, in synthesis, is their account of this decline.

Formerly the strengths of the Networks included their geographic diversity, which enabled them to understand and address the considerable differences in kidney failure patterns and lifestyles among patients in the eighteen regions; their employment of distinguished medical experts as advisors; and their access to data from dialysis clinics with which to perform independent research projects on quality of care. Much of this work was paid for by a multimillion-dollar fund, raised through a blanket $0.50 tax on each dialysis treatment established by Congress in the 1980s, to pay for the ESRD Networks' research and regulation functions.

In recent years, however, the ESRD Networks have been subsumed under a handful of large Quality Improvement Organizations (QIOs), which have no regional expertise or specific knowledge of dialysis. These QIOs, though technically nonprofit entities, focus on cost-cutting rather than dialysis quality, in large part because CMS awards contracts to oversee the dialysis industry on the basis of lowest bid rather than best performance. Betty Smith, one of the former ESRD Networks executives I interviewed, related how the chief executive of the new QIO that had taken over her Network repeatedly told the QIO's board, "We bid to win, and we manage to profit," although his organization was a 501(c)(3). "I was sitting there looking around the room," Smith remembers, "saying [to myself], when is somebody gonna jump up and say, 'Wait a minute! We're a not-for-profit organization!'" With the arrival of Thomas Scully, former DaVita board member, as head of what is now CMS, dialysis companies were exempted from supplying data from their operations, which they had historically shared with the Networks. "He [Scully] totally drove that," Smith remembers, "because he was corporate—he came from DaVita. So it was all about what makes it easier and better for the corporations, and getting the Networks out of the way, taking away our ability to collect local data for quality."

All four of these former ESRD Networks executives strongly question how CMS is using the $0.50 per treatment facility tax, which one executive estimated at about $40 million annually, and evidently suspect malfeasance. When one of them asked a CMS official how the funds were being spent, the official claimed that a substantial portion was being used to develop a data collection infrastructure for the dialysis industry known as CROWNWeb, a project with a history of incompetence and waste (CMS went through three contractors before getting a workable product, the first two prototypes having been so flawed that they had to be scrapped). Regardless, CROWNWeb was completed more than a decade ago, yet as one former ESRD Networks executive observed, "the gap between the aggregate tax on dialysis facilities and the aggregate funding of Networks has only widened." Calling the entire saga of the missing dialysis funds "egregious," the executive concluded: "CMS has offered no transparency on this matter." Betty Smith concurs. "The last contract that I signed [before retiring], we were getting about 22 cents a treatment," out of the 50 cents the Network should have been receiving. And what is CMS doing with the balance? "As far as I have ever been able to tell, that other money—they do whatever they want with it, and don't report it to anybody."

· 10 ·

The Wisdom of the Kidney

EMANUEL GONZALES, a dialysis technician in California, has known all his life that dialysis in America cuts along racial and ethnic lines. He grew up in a Latino neighborhood in La Puente, California, where the prevalence of kidney failure was well above the national average. His father, Vince, fifty-eight, has been on dialysis since Gonzales was eight years old. As generation after generation enters dialysis clinics, many children in such neighborhoods grow up believing the arc of their lives, too, will end in one of those gleaming gray chairs, watching the blood leave their bodies.

For a time, Emanuel Gonzales thought he would escape this fate. He was accepted at Wheelock College, and became the first member of his family ever to attend university. But midway through his freshman year, the Great Recession hit the family's finances, and his father's health declined. After completing his first year of college, Gonzales returned home, and spent the money he'd saved for his education to train as a dialysis tech. He has lived in the San Gabriel Valley ever since, where he treats patients at several Fresenius clinics, and accompanies his father to a DaVita unit near the family home.

"Every time that I go in to my work and I care for my patients, I see my dad in them," Gonzales says. "I think about their family members that are going through the same thing I did growing up. There are children in the waiting rooms, teenagers, or grade schoolers like I was. Their parents—my patients—are already starting to worry about those children ending up on dialysis, too."

Determined to break this cycle of disease and harmful care, Emanuel Gonzales joined SEIU-UHW, the labor union of healthcare workers, which five years ago made fixing kidney dialysis in California, and in America, its top priority. "So many of our members were being traumatized by their inability to care for their patients, and by frankly dangerous working conditions," says Cass Gualvez. "Many had PTSD-like symptoms. We all saw this was an emergency." In 2018, 2020 and again in 2022, SEIU-UHW organized California ballot initiatives in an attempt to require safer conditions and better hygiene in dialysis clinics. SEIU-UHW brought patients and workers to Sacramento to educate state lawmakers on kidney disease, and to Washington, DC, to lobby against new legislation being pushed by Big Dialysis to protect its profit-maximizing practices. Emanuel Gonzales took part, and discovered a talent for oratory. He is now one of the union's most popular and effective speakers.

In a talk Gonzales gave in Sacramento, he described his childhood with a father on dialysis, and how some of his earliest memories were clouded by his father's condition. He told of the day that Vince, a model of Latin machismo who never showed fear or weakness, came home from the clinic with a strange, frozen expression that Emanuel Gonzales had never seen before. Vince said that he'd just seen his friend in the next chair die of cardiac arrest, and he announced that he wanted to stop dialyzing: he was giving up. "As I told my story to the members of the legislature, I began to cry," Gonzales remembers. "All those emotions of what my father had been through, myself growing up in a dialysis family, and what so many other people in my neighborhood have suffered . . . it was overwhelming."

Through his tears, Gonzales saw his father in the front row, with the same cold, stony face he'd worn years before, when he'd told his young son that he would rather die than dialyze. "I thought he was angry with me, or embarrassed by how I was showing my emotions," Gonzales remembers. "But then, he started crying, too. Later on, he came up on stage and stood next to me. He said, 'Thank you, son, for standing up for me—standing up for all of us on dialysis.' It was very powerful."

Despite criticism of his union activities by some supervisors and coworkers, Emanuel Gonzales still works at multiple Fresenius clinics, and continues to call out their shortcomings. (Most recently, after working as a volunteer in several of Fresenius's COVID-19 units, he publicly denounced the firm for failing to vaccinate its staff, and for telling workers to get their shots at a hospital instead, on their own time.) Gonzales remains an activist and leader at SEIU-UHW, and he made an unsuccessful run for a seat in the US House of Representatives in 2020. "I may run again in the future," he says. "I haven't ruled that out. But one thing's for sure: I'm staying in the fight for better dialysis."

❑

DIALYSIS WORKERS I've met cry a lot. They may begin the interview dispassionately enough, describing how they open their clinic at 4:00 a.m., watch over pod after pod of patients as they crank through the shifts. So far they remain composed. They are, after all, professionals in a hard job, where blood, distress and death are constant companions. But stay with them a while longer, probe deeper. Ask about their favorite patients, the ones they care about, or miss, the most. You'll find that everyone has a Mr. Popcorn Man story, a breaking point where the contradictions of their work hit home. As they remember this story, they falter. Their eyes glisten, their voices catch. And as the memories unfurl behind their eyes, you see them break down.

While I was in Los Angeles in 2018 to interview SEIU-UHW patient and worker advocates, I watched tears roll down Emerson Padua's face as he stood with one of his patients, Amar Bajwa, and admitted that he felt unable to dialyze Bajwa properly. "My company's focused on making more profits instead of taking better care of patients, and it's a huge problem," he sobbed. "I can't take care of Amar, and it kills me."

Bajwa, a thin, thoughtful Indian man with a neatly trimmed gray mustache, whose dark skin had a yellowish cast from his disease, laid a consoling hand on Padua's shoulder. For a moment their roles seemed reversed: Padua was the sufferer, whose pain Bajwa sought to ease.

Emanuel Gonzales weeps as he speaks of growing up with kidney disease in his family. Even SEIU-UHW executive committee member Cass Gualvez, who leads the union's dialysis initiatives, loses her composure near the end of our talk. During the union's campaign for better dialysis, she says, "four of our patient leaders, who've been with us to Sacramento, who've talked to the press, have died. Workers and patients, they are literally fighting for their lives." She stops and looks down, as if she still can't quite believe what she's seen. She dabs her eyes, blotching her neat mascara. Then she looks me in the face, as if willing me to understand. "I wish change could happen faster," she breathes.

For the past five years, SEIU-UHW has fought a highly public battle against what they see as the depredations of Big Dialysis, which has made California a strategic front in the fight for better dialysis in the United States. "We realized that our dialysis workers were the victims of systematic understaffing, overwork, and terrible conditions in their clinics," says Cass Gualvez. "These conditions make it impossible for them to take proper care of their patients, in this state and nationwide."

SEIU-UHW began its initiative by documenting the unsanitary conditions in many California clinics: flies, cockroaches, mice, crusts of blood on dialysis stations, defective water purification. The union's review of inspection reports issued by the California Department of Public Health between January 1, 2017, and June 25, 2020, revealed 5,190 deficiencies, which included numerous failures to follow physician prescriptions for dialysis treatment. (Union officials note that, as inspections happen far less often than required by federal law, conditions are probably worse.) SEIU-UHW researchers also discovered that deaths from cardiac events during dialysis were alarmingly frequent, and were on the rise. Infections were also increasing; between 2016 and 2020, 4,400 Californians died of infection—a complication of dialysis whose risk can be minimized with proper sterile procedure, but which becomes more likely when clinic managers increase time pressure on their employees, and shorten the interval between patient shifts. "Wiping bloodstains off the chair before the new patient sits in it is part of our responsibilities," one California dialysis tech told me, "but often we just don't have the time."

The union's analysis of 9-1-1 calls made from California dialysis facilities was particularly disturbing. Between 2012 and 2017, dialysis workers frequently called 9-1-1 to request help with patients who had chest pains, had stopped breathing or were in cardiac arrest. (During this five-year period, twenty facilities alone made 2,457 calls to 9-1-1.) Many of these calls suggested that workers were incapable of performing rudimentary emergency procedures such as CPR.

To raise public awareness of the dialysis problem, SEIU-UHW organized marches and sit-ins, encircling substandard units with a wall of workers, patients and their families, some holding photos of relatives who died there. Union representatives testified at committee hearings in Sacramento, and held a major rally on the capitol lawn. Gradually they won over influential lawmakers to their cause, including California governor Gavin Newsom. At which point they began a series of legal challenges to Big Dialysis.

The first was Proposition 8, a 2018 ballot initiative that aimed to cap the profits of dialysis companies at 115 percent, and require the residual earnings to be refunded to patients and insurers, or to be invested in better care through patient education, staff training and higher wages. Prop 8 would also have prevented dialysis companies from discriminating against patients based on their insurance status—an attempt to end the celebration of HIPPERs and the derogation of everyone else.

In response, a lobbying group bankrolled by DaVita and Fresenius called "Dialysis Is Life Support" denounced Prop 8 as a serious threat to California dialysis patients: the proposed earnings cap, the group claimed, would make dialysis so unprofitable that many units would be forced to close, leaving thousands of patients without care. (This threat to shut unprofitable facilities has been a popular negotiating ploy of Big Dialysis since NMC's vigorous lobbying efforts in Congress during the 1970s.) The dialysis lobby mounted the most expensive ballot campaign in California history, spending more than $110 million. It flooded television and radio with scare-tactic ads featuring anguished patients saying they feared being left to die if the initiative passed.

Big Dialysis also fought the union's activities in more pointed and personal ways. "When I started in the industry twenty-one years ago, it was all about patient care," Emerson Padua told a group of dialysis patients and healthcare workers, as he stood on the statehouse steps in Sacramento. "Now they have us so short-staffed, that I'm like a part-time janitor, part-time social worker, part-time dietician and part-time inventory technician." One day after his speech, DaVita fired Padua. "I've worked there sixteen years, and they treat me as disposable," Padua told me later. In all, dialysis firms fired twenty-three workers who were involved in the California unionization effort. Megallan Handford says he saw a video on the DaVita intranet of himself addressing the state legislature in Sacramento; someone had drawn a red X across his face, and added subtitles that accused him of betraying his honest, hard-working colleagues. California dialysis workers tell me that Kent Thiry made video appearances of his own, in which he reviled labor unions as un-American, and affirmed his firm's right to dictate all aspects of dialysis care . . . as well as to fire any Villager who objected.

In the end, Proposition 8 was defeated. "That's $110 million that the industry has spent in lobbying, which they should have spent on their suffering patients and overstretched caregivers instead," Cass Gualvez told me after the vote. "That they can afford such a big lobbying bill shows just how much excess profits the big dialysis corporations are making."

Within months, the union supported a new legislative push, this time spearheaded by state assemblymember Jim Wood, chair of California's Health Committee, which targeted what he called a "self-serving scam" being perpetrated by the dialysis companies on patients and taxpayers alike. Wood was referring to the arrangement that large dialysis companies have with the American Kidney Fund, the nonprofit foundation that helps pay dialysis patients' bills, but is also alleged by some sources to be enabling dialysis firms to steer patients away from government insurance and into private healthcare plans. This behavior threatens to destabilize Affordable Care Act risk pools, and, according to one estimate, drains California's healthcare system of more than $1 billion per year.

Once again, Big Dialysis turned the issue on its head, branding the proposed new legislation as a threat to patient safety, and claiming that reducing the influx of private insurance dollars would harm patients, particularly low-income patients—the very patients who, in reality, often suffer most from being guided into private insurance. Governor Newsom approved the law in October of 2019, but it was blocked two months later by a federal judge, who, citing the argument made by the dialysis industry, expressed concern that it might cause needy patients to be denied care.

In early 2020, the union and its allies announced a second ballot initiative, Proposition 23, which in addition to preventing clinics from discriminating against publicly insured patients and from closing clinics without state approval; would also have required clinics to publish all infection incidents; and to have a physician on-site when patients were being treated, in order to stem the tide of emergency deaths that are all too common in dialysis. The industry spent another $105 million to oppose Proposition 23, paying generous "consulting fees" to certain organizations to ensure they condemned the measure. Seventy-five thousand dialysis industry dollars went to a political consulting firm owned by Alice Huffman, president of the California chapter of the NAACP, part of about $1.7 million that Huffman's firm collected in such contributions in 2020 alone. Sure enough, the NAACP and numerous other groups condemned Proposition 23, which was voted down in November of 2020. Alice Huffman resigned that same month amid conflict of interest accusations.

Despite these setbacks, SEIU-UHW brought a third ballot initiative in November 2022, which was once again voted down. Undeterred, the union started a vigorous post–COVID-19 push to organize California dialysis workers, who report chronic understaffing at both Fresenius and DaVita clinics, and say they received minimal financial rewards for the risks they ran treating immunocompromised patients during the pandemic. "One worker told me, 'I walked by their Healthcare Heroes sign every day, but they only gave me a 20-cent raise,'" Gualvez says. Since November 2022, SEIU-UHW workers have unionized eleven dialysis clinics throughout California, the first dialysis facilities in the state to unionize. In the face of intense opposition from management, more units seem poised to follow.

The union has also launched a direct legal challenge to the business model of Big Dialysis. On January 11, 2022, SEIU-UHW and the National Health Law Program, a public interest law firm that defends the health and civil rights of disadvantaged individuals, filed an administrative complaint with the HHS Office of Civil Rights. Drawing on the extensive body of medical research that demonstrates the numerous and predictable harms caused by short-duration, high ultrafiltration rate (UFR) treatments—John Agar's "bazooka dialysis"—the union alleged that, compared to white patients, Latino and Asian American patients in California are disproportionately exposed to this detrimental form of care, and therefore to poor outcomes and the risk of fatality. This complaint was brought against Fresenius, DaVita and Satellite, who run the majority of the state's dialysis facilities. At last, the same argument is being made in a court of law that nephrology experts, in the United States and abroad, have been making for decades: that dialysis as commonly practiced by corporate America, which is based on high UFR, short treatment times and a fixation with Kt/V, is inherently harmful, and sometimes lethal.

One of the plaintiffs in the union's lawsuit is Roopa Bajwa, the wife of Amar Bajwa, the patient from India whom I interviewed in Los Angeles in 2018. On July 27, 2021, Bajwa died of heart failure while on dialysis. That morning, he had gone through his usual routine and prepared his own breakfast, and seemed to his family to be in good health. But the chronic low blood pressure and cramps that he routinely suffered during his treatments, classic symptoms of bazooka dialysis, were taking their toll. "I miss him so much, and the energy he had to make a difference," says Roopa Bajwa. Despite his tragic and possibly premature death, this lawsuit may allow Amar Bajwa to continue making a difference in dialysis.

❑

LEONARD STERN in New York City is part of another kind of dialysis revolution, less confrontational than the efforts of the California labor union, but no less transformative. After leaving the dialysis clinic run by DaVita, Stern began treating patients at their homes, in private practice. Because assisted dialysis care of this kind isn't covered by Medicare, most of Stern's patients are wealthy New Yorkers who pay for their care out of pocket. One of his first experiences with home dialysis involved an elderly Jewish man we'll call Martin, whose story captures why home dialysis is superior for many patients.

Martin started dialysis in a DaVita center, but couldn't tolerate it. "The water quality, the flow rate, everything about the treatment in clinic was hurting him," says Stern. "He became very depressed, stopped eating, his blood pressure dropped, and had to be hospitalized a few times. So I worked out the mechanics of dialyzing him at home." After the shift to home treatment, Martin's mood improved, though he still had little appetite.

"Dad won't eat," his daughter Jane told Stern. "He wants a pastrami sandwich, but the dietician in the dialysis center always said he couldn't have that, because it's high-sodium."

"Get him a pastrami sandwich!" Stern responded. "He's not going to eat the whole thing, he's only going to eat a little bit." Stern told his technician that if Martin's blood pressure rose after eating the pastrami, he was to dialyze a few minutes longer, to remove the extra fluid.

"For something like dialysis you need to be flexible, because you're always treating the person, you're not treating numbers," Stern observes. "So the rigidity of a DaVita dietician who follows the letter of the law, and forbids pastrami because it's high-salt, is wrong. This man had eaten pastrami all his life. He needed a comfort food to get him out of his state of despair. A few bites of the pastrami sandwich made a world of difference."

Martin quickly recovered his zest for life. Within three months, he was unrecognizable from the forlorn, demoralized old man that Stern had first met.

"Now when I make a home visit for a checkup, he's sitting there on his dialysis chair almost like a throne, being treated by a technician," Stern remembers the scene. "One of his four kids is visiting, his grandkids are there, his wife makes food. And he's advising his son on business issues. He's come back to life."

Several years later, Martin passed away peacefully at home, surrounded by his family. "To this day I have memories of those visits," Stern says. "And of his wife feeding me—feeding me too much, actually! I was part of the family. Even several years after Martin passed away, I'm still a part of the family."

This recovery of an active, productive life is precisely what Congress had in mind with its original dialysis legislation back in 1972. Stern points out that Martin's treatment cost society substantially less than if he'd dialyzed in a clinic. "The home dialysis patient pays for the real estate and the utilities. We save on their transportation, which at a clinic often requires a costly transportation service to do the driving."

Stern is now carrying out a pilot staff-assisted home dialysis project, to demonstrate the cost-effectiveness of this style of treatment, and to convince Medicare to cover it. He plans to launch a home dialysis business that caters to middle-income and poor patients in the New York area—including Dominicans in Washington Heights and the West Bronx.

"Staff-assisted home dialysis should not be just for rich people," Stern says with a shrug, as if his suggestion were self-evident. "The rich person with a gold-plated sink in their bathroom can afford the level of care that they can pay for. What really matters to me is the other person, who doesn't have the gold-plated bathroom, who's no different: he's a human being. He should get the same care. And we can do that. Instead, right now we have a huge disparity, because some Americans think that people don't have a basic right to healthcare. Which is an anathema to me."

❑

STERN IS hardly the first nephrologist to be outraged by dialysis in America. In the early 1970s, Belding Scribner and colleagues condemned the abuses of corporate dialysis, and the commonly accepted perception of dialysis patients as invalids, worthy only of "adequacy" rather than true rehabilitation. In subsequent decades, the influential research nephrologist Carl Kjellstrand deplored the "unphysiology" of fast, thrice-weekly dialysis, which he said was far more harmful to the patients' bodies than the urea in their blood. "The prevailing attitude of doctors and staff at many clinics is that of denial," Kjellstrand observed in 1994, "that the situation is so bad that it must not be dealt with." From the 1990s through the 2010s, Thomas Parker, another leading researcher, delivered a series of rousing calls for change. At a 2013 conference of nephrology nurses, Parker demanded the reform of US dialysis, where he said gross wrongdoing went unchallenged by most renal professionals. Parker told the story of Rosa Parks, whose act of courage on a city bus in Montgomery, Alabama—Parks refused the driver's orders to give up her seat to a white passenger, for which she was arrested—helped to alter society's thinking about segregation, and furthered the civil rights movement. Parker then urged his fellow dialysis workers to rise up against injustice in their industry, repeating the words that Martin Luther King, Jr., spoke when he learned of Rosa Parks's brave stand in Montgomery: "There comes a time when change must occur."

A number of signs, subtle but pervasive, suggest that, after decades of injustice and the recent grim caesura of COVID-19, change is finally coming in American dialysis. In January 2021, the HHS Civil Rights Office opened an investigation into civil rights violations alleged by Vanessa Winters, who was discharged and claims she was blackballed by dialysis units in the Baltimore area run by the MANA group, a local nephrology practice, in joint venture with DaVita. Law firms continue to bring whistleblower cases against Big Dialysis, and are weighing the possibility of filing new lawsuits that allege patient harm, civil rights and antitrust violations, and other wrongdoing.

A firm called Renalogic, which advises private companies, governmental entities and tribal enterprises on how to contain the costs of dialysis treatment for members of their employee health plans, is documenting the systemic harm to the national healthcare system that, they assert, high charges to such health plans by Big Dialysis are causing.

Dialysis companies are pushing back: between late 2018 and early 2019, DaVita filed five federal lawsuits against private health plans, in a coordinated effort to force them to pay dialysis claims at high, "most favored" rates. In November 2020, the US Court of Appeals for the Ninth Circuit, following Renalogic's reasoning, decided one of these suits in favor of Renalogic's client, the California-based organic food producer Amy's Kitchen, ruling that the firm was justified in paying lower dialysis rates than those demanded by DaVita. The US Supreme Court heard another of these suits, *DaVita v. Marietta Memorial Hospital*, and on June 21, 2022, ruled against DaVita once more.

"DaVita's stock price dropped almost 15 percent on this news, which demonstrates the extent to which Big Dialysis uses private plans to fund their profits," says John R. Christiansen, executive vice president of Legal Risk and Strategy at Renalogic. "Because so much money is at stake, we expect to see more litigation aimed at maintaining Big Dialysis profits in the coming years, along with lobbying efforts to get Congress and regulatory agencies to implement laws that keep dialysis profits high." Sure enough, just over a month after DaVita lost the Supreme Court case, a bipartisan group of seventeen House members, all of whom have received campaign donations from DaVita's PAC since January 2021, introduced the "Restore Protections for Dialysis Patients Act," which would forbid any group health plan from limiting, restricting or conditioning its reimbursement of dialysis services. A reporter at *Politico* obtained a document authored by DaVita's chief legal officer and one of its top lobbyists, whose language was so similar to the proposed legislation that some of it appears to have been cut and pasted into the text of the proposed law.

"This law claims to be protecting patients and Medicare, but in reality does neither," says Kevin Weinstein, CEO of Renalogic. "What it does is seek to protect the profits of large dialysis companies, at the expense of self-funded plans and their members, who would end up paying more for the same treatments that they're receiving right now. This willful and skillful misinformation campaign is typical of the historic rapacious behavior of large dialysis companies."

The most momentous legal development of all, however, at least for patient health, may be the SEIU-UHW civil rights lawsuit against bazooka dialysis in California. If this suit progresses through the courts, other states will likely challenge the industry status quo in similar ways.

As in the 1960s and 1970s, when the apparent miracle cure of dialysis received a critical examination in the press, Big Dialysis has recently drawn several hard-hitting investigations in prominent venues, including the *New England Journal of Medicine*, ProPublica and *Scientific American*. Even comedians have zeroed in on dialysis. John Oliver devoted an episode of his popular show *Last Week Tonight* to lampooning what he presented as the greed and cult-like craziness of the industry. Matt Stone and Trey Parker, creators of *South Park*, made a spoof of a local TV news program they set in Cheyenne, Wyoming, which cast a deep-fake Mark Zuckerberg as a huckster selling dubious dialysis treatments. ("At these prices," the sham Zuckerberg trumpets, "you can't afford *not* to get dialysis!") And in late 2021, a well-known documentary film company began making a sweeping exposé of the dialysis industry.

As in the early days of dialysis, this media coverage appears to be drawing attention from politicians and policy makers. In May 2022, staff members of a committee of the US House of Representatives began discreetly contacting experts with knowledge of the UFR issue, suggesting that a congressional investigation, and even hearings, may follow. Perhaps more significantly, in 2019, President Donald Trump signed "Advancing Kidney Health," an executive order calling for better diagnosis and treatment of early-stage kidney disease, an 80 percent increase in transplants by 2030, and more widespread use of home dialysis. The originator of the order, which was applauded by the nephrology community, probably wasn't Trump (though Melania Trump was hospitalized in 2018 for a kidney operation), but his head of HHS, Alex Azar. As a former pharma lobbyist and president of US operations for the drug giant Eli Lilly, on whose watch the firm's insulin prices doubled, Azar himself seemed an unlikely person to challenge the business practices of corporate dialysis. But Azar had learned about the industry's endemic problems from personal experience: his father had been on dialysis for several years before receiving a living donor transplant.

"Americans [should] start paying for kidney health rather than kidney disease," Azar said in a speech before the National Kidney Foundation, "and pay for Americans with kidney disease to actually get good outcomes, rather than the endless, life-consuming procedures that you all know so well."

There's room for hope, when people like Alex Azar recognize what Alonzo Plough saw decades ago: that allowing people to reach the precipice of death before treating them is both cruel and ruinously expensive. That both fiscally and morally, offering preventive medicine and long-term management of kidney disease to intercept people before they reach that precipice makes far better sense.

Since the executive order was issued, CMS has begun to revise a number of payment policies, including its ESRD Quality Incentive Program. In December 2021, CMS issued a call for public comment from members of the nephrology community, which may signal further policy changes. Several new bipartisan laws to improve kidney care are now before Congress; one of them, the Improving Access to Home Dialysis Act, would further Leonard Stern's plan to provide assisted home dialysis to the masses, by authorizing Medicare to pay dialysis workers who help patients in their homes. "The law apparently has only a 3 percent chance of being passed, but it would make all the difference," says Stern. Transplants are becoming easier to obtain and the transplantation process less racially biased, thanks to shifts in the HHS allocation policies for donor kidneys and pancreases that were finalized in 2014 and 2021. The Living Donor Protection Act of 2021, a new law that would offer financial incentives and other assistance to living donors, has received strong bipartisan support in the House and the Senate.

Milda Saunders, the Chicago internist, is upbeat about the future. "Dialysis is on people's minds as never before. Five years ago, for instance, nobody knew what GFR [glomerular filtration rate] was, and today it's being widely debated." Many medical centers have changed the way they estimate GFR, she continues, leading clinicians to learn more about the measure. Major organizations are publicly confronting systemic bias in kidney health, often for the first time. "I was recently at a NIDDK [National Institute of Diabetes and Digestive and Kidney Diseases] conference on structural racism," Saunders says. "I mean, wow, NIDDK had a conference on *structural racism*—that's amazing!" She mentions two drugs with promising new applications in renal care—SGL2 inhibitors and nonsteroidal mineralocorticoid receptor antagonists—which may help physicians to prevent further damage to their patients' kidneys, so they don't fail. "We're all human, and if we doctors have a treatment to prevent something, then we're more likely to pay attention to it. If all we can do is just watch the decline, then we don't."

Thus at the big-picture level of policy and regulation, there are indications that American dialysis may be starting to catch up to the rest of the world. Of course, wholesale change can only come with the help of, or despite, Big Dialysis, with its thousands of facilities across the nation and its entrenched Beltway power.

On the day-to-day level, life on dialysis hasn't changed much. Most of the patients we've met in this book continue the dialysis grind, focusing on survival. Several have passed away since I interviewed them. Even on the blood floor, though, a faint breeze of change sometimes comes. Gerald Thompson continues to dialyze at his home in Memphis, with help from Sherry, and from a DaVita nephrologist whom both say is committed and compassionate. Justin Charles Evans remains at his new DaVita center in Atlanta, and is happy with the staff, if not with the shorter, sharper treatments. After two blissful years off dialysis, Carrie Brito's kidneys failed for good, and she has had to resume treatment. Thanks to a determined effort by her nephrologist at the Baylor University Medical Center in Dallas, she was accepted in the DaVita facility in Kaufman, Texas, just down the street from her old Fresenius unit—the same DaVita unit that she says once declined to treat her. Memories of her previous termination still weigh heavily, and she says that members of the staff in the new clinic have a poor bedside manner. "At least they're treating me," she says with a bitter laugh. "They're keeping me alive. That's a start."

That Thompson, Evans and Brito are all receiving care from DaVita, the company that has received so much criticism in this book, is in itself encouraging. Despite the negative environment that the company's culture can create for patients and workers, in any given center, one strong, principled nephrologist, nurse or tech can make a huge difference in a patient's life. Megallan Handford, Emanuel Gonzales and Emerson Padua still work in Big Dialysis, and find ways, within the constraints of the fast food model, to practice medicine effectively and humanely. And some senior American nephrologists continue to condemn industry norms and champion patient-centered care, an honor roll of doctors who keep faith with Hippocrates and Maimonides: Leonard Stern, Steven Rosansky, Brent Miller, Steven Bander, Jesse Goldman, Robert Lockridge, Jeffrey Berns, Thomas Golper, Jeffrey Wallach, Daniel Coyne, J. Clint Parker and a few others.

Cornelius Robbins says he's grateful every morning for his transplant. "Free at last! But a lot of people are still back in those centers, because they don't know how to get on the list." Unwilling to wait for public policy to fix Big Dialysis's transplant inequities, Robbins and several fellow transplant recipients have begun visiting clinics in central Georgia, catching patients as they arrive and leave (staff won't allow Robbins and the others to enter the building) and explaining the transplant facts of life. "Patients may trust us more than someone at the clinic, because we've been through it. They know we're giving them the straight story."

Among several dialysis patients and family members I've met, the urge to advocate has grown strong. Sherry and Gerald Thompson are determined to help other dialysis patients, after experiencing the deadly cycle of termination and blackballing in for-profit dialysis, a trap whose existence, before Gerald fell ill, neither of them could have imagined happening in modern-day America. "It is terrifying to be in the position that someone else is in control of your life, and there's nothing you can do about it," Sherry says. "And you have to do what they say, or you're going to the whipping post, or we're going to sell you off. And [when that happens] guess what, nobody else wants you because you're a damaged slave now, and they're not gonna take you."

Gerald nods, too moved to speak. Sherry lays her hand on his arm. "It's got to stop," she continues. "We're going to do what we can to make that happen. That's our goal. We don't want anybody to feel this way. We don't want anybody to go through the abuse."

For William Sarsfield, years spent at his wife's side have taught him the pivotal role of psychology in dialysis. "What I've learned from this whole damn thing is, dialysis is mind over matter." As Leonard Stern used modernist art to lift his patients' spirits, so Sarsfield plans to use music, by convincing local bands he knows to play benefits at Texas dialysis clinics, in order to raise community awareness about kidney disease, but especially to energize the patients. "Music heals the soul. We have to help dialysis patients mentally, to accept their treatment and start getting their lives back, not just maintaining life and being milked for money until they end up in a pine box." Belding Scribner said the same thing a half century ago: dialysis must aim to achieve rehabilitation, not mere adequacy.

Justin Charles Evans, too, is determined to change dialysis. He has retained a lawyer, and plans to file suit against DaVita for the poor care he says he has suffered at two of its clinics. And together with Arlene Mullin and other members of Dialysis Advocates, and civil rights activists like Chili Most in Los Angeles and Rev. Ronald Wright in Dallas, he is organizing a demonstration against the human harm endemic in this industry.

"A lot of people think stuntmen are daredevils, but that's wrong. We're experts at calculating risks. Right now I'm taking a calculated risk with my life, by calling out DaVita. I love life, and thank God for every day I'm alive. But this abuse has *got* to stop. Not just for me, but for everybody on dialysis. The world needs to know this is going on."

As she has been for the past twenty-four years, Arlene Mullin remains at the heart of dialysis advocacy in America—she is "Queen Arlene" to many grateful patients. She still takes calls from patients in trouble, though at seventy-three, she has begun to think about life after advocacy. She recently remarried, and now lives in a spacious house in Tallahassee, Florida—a far cry from the borrowed trailer home in southern Georgia she inhabited when I met her. Sherry Thompson and

William Sarsfield have both joined the board of Dialysis Advocates, together with former NBA player Clem Johnson and Mullin's longtime friend Bill Summers, a retired Marine.

"For many years I fought this battle alone," Mullin says. "People called me crazy, and some days I believed them. But America is finally starting to hear the voices of dialysis patients. The battle isn't over. Many, many patients are still being hurt and killed. But for the first time, I'm beginning to feel that change might happen."

She cracks a grin. "Maybe someday I'll get to retire!" Since I met her years ago, Mullin has laughed readily, even in dark moments. But this is one of the few times I've actually seen her smile.

❑

IN 1972, as Congress promised dialysis and rehabilitation for all kidney failure patients in America, on the other side of the planet, Australia was passing its own law to guarantee universal dialysis coverage. Since then, Australia and America have traveled very different paths, in dialysis and in healthcare as a whole. The treatment philosophy that John Agar followed for decades, until his retirement in 2020, emphasizing life quality as the main goal of good dialysis and home treatment as the best option for most patients, is practiced today at centers throughout Australia and New Zealand. Leonard Stern's dream of high-quality home dialysis for the masses is already a reality, Down Under.

Many of Agar's patients dialyze at home, not because they live in the bush—a higher percentage of Australians than Americans live in cities—but because they've developed the independence and confidence required to treat themselves. Agar, his nephrologist colleagues and his team of nurses train patients to cannulate themselves and run their own machines, according to the treatment plan that best fits their individual physiology and lifestyle. (Nurses and technicians are always on call, if patients get into trouble.) For most of Agar's patients and their families, dialysis is less an alien ordeal than a challenge of everyday life. "Our patients take charge of their own health," he says. "We don't even allow their partners to cannulate. In fact, for most of our patients who dialyze at home, if somebody comes near their fistula, they'll beat him with a cricket bat. 'Get away from my fistula! I'm the only one who looks after that.' Patients gain a huge sense of responsibility and accomplishment. They're not helpless victims in this process. They're in charge."

He introduces me to Dale Darcy, who has been his patient for twenty-four years. "Dale is a real gun," Agar says. "He's a bit naughty sometimes, though I tend to encourage his limit-pushing. And Dale knows the limits of my limits!"

On Zoom with Darcy in his home in a suburb of Geelong, his two young daughters flit in and out of the frame, and his wife Michelle stops by to say hello on her way out the door. Darcy works as an engineer and handyman at a wildlife park that's part of the Royal Melbourne Zoo. "I like to pat the rhinos, but my biggest thrill is making a gate that can hold them." When he first started dialysis, Darcy used to load his dialysis machine, a generator and a tent into the bed of his ute (pickup), and go swimming and pig shooting up on the Murray River for a week at a time. When he needed to dialyze, he'd hammer a nail into a tree and hang the bags of dialysate from it. He's stopped camping on the Murray since his children arrived, but he still practices jujitsu, as a brown belt. "I've got a fistula in my arm, so I've gotta be careful. Sometimes they'll put me in an arm bar. When that happens, I just have to tap out."

Darcy's knowledge of his body, and the warning signs of his disease, are striking. "When I have high potassium, I see these blue stars when I close my eyes. No one would believe me if I told them, but that just means they haven't done a medical study to prove it—I know that's high potassium. And I can tell by my fistula when I've got high blood pressure, because it goes hard as a rock. If I've got extra fluid on, I get puffy under the eyes. And when I get the shakes, I know I've got an infection, and it's straight into hospital."

I ask if he found it difficult to learn to cannulate himself: to insert those long needles into his own arm. "Well, I already knew it hurt, because the nurses had been doing it to me," he replies. "So I thought, 'Well, it's still gonna hurt, but now I'm in control. If it hurts too much, I can sort of back off a bit, whereas the nurses wouldn't—they'd just push it in. So you've just gotta get over it psychologically."

Another of John Agar's patients, Andrew O'Dwyer, was a longboard surfer who lived in Anglesea, a town on the Surf Coast southwest of Geelong. He surfed every day that the conditions permitted, sometimes twice daily. "I was always conscious of the fact that his fistula might not heal properly, being wet all the time," says Agar today. "But he said, 'Look, John, I just put a Band-Aid on it,' and that was that. He was aware that he was taking risks, but he continued to surf. He was on home dialysis for ten or twelve years. And he surfed all that time."

"That's the whole beauty of home dialysis: being prepared to trust your patient," Agar continues. "And the trust comes from both sides. The patient needs to be able to trust themself, and build their own confidence in what they are doing. But the care team also has to be prepared to let go, and let the patient learn, and sometimes make errors. To build this mutual trust, I think doctors and patients need to feel they're on the same level: just two human beings working together to get a good outcome. That's what I find is often lacking in US dialysis, and US medicine generally. American doctors are very aware and actually quite jealous of their exalted status, and patients revere them like gods."

Andrew O'Dwyer, the surfer, died on home dialysis. The coroner for the State of Victoria concluded that he had set his machine incorrectly. "Andrew lived on his own terms, and dealt with his disease on his own terms," says Agar. "Home dialysis allowed him the freedom to do this. I don't think he'd have had things any other way."

Dialysis done right is a series of choices, guided by the care team but ultimately made by the patient. Including one final choice: when to stop. Agar remembers Edna Kent, an elderly Irish Australian patient he treated for eighteen years. Shortly before her eighty-sixth birthday, after her husband and all her other close relatives had passed away, Kent announced she wanted to stop her dialysis treatments.

"Of course, I talked it over with Edna for months, making sure she was clear on what she was doing," says Agar. "But she was immovable. She said she'd done all she had ever wanted to do, except to die well."

In a series of conversations that it's hard to imagine taking place in a US facility, Agar and Kent planned how her life would end. "She said she wanted an Irish wake, and she was going to host it," Agar says. "She invited all her friends, including her nurses Rosie and Janeane, and everyone else from the clinic. She bought star fruits, bananas, papayas—all the forbidden fruits for dialysis patients, because of their high levels of potassium. She threw a potassium party for us! She must have eaten a dozen star fruits. We talked, laughed, reminisced. She lay down on her bed, and said goodbye. People were weeping. I blubbered shamelessly. But many of us were smiling too. In a few hours, she drifted quietly into a coma, and died. Edna chose her own way out, and she went in style."

Tears shine in Agar's eyes as he recalls the scene. "Yah, look," he continues eventually, in a gruff voice, as if to mask his emotion. "We let people dialyze to live, rather than living to dialyze."

Edna Kent's decision, and the manner in which she carried it off, recall the ancient Stoics, who believed that the ability to decide how our life will end is central to human liberty and dignity. "What is freedom, you ask?" wrote Seneca. "To be a slave to no situation, to no necessity, to no chance events." To Seneca and other Stoics, keeping an "open door" on the Beyond, and choosing the right time to pass through it, were integral parts of a life well lived. But in addition to such grand Mediterranean equanimity, there is also a festive air about Edna Kent's Irish wake, a sprinkling of wit and star-fruit humor worthy of Flann O'Brien or Oscar Wilde, that, in the closing act of her life, shows a rare kind of courage. Courage that not only transcends the fear of death, but also affirms a powerful love of life.

❏

"Mental integrity is a sine qua non of the free and independent life," wrote Homer Smith, the pioneer of kidney physiology. "But let the composition of our internal environment suffer change, let our kidneys fail for even a short time to fulfill their task, and our mental integrity, our personality, is destroyed."

Dialysis patients, tethered to their machine, understand all too well how kidneys shape human independence. They know the mental fog that rolls in when poisons and fluids build in their blood—or when high-speed dialysis itself roils their inner sea. Maintaining a stable internal milieu is equally necessary to all vertebrates and invertebrates, and to countless other organic entities: termite colonies and beehives; cloud forests and wetlands; and to our planet as a whole, which in many ways behaves like one complex organism. At each unit of scale, when a system loses the sustaining balance of its individual elements, it rapidly disintegrates.

Smith's observations about equilibrium also apply to human communities, which require their own form of homeostasis to thrive. A society works when the often competing cultures and faiths of its members, their economic needs and political convictions, remain in balance; and when, ultimately, a people's desire to cooperate is stronger than their will to fight. Conversely, when toxins like race hatred, fearmongering, religious extremism and economic disparity accumulate in a community's bloodstream, they can overwhelm the balancing tendencies—mutual respect and trust, confidence in justice, the instinct to shield the weak and confront the strong—that protect our equilibrium. In such times, as Homer Smith said of the body, a society loses its mental integrity, and its personality is destroyed. The ancient Greeks recognized the danger of such imbalances long ago, in the human body and the body politic alike. Around 500 BC, medical writer and philosopher Alcmaeon of Croton expressed the secret of health in political terms, as a balance of opposites: "The equal balance (*isonomia*) of the powers—wet, dry, cold, hot, bitter, sweet and the rest—maintains health. But the absolute rule [by one] among them produces disease."

Writing this book, I've begun to see America's many problems as a progressive loss of homeostasis. That we allow some of our most defenseless citizens to be herded together and bled for profit, that we watch mutely as money taints medical ethics, that we accept and even celebrate greed when it's airbrushed with the discredited ideologies of long-dead economists... dialysis in America is symptomatic of a chronic, society-wide condition, of which opioid pushing, mass shoot-ings, rampant homelessness, endless wars and our dire failures during the pandemic are further signs. America's kidneys are failing.

What would a nation's kidneys be? Something hidden away deep within our neighborhoods and our homes, a reservoir of calm, trust and long-term thinking that we rarely notice until it's gone. Some-thing apparently insignificant, even a little contemptible and urine-scented—the simple child of the Passover seder, the homeless man on the sidewalk who greets us with a knowing smile—that turns out to be the true measure of our humanity. In a society with sound kidneys, businesses and universities would live by their mission statements (or might not need them at all). Churches would put their holiest Words into practice each day. Politics would be concerned with the abiding welfare of the polis, not with personal and group power. Success would be understood not as dominion over antagonists, but as enduring, joy-ful coexistence: homeostasis, in a word.

Though I'm only guessing what America's kidneys are, I do have a strong sense of what they sound like. Over the years of conversations that have gone into this book, dialysis patients have taught me things about balance, poise and strength that no one else seems to know. Per-haps, lacking equilibrium themselves, people without kidneys can best explain why it matters. Some dialysis patients I've met are like those folktale figures who have lost the most, who yet have the most to give; the legendary ones with every reason to be bitter about the course of their lives, who yet savor life's sweetness. The fragile ones, with a fearful strength.

Listening hard to dialysis patients in America, caring for them hon-orably and well, is a way to regain our collective homeostasis. Being more like them is a path to finding our better selves.

EPILOGUE AND ANNOTATIONS

As EXPLAINED IN the first chapter of this book, before publication, I shared excerpts with a number of organizations, and invited them to comment. These organizations included DaVita, Fresenius, Satellite and the Mid-Atlantic Nephrology Associates; the American Kidney Fund, CMS, the ESRD Networks, the Washington University School of Medicine, and Tenet Healthcare. In response, DaVita made a number of objections, which I summarized in the first chapter of this book. The American Kidney Fund also made a series of objections, which are summarized in chapter 7. As of the time this book went to press, there was no indication that DaVita or the American Kidney Fund had changed their positions. The other organizations with whom I shared passages either did not respond or chose not to comment. As of the time this book went to press, there was no indication that they had changed their positions, either.

The following notes aim to help readers explore the medical, social and legal underpinnings of my narrative. They identify peer-reviewed literature, clinical reports, legal complaints, judicial opinions, data from government healthcare bodies, and other materials that I've relied on. They also cite journalism that I found particularly helpful. I have not annotated details that can easily be verified via search engines and other familiar Internet resources. For brevity, I have employed generally accepted abbreviations for scholarly publications, and have shortened some citations in ways that, hopefully, leave them readily comprehensible. I supply URLs to documents that might otherwise be difficult to locate on the web.

These notes signpost a few pathways into the broad landscape of learning related to the rise of nephrology, not only as a branch of medicine, but also as a phenomenon of great significance for public health, corporate culture, economics, government regulation and the law. I hope their breadth, if not their comprehensiveness, conveys the importance of dialysis as one of the first instances of high-tech medicine, and as an object lesson in the problems that can arise when health systems operate within a predominantly for-profit ethos.

Much of the information in this book also derives from hundreds of interviews I carried out over a six-year period, with dialysis patients, nephrologists, nurses, techs and other clinic workers, medical researchers, scholars of economics and public health, prosecutors, whistleblower attorneys, government and private investigators, congressional staffers, stock analysts, and experts in many other fields. I would have liked to acknowledge, by name, everyone who aided and guided my work, but many people agreed to speak with me on condition of anonymity. So to all of my sources, the named and the nameless: thank you. My deepest gratitude of all goes to the dialysis patients I consulted: your generosity, courage and wisdom made this book possible. And to Amar Bajwa, Gregg Hansen, Tangi Foster, Nancy Spaeth and others who have died during its writing: you are remembered.

NOTES

vii **"Of all the forms of inequality":** See the discussion of King's exact words and their context in Quote Investigator, "Of All the Forms of Inequality" (https:// quoteinvestigator.com/2015/10/22/mlk-health).

2. THE INNER SEA

5 **When a lobe-finned fish:** An excellent and entertaining introduction to the evolution of tetrapods from lobe-finned fish is Neil Shubin, *Your Inner Fish* (New York, 2008). See also Homer W. Smith, *From Fish to Philosopher* (New York, 1961); Homer Smith, *Kamongo Or, the Lungfish and the Padre* (New York, 1949); and Neil Shubin, *Some Assembly Required* (New York, 2020).

6 **Starting in early sea creatures:** Shubin, *Your Inner Fish*; and more specifically, Melanie P. Hoenig and Mark L. Zeidel, "Homeostasis, the Milieu Intérieur, and the Wisdom of the Nephron," Clin J. Am Soc Nephrol (2014); Jeroen P. Kooman, "Geology, Paleoclimatology and the Evolution of the Kidney," Blood Purif (2012); and Robert L. Chevalier, "Evolutionary Nephrology," Kidney Int Rep (2017).

6 **concept of the *milieu intérieur*:** A good introduction to Bernard and his conception of *milieu intérieur* in Charles G. Gross, "Claude Bernard and the Constancy of the Internal Environment," Neuroscientist (1998). Further references to Bernard and his seminal work can be found in the annotations to Chapter 4. See also Peter Wise, "Claude Bernard and the Milieu Intérieur," in Todd Ing, Mohamed Rahman et al., eds., *Dialysis* (Singapore, 2012); and Laura Keogh, David Kilroy et al., "The Struggle to Equilibrate Outer and Inner Milieus," Ann Anat (2021).

7 **have a sense of smell:** Jennifer Pluznick, personal communication. See also Jennifer L. Pluznick, Dong-Jing Zou et al., "Functional Expression of the Olfac-

tory Signaling System in the Kidney," Proc Natl Acad Sci USA (2009); and Nicholas M. Dalesio, Sebastian F. Barreto Ortiz et al., "Olfactory, Taste, and Photo Sensory Receptors in Non-sensory Organs," Front Physiol (2018).

7 **Twenty percent of the blood:** Arthur C. Guyton and John E. Hall, "Local and Humoral Control of Tissue Blood Flow," in *Guyton and Hall Textbook of Medical Physiology*, 12th ed. (Philadelphia, 2011), table 17-1, p. 192. More generally on renal physiology, see the useful primer by Rachel Casiday and Regina Frey, "Maintaining the Body's Chemistry: Dialysis in the Kidneys," publication of the Department of Chemistry, Washington University in St. Louis (2021).

9 **diabetes, obesity and hypertension:** Regarding diabetes: CDC, "National Diabetes Statistics Report" and "The Facts, Stats, and Impacts of Diabetes"; and Eberhard Standl, Kamlesh Khunti et al., "The Global Epidemics of Diabetes in the 21st Century," Eur J Prev Cardiol (2019). Regarding obesity: Harvard T. H. Chan School of Public Health, "An Epidemic of Obesity: U.S. Obesity Trends" (archived at https://web.archive.org/web/20220706202201/ https://www.hsph.harvard.edu/nutritionsource/an-epidemic-of-obesity/); and CDC, "Adult Obesity Facts." Regarding hypertension: "Estimated Hypertension Prevalence, Treatment, and Control among U.S. Adults," from the CDC Million Hearts initiative (https://millionhearts.hhs.gov/data-reports/hypertension-prevalence.html) (2021); and Paul Muntner, Shakia T. Hardy et al., "Trends in Blood Pressure Control among US Adults with Hypertension," JAMA (2020).

9 **newly identified as having renal failure:** USRDS Annual Data Report 2021, "Incidence, Prevalence, Patient Characteristics, and Treatment Modalities," Highlights (https://adr.usrds.org/2021/end-stage-renal-disease/1-incidence-prevalence-patient-characteristics-and-treatment-modalities). See also Nilka Rios Burrows, Israel Hora et al., "Incidence of End-Stage Renal Disease Attributed to Diabetes among Persons with Diagnosed Diabetes," CDC Morbidity and Mortality Weekly Report (2017).

9 **about 37 million adults:** For a good overview by the NIH, see "Kidney Disease Statistics for the United States." See also USRDS Annual Data Report 2021, "CKD in the General Population" (https://adr.usrds.org/2021/chronic-kidney-disease/1-ckd-in-the-general-population).

9 **patients on dialysis dropped:** See the analysis by Duaa Eldeib, "They Were the Pandemic's Perfect Victims," ProPublica (2021). Exhaustive epidemiological data can be found in the USRDS Annual Data Report 2021, "Incidence, Prevalence, Patient Characteristics, and Treatment Modalities."

9 **medical science devised dialysis:** For references to the following material, see Chapter 4, section beginning "World War II brought a flood of soldiers...."

10 **"I took to nephrology immediately":** Information and quotations here and following: Leonard Stern, personal communication.

10 **"a field of infinite promise":** This and quotations following: John Agar, personal communication.

11 **"survival rate in the United States":** Leonard Stern, personal communication.

On the question of higher patient mortality and rates of infection and cardiac problems in the United States than in other countries, see Aminu K. Bello, Ikechi G. Okpechi et al., "Epidemiology of Haemodialysis Outcomes," Nat Rev Nephrol (2022); Robert N. Foley and Raymond M. Hakim, "Why Is the Mortality of Dialysis Patients in the United States Much Higher than the Rest of the World?" J Am Soc Nephrol (2009); Carl Kjellstrand and Christopher R. Blagg, "Differences in Dialysis Practice Are the Main Reasons for the High Mortality Rate in the United States Compared to Japan," Hemodial Int (2003); Bruce M. Robinson, Jinyao Zhang et al., "Worldwide, Mortality Risk is High Soon After Initiation of Hemodialysis," Kidney Int (2014); and Eric Weinhandl, "Troubling Health Trends in the New USRDS Annual Data Report," Nephrol News Issues (2018). See also excellent reporting in ProPublica: Robin Fields, "In Dialysis, Life-Saving Care at Great Risk and Cost," ProPublica (2010); and additional resources by Fields and other ProPublica reporters in "Dialysis: High Costs and Hidden Perils of a Treatment Guaranteed to All," ProPublica (2010–2012).

3. DIALYSIS IN AMERICA

13 **Fresenius, the North American subsidiary:** Fresenius Medical Care North America, which is the North American subsidiary of Fresenius Medical Care AG, a company based in Bad Homburg, Germany, that is the world leader in treating people with chronic kidney failure. Fresenius Medical Care AG is, in turn, a subsidiary of Fresenius SE & Co. KGaA, also called the Fresenius Group, together with three other subsidiaries: Fresenius Helios (operates private hospitals); Fresenius Kabi (produces drugs, nutrition products and medical devices); and Fresenius Vamed (plans, develops and manages healthcare facilities). For details, see https://www.fresenius.com/group-overview. Except where otherwise indicated, every mention of "Fresenius" in this book refers to the dialysis-related US operations of Fresenius Medical Care North America.

13 **Kaufman County Poor Farm:** Martha Doty Freeman, "Indigent Care in Texas," Index of Texas Archaeology: Open Access Gray Literature from the Lone Star State (2008); Kathey Kelley Hunt, "Kaufman County Poor Farm," Kaufman County Historical Commission (2008).

13 **Civil War memorial:** "Kaufman County Confederate Soldiers Monument" (https://www.hmdb.org/m.asp?m=63755); Patrick Strickland "In Small-Town North Texas, Some Confederate Monuments Still Stand Tall," *Dallas Observer* (March 2, 2021).

14 **"racism here is unquestioning":** Quotations here and following: Carrie Brito, personal communication.

14 **"fistula," in her left arm:** For an excellent overview of the procedures involved in various forms of dialysis, see Dori Schatell and John Agar, *Help, I Need Dialysis!* (Madison, WI, 2021). For a more detailed account, see

the Medical Education Institute, *Core Curriculum for the Dialysis Technician* (Madison, WI, 2017). Eighty-eight percent of renal failure patients in America who dialyze perform hemodialysis as described here; see USRDS Annual Data Report 2021, "Incidence, Prevalence, Patient Characteristics, and Treatment Modalities," figure 1.6 (https://adr.usrds.org/2021/end-stage-renal-disease/1-incidence-prevalence-patient-characteristics-and-treatment-modalities). An entirely different form of dialysis—peritoneal—involves filling the abdominal cavity with dialysate and using the peritoneum, the abdominal lining, to filter the blood. (See a fuller description in Chapter 4.) Only 12 percent of dialysis patients in America use this treatment modality, primarily at home. Hemodialysis is the core business of the US dialysis industry, and the focus of this book. In addition to fistulas, two other methods exist to connect a dialysis patient's bloodstream to the machine: catheters and grafts. According to nephrology best practices, these methods are to be avoided where possible, because they are associated with a higher risk of infection and blood clotting than when a fistula is employed.

14 **treatments are likely too short and fast:** The literature on why short treatment times, elevated UFR and high blood pump speed are harmful is too extensive to describe here in anything but extreme synthesis. Important studies include Damien Ashby, Natalie Borman et al., "Renal Association Clinical Practice Guideline on Haemodialysis," BMC Nephrology (2019); Steven M. Brunelli, Glenn M. Chertow et al., "Shorter Dialysis Times Are Associated with Higher Mortality among Incident Hemodialysis Patients," Kidney Int (2010); Charles Chazot, Cyril Vo-Van et al., "Even a Moderate Fluid Removal Rate During Individualised Haemodialysis Session Times Is Associated with Decreased Patient Survival," Blood Purif (2017); Jennifer Flythe, Gary C. Curhan et al., "Shorter Length Dialysis Sessions Are Associated with Increased Mortality, Independent of Body Weight," Kidney Int (2013); Yuntac Lim, Gyeonghun Yang et al., "Association Between Ultrafiltration Rate and Clinical Outcome Is Modified by Muscle Mass in Hemodialysis Patients," Nephron (2020); Mark R. Marshall, B. G. Byrne et al., "Associations of Hemodialysis Dose and Session Length with Mortality Risk in Australian and New Zealand Patients," Kidney Int (2006); Christopher W. McIntyre, James O. Burton et al., "Hemodialysis-Induced Cardiac Dysfunction Is Associated with an Acute Reduction in Global and Segmental Myocardial Blood Flow," Clin J Am Soc Nephrol (2008).

Nephrologists have warned of the dangers of short, high-speed dialysis treatments for decades. A good historic overview of their concerns is in Dori Schatell, "Not. Enough. Dialysis." Home Dialysis Central (June 19, 2018) (https://homedialysis.org/news-and-research/blog/266-not-enough-dialysis). See also Carl M. Kjellstrand, "Short Dialysis Increases Morbidity and Mortality," in Contrib Nephrol (1985); and the comprehensive review of the issue in Eli A. Friedman, ed., *Death on Hemodialysis* (Dordrecht, Netherlands, 1994). For an accessible explanation of the risks of high blood pump speed (also called "flow rate"), see John Agar, "Don't Flog the Fistulas," Home Dialysis Central (March 14, 2014) (https://homedialysis.org/news-and-research/blog/38-dont-flog-fistulas-slow-hemodialysis-blood-flow).

15 **weighs 120 pounds:** Details of Brito's treatment derive from a review of extensive medical records that she supplied, as well as personal communication with Brito, John Agar, William Sarsfield and Arlene Mullin.

15 **a 2011 memo to clinicians:** Fresenius Medical Care Internal Memo on Dialysis Treatment Time and Ultrafiltration Rate, dated June 23, 2011. In this document, the Fresenius Medical Care North America Medical Office recommends to medical directors and attendings a minimum treatment time of four hours and an ultrafiltration rate target of ≤ 10 ml/kg/hr for incident patients. For the dangers, and the routine application, of short, high-speed dialysis, see also references in the earlier note **treatments are likely too short and fast**, and the administrative complaint filed by California labor union SEIU-UHW with the HHS Office of Civil Rights, both in San Francisco and in Washington, DC, titled "Re: High-Speed Hemodialysis Has a Disparate Impact on Latino and Asian American Patients" (https://healthlaw.org/wp-content/uploads/2022/01/2022-01-11-HHS-Complaint-final.pdf).

15 **blood pressure spikes to dangerous levels:** This scene and subsequent events at the clinic: Carrie Brito, William Sarsfield and Arlene Mullin, personal communication, together with detailed documentation, videos and voice recordings compiled by Brito.

16 **blood on her dialysis chair:** Brito, Sarsfield and Mullin, personal communication; detailed documentation, videos and voice recordings compiled by Brito. CMS Form 2567 Statement of Deficiencies and Plan of Correction, a report of an unannounced inspection of the Kaufman facility on July 30, 2018, confirms some of Brito's assertions regarding sanitation hazards and other problems at the clinic.

17 **sign a behavioral contract:** Fresenius Medical Care Conditions of Care Agreement, which Brito signed and dated on December 17, 2016.

17 **her care was being terminated:** Fresenius Medical Care Patient Discharge Letter 30 Day Notice, dated January 19, 2017.

18 **A woman answered:** William Sarsfield, personal communication.

18 **home in Albany, Georgia:** This section on Arlene Mullin's work at Dialysis Advocates is based on my personal observation, as well as personal communication with Arlene Mullin, Carrie Brito, William Sarsfield, Marie DeFrancesco-Malviya, Pat Reilly, Chili Most, Ronald Wright, Clem Johnson, David Barbetta and Marcel Reid.

19 **advice of their legal counsel:** Carrie Brito and William Sarsfield, personal communication.

19 **dangerous, even deadly:** For the higher mortality of dialysis patients treating in ERs, see Lilia Cervantes, Delphine Tuot et al., "Association of Emergency-Only vs Standard Hemodialysis with Mortality and Health Care

Use among Undocumented Immigrants with End-Stage Renal Disease," JAMA Intern Med (2018); and End Stage Renal Disease (ESRD) Network Program, ESRD National Coordinating Center, summary annual report (2018), especially p. 9 (https://esrdncc.org/contentassets/187eeba04ded4b7d a4880050bdff04c7/2018summaryannualreport508.pdf). Quotation of Robert Bear, personal communication.

20 **a specialist at Baylor:** Carrie Brito, personal communication.

21 **James Kasiewicz was involuntarily discharged:** Fresenius Medical Care, Notice of Discharge, January 15, 2016. This and subsequent details of James Kasiewicz's experiences are recorded in documentation contained in Arlene Mullin's case file on Kasiewicz.

21 **In an anguished written statement:** statement by James Kasiewicz, November 2, 2016.

21 **Justin Charles Evans:** Information here and following from Justin Charles Evans, personal communication, and documentation as noted below. See also Chapter 9 for a fuller account of Evans's experiences.

21 **letter to Johnny Isakson:** Letter of Justin Charles Evans and co-signatories to Senator Johnny Isakson, July 21, 2017.

21 **discharged him and harassed:** Details from Justin Charles Evans's written chronicle of the events, which he memorialized as they happened; voice recordings he made of conversations with patients and workers at his facility; as well as my personal communication with Justin Charles Evans and the registered nurse involved (who spoke on condition of anonymity).

22 **escorted him off the premises:** Incident Report / Investigation, Sandy Springs Police Department, Officer H. N. Hunt, Case Number 2017-017361, December 29, 2017.

22 **add the gun accusation:** Personal communication with the registered nurse involved (who spoke on condition of anonymity), and Evans's recorded conversation with this nurse.

22 **a letter to Esperanza:** Sources for this and subsequent information, including extended quotations, are undated written statements by the parties involved (I have used assumed names), and personal communication with Arlene Mullin.

22 **"very highly respected nephrologist":** Joanne Bargman, personal communication.

23 **termination of multiple patients:** This and the subsequent quotation are in an email from Jesse Goldman dated March 5, 2019. Related email correspondence from Goldman on February 21, 2018.

23 **higher reimbursements than does government insurance:** See "The Exorbitant Cost of End-Stage Renal Disease ('ESRD')," a white paper by Dialysis Pro Cost Containment (November 1, 2016); Peace Officers' Annuity and Benefit Fund of Georgia, et al. v. DaVita Inc., Kent J. Thiry et al., case number 1:17-cv-00304, US District Court for the District of Colorado, class action complaint (filed January 12, 2018); Riley J. League, Paul Eliason et al., "Variability

in Prices Paid for Hemodialysis by Employer-Sponsored Insurance in the US from 2012 to 2019," *JAMA Network Open* (2022); Christopher P. Childers, Jill Q. Dworsky et al., "A Comparison of Payments to a For-profit Dialysis Firm from Government and Commercial Insurers," *JAMA Intern Med* (2019). See also Jenny Gold, "First Kidney Failure, Then a $540,842 Bill for Dialysis," Kaiser Health News (July 25, 2019); analysis by the Affordable Healthcare Coalition of North Carolina, "Does DaVita Charge $17,871 for a Single Dialysis Treatment?" (June 7, 2019); Freakonomics podcast hosted by Stephen J. Dubner, "Is Dialysis a Test Case of Medicare for All?" (April 7, 2021); and Reed Abelson and Katie Thomas, "Top Kidney Charity Directed Aid to Patients at DaVita and Fresenius Clinics, Lawsuit Claims," *New York Times* (August 2, 2019).

23 **treat them as VIPs:** Personal communication with numerous clinic staff, patients and family members, including Megallan Handford, Emanuel Gonzales, Marie DeFrancesco-Malviya and Gregg Hansen. See also the discussions in later chapters regarding HIPPERs ("high-paying patients").

23 **"The biggest mistake we ever made":** For this and what follows, Gerald and Sherry Thompson, personal communication.

24 **"According to a culture":** Robert Bear, personal communication.

24 **he notes, certain managers:** Leonard Stern, personal communication.

24 **cut corners on supplies:** For this and what follows, personal communication with numerous current and former dialysis workers, including Megallan Handford, Emerson Padua, Emanuel Gonzales and Arlene Mullin.

24 **decades of settled medical science:** For this and what follows, see references in the earlier note **treatments are likely too short and fast**.

24 **"bazooka dialysis":** John Agar, personal communication.

25 **Nephrologists who order longer treatments:** Brent Miller and Leonard Stern, personal communication.

25 **"If you're working for patients":** Megallan Handford, personal communication.

25 **The term "moral injury":** Jonathan Shay and James Munroe, "Group and Milieu Therapy for Veterans with Complex Posttraumatic Stress Disorder," in Philip A. Saigh and J. Douglas Bremner, eds., *Posttraumatic Stress Disorder* (Boston, 1998); and Jonathan Shay, "Moral Injury," Psychoanal Psychol (2014).

25 **applied to doctors:** Simon G. Talbot and Wendy Dean, "Physicians Aren't 'Burning Out.' They're Suffering from Moral Injury," *STAT News* (2018); and Wendy Dean, Simon Talbot et al., "Reframing Clinician Distress," Fed Pract (2019).

25 **as many as seventeen patients:** For this and what follows, Megallan Handford, personal communication.

26 **"workers are stretched so thin":** Cass Gualvez, personal communication.

26 **frequently precede involuntary discharges:** For this and what follows: Arlene Mullin, personal communication, and case files on individual patients she has advocated for, as well as my own conversations with numerous patients.

26 **"not about the patients":** Kent Thiry, "Energizing a Firm with Mission & Values," speech at UCLA Anderson School of Management (April 10, 2009) [video]. Quotation starts at 1:10:10.

27 **Thiry's fast food analogy:** For several views of how the fast food approach is being applied in medicine, see Roy M. Poses, MD, "Would You Like Fries with That?—The Fast Food Model for the Corporate Physician," Health Care Renewal (2011); Alex Kacik, "Health Systems Revamp Their Approach to Retail Clinics," *Modern Healthcare* (2021); Patrick Clark, "The Mall of the Future Will Offer Dinner, Movies, and a Colonoscopy," Bloomberg Business (2016); and Brian Solomon, "Drive-Thru Health Care: How McDonald's Inspired an Urgent Care Gold Rush," *Forbes* (2014).

Just how deeply ingrained, and unexceptional, the medicine-as-fast-food paradigm has become is clear from Atul Gawande's recommendation to healthcare companies, in a widely discussed essay, that they emulate the methods and mentality of the Cheesecake Factory in order to achieve good, consistent results at low cost: "Big Med: Restaurant Chains Have Managed to Combine Quality Control, Cost Control, and Innovation. Can Health Care?" *New Yorker* (2012). Gawande seems not to recognize that large healthcare organizations have been applying the fast food model since the 1960s, often with very different results from those he envisions. Among the numerous reactions to Gawande's essay, which predictably struck a nerve, here are two: Steve Denning, "How Not to Fix US Health Care: Copy the Cheesecake Factory," *Forbes* (2012); and Ruben J. Nazario, "Health Care Isn't Cheesecake," *Today's Hospitalist* (2012).

27 **early for-profit hospital chains:** Excellent analysis of HCA, NME and other early for-profit hospital companies can be found in Maggie Mahar, *Money-Driven Medicine* (New York, 2009); and Henry Scammell, *Giantkillers* (New York, 2005), which includes a revealing insider account of litigation against HCA from the perspective of whistleblower James F. Alderson. Specific to NME (and Tenet) are Stephen Klaidman, *Coronary* (New York, 2007); and Joe Sharkey, *Bedlam* (New York, 1994). For HCA, see "Largest Health Care Fraud Case in U.S. History Settled: HCA Investigation Nets Record Total of $1.7 Billion," Department of Justice press release (June 26, 2003) (https://www.justice.gov/archive/opa/pr/2003/June/03_civ_386.htm); and Kurt Eichenwald, "HCA Is Said to Reach Deal on Settlement of Fraud Case," *New York Times* (December 18, 2002).

27 **He calls his firm a "Village":** For backgrounders on DaVita and Thiry, see Luc Hatlestad's superb article, "The Strangest Show on Earth," *5280* (2012); Robert L. Shook, "All for One and One for All," in *Heart & Soul* (New York, 2010); Bill George and Natalie Kindred, "Kent Thiry: 'Mayor' of DaVita," Harvard Business School case study 9-410-065 (2011); Jeffrey Pfeffer, "Kent Thiry and DaVita: Leadership Challenges in Building and Growing a Great Company," Stanford Graduate School of Business case study OB-54 (2006); and Charles O'Reilly, Jeffrey Pfeffer et al., "DaVita: A Community First, a Company Sec-

ond," Stanford Graduate School of Business case study OB-89 (2014). See also John Oliver's 2017 show on HBO, *Last Week Tonight*, season 4, episode 12, "Dialysis" (2017), which is both hilarious and trenchant.

28 **I almost vomited:** Leonard Stern, personal communication.

28 **a third of its stock:** DaVita Inc., SEC Schedule 13D/A (August 3, 2021) (https://www.sec.gov/Archives/edgar/data/927066/000119312521236271/d212960dsc13da.htm).

28 **over half a billion dollars:** Calculated from DaVita financial statements from the years 2000 to 2020, including Thiry's salary, bonus, stock awards, profits on stock-based compensation, and other compensation.

28 **"the real heroes of business":** Bill Taylor, "Need a Hero? Check Out DaVita's Kent Thiry," *Washington Post*, Panel on Leadership (2010) (http://views.washingtonpost.com/leadership/panelists/2010/07/need-a-hero-check-out-davitas-kent-thiry.html).

29 **CEO of Total Renal Care:** See references in the earlier note **He calls his firm a "Village,"** especially Shook, "All for One and One for All."

29 **manipulated its financial statements:** Shook, "All for One and One for All"; Sharon Bernstein, "Total Renal Faces Lawsuit over Earnings," *Los Angeles Times* (February 24, 1999); New York County Clerk (May 13, 2022), Index No. 653594/2018, NYSCEF Doc. No. 1029, Exhibit 1, sv "Total Renal Care" (https://www.renrensettlement.com/Content/Documents/Ex%201%20to%20Mackintosh%20Affirmation%20ISO%20Revised%20App.pdf); and "Vultures Who Circle," This is Money.co.uk (March 16, 1999) (https://www.thisismoney.co.uk/money/news/article-1582864/Vultures-who-circle.html).

29 **and are still rising:** Historical–CMS: The National Health Expenditure Accounts; and Statista.com, Gross Domestic Product (GDP) of the United States at Current Prices from 1987 to 2027.

29 **had grown twenty-eight times:** On the high burden of kidney disease and renal failure in the United States compared with other nations, see USRDS Annual Data Reports, ESRD, International Comparisons. For the 10,000 patients on dialysis in 1972, see Richard A. Rettig, "Origins of the Medicare Kidney Disease Entitlement," in Kathi E. Hanna, ed., *Biomedical Politics* (Washington, DC, 1991). For the 281,339 patients on dialysis in 2000, see USRDS Annual Data Report 2020, figure 1.6–Number of Prevalent ESRD Patients, by Modality, 2000–2018 (https://adr.usrds.org/2020/end-stage-renal-disease/1-incidence-prevalence-patient-characteristics-and-treatment-modalities).

29 **experiment with "Medicare for All":** Rettig, "Origins of the Medicare Kidney Disease Entitlement." End-stage renal disease (ESRD) is not the only universal medical entitlement: patients with amyotrophic lateral sclerosis (ALS, also known as Lou Gehrig's disease) have similar coverage (http://www.alsa.org/als-care/resources/medicare-information.htm). But ALS sufferers represent a far smaller (and therefore less costly) patient population.

29 **Thiry calls them "sticky":** DaVita Inc. Analyst/Investor Day (May 25, 2017)
    (https://ffj-online.org/wp-content/uploads/2017/09/DaVita_InvestorDayTscript
    _Aug17.pdf).

30 **dialysis company named Vivra:** Shook, "All for One and One for All"; Char-
    lotte Snow, "Feds Probe Vivra: Investigation Relates to Dialysis Firm's Lab
    Practices," *Modern Healthcare* (January 6, 1997); Milt Freudenheim, "Swed-
    ish Holding Company to Buy U.S. Dialysis Provider," *New York Times* (May 6,
    1997); "Vivra's Ex-Venture, Renal Unit Are Focus of U.S. Billing Probe," *Wall
    Street Journal* (December 30, 1996); and "Gambro Healthcare, Inc. Agrees to
    Pay $53 Million for Overcharging Medicare, Medicaid & Tricare," Department
    of Justice press release (July 13, 2000) (https://www.justice.gov/archive/opa/
    pr/2000/July/399civ.htm).

30 **Success in the dialysis business:** Here and following, I was helped by conver-
    sations with David Barbetta and Steven Bander. Barbetta was a senior financial
    analyst in DaVita's mergers and acquisitions department, before he resigned
    and filed a False Claims Act whistleblower complaint against the firm (see
    Chapter 8 for details). Barbetta's complaint is captioned: United States et al.
    ex rel. David Barbetta v. DaVita Inc. and Total Renal Care Inc., case num-
    ber 1:09-cv-02175-WJM, US District Court for the District of Colorado, first
    amended complaint (December 23, 2011). See also the United States complaint
    in intervention in the same case (October 22, 2014). Bander was the chief med-
    ical officer of Gambro, before blowing the whistle on his employer; his second
    amended complaint is United States ex rel. Steven J. Bander v. Gambro Health-
    care US Inc., case number 4:01-cv-00553-DDN, US District Court for the East-
    ern District of Missouri (filed November 30, 2004).

30 **the corporate culture:** For this and what follows, see references in the earlier
    note **He calls his firm a "Village."**

30 **Thiry has told the story:** Shook, "All for One and One for All"; and Hatlestad,
    "The Strangest Show on Earth."

30 **"famous for their dedication":** Hatlestad, "The Strangest Show on Earth."

31 **several of his former executives:** For this and what follows, see Shook, "All for
    One and One for All."

31 **an imaginary American hometown:** For this and what follows: Hatlestad,
    "The Strangest Show on Earth"; and images of DaVita headquarters available
    on the Internet.

31 **a large wooden bridge:** For the bridge and the quotation of Thiry about its sig-
    nificance, see George and Kindred, "Kent Thiry: 'Mayor' of DaVita."

31 **The atmosphere at a Nationwide:** Regarding Nationwide conferences, see
    Hatlestad, "The Strangest Show on Earth"; and Kent Thiry's speech at UCLA,
    "Energizing a Firm with Mission & Values," starting at 1:08. A DaVita in-house
    video titled "Musketeer Skit" (no date), starting at 7:02, records employee
    behavior at a Nationwide.

31 **Barbir, a former dialysis nurse:** Daniel Barbir, personal communication,

shortly before settling his lawsuit against DaVita and Gambro in June 2015. Barbir was a dialysis nurse at Gambro facilities in Georgia that were taken over by DaVita. Together with Alon Vainer, a nephrologist at these same facilities, Barbir alleged a range of fraudulent billing schemes. See United States ex rel. Alon J. Vainer and Daniel D. Barbir v. DaVita Inc. and Gambro Healthcare Inc., case number 1:07-cv-2509, US District Court for the Northern District of Georgia, Atlanta Division, fourth amended complaint (July 25, 2011). For quotations and descriptions from Barbir that follow, Daniel Barbir, personal communication. See also Kent Thiry's speech at UCLA, "Energizing a Firm with Mission and Values," starting at 1:08; and Oliver, *Last Week Tonight*, "Dialysis."

4. WHO LIVES, WHO DIES

33 **"Superficially, it might be said"**: Homer W. Smith, *From Fish to Philosopher* (New York, 1961).

34 **embalm a dead pharaoh**: For this and what follows, see Mohamed E. Salem and Garabed Eknoyan, "The Kidney in Ancient Egyptian Medicine," Am J. Nephrol (1999); Giovanni Maio, "The Metaphorical and Mythical Use of the Kidney in Antiquity," Am J Nephrol (1999); and Hope W. Hogg and Grafton E. Smith, " 'Heart and Reins' in Ancient Literature of the Near East," J Manchester Univ Egyptian Oriental Soc (1911).

34 **linked kidneys with sex**: For this and what follows, see Athanasios Diamandopoulos, Andreas Skarpelos et al., "The Use of the Kidneys in Secular and Ritual Practices According to Ancient Greek and Byzantine Texts," Kidney Int (2005); Athanasios Diamandopoulos and Pavlos Goudas, "The Role of the Kidney as a Religious, Cultural and Sexual Symbol," Am J Nephrol (2002); and Maio, "The Metaphorical and Mythical Use of the Kidney in Antiquity."

35 **The Hebrews saw kidneys**: For this and what follows, see Garabed Eknoyan, "The Kidneys in the Bible," J Am Soc Nephrol (2005); Joel D. Kopple, "The Biblical View of the Kidney," Am J Nephrol (1994); and Shaul G. Massry and Miroslaw Smogorzewski, "The Influence of Judaism and Jewish Physicians on Greek and Byzantine Medicine and Their Contribution to Nephrology," Am J Nephrol (1997).

35 **"For you formed my kidneys"**: Psalm 139:13–14.

35 **"His archers surround me"**: Job 16:13.

35 **basic processes break down**: A useful overview of this deterioration is found in Robert Thomas, Abbas Kanso et al., "Chronic Kidney Disease and Its Complications," Prim Care (2008). I also drew on personal communication with John Agar, Leonard Stern and Steven Bander.

36 **taken such a toll**: Duaa Eldeib, "They Were the Pandemic's Perfect Victims," ProPublica (2021).

36 **first wave of COVID-19**: Important sources from the large body of literature concerning the impact of the pandemic on end-stage renal disease

(ESRD) patients, and how COVID-19 can cause acute kidney injury, include: USRDS Annual Data Report 2021, figure 13.10 (https://adr.usrds.org/2021/supplements-covid-19-disparities/13-covid-19-supplement); USRDS Annual Data Report 2021, Supplements: COVID-19; Racial and Ethnic Disparities: Chapter 13, COVID-19 Highlights (https://adr.usrds.org/2021/supplements-covid-19-disparities/13-covid-19-supplement); C. John Sperati, "Coronavirus: Kidney Damage Caused by COVID-19," *Johns Hopkins Medicine* (March 1, 2022); and Sachin Yende and Chirag R. Parikh, "Long COVID and Kidney Disease," Nature (2021).

36 **French physiologist Claude Bernard:** On Claude Bernard and his life and work, here and following, see references in the Chapter 2 note **concept of the milieu intérieur.** See also Charles G. Gross, "Claude Bernard and the Constancy of the Internal Environment," Neuroscientist (1998); and Cheralathan Arunachalam and Alexander Woywodt, "Turbid Urine and Beef-Eating Rabbits," NDT Plus (2010).

37 *Lectures on the Phenomena***:** Quotations here and following from Claude Bernard, *Leçons sur les phénomènes de la vie, communs aux animaux et aux végétaux* (Paris, 1878).

38 **Scottish physicist Thomas Graham:** J. Stewart Cameron, "Thomas Graham (1805–1869)," in Todd Ing, Mohamed Rahman et al., eds., *Dialysis* (Singapore, 2012); and Jaime Wisniak, "Thomas Graham," Educación Química (2013).

38 **read before the Royal Society:** Thomas Graham, "Liquid Diffusion Applied to Analysis," read before the Royal Society on June 13, 1861.

38 **John Jacob Abel devised:** For a review of Abel's work, see Charles R. P. George and Garabed Eknoyan, "John Jacob Abel," in Ing, Rahman et al., eds., *Dialysis*; and Garabed Eknoyan, "The Wonderful Apparatus of John Jacob Abel Called the 'Artificial Kidney,'" Semin Dial (2009). Regarding hirudin, see Doreen A. Wüstenhagen, Phil Lukas et al., "Cell-Free Synthesis of the Hirudin Variant 1 of the Blood-Sucking Leech *Hirudo medicinalis*," Sci Rep (2020).

39 **called "crush syndrome":** Dilini Peiris, "A Historical Perspective on Crush Syndrome," J Clin Pathol (2017). For a World War I precursor, trench nephritis, see Gregory M. Anstead, "The Centenary of the Discovery of Trench Fever," Lancet (2016).

39 **Willem "Pim" Kolff:** For this section on Kolff's life and times, see Eli A. Friedman, "Willem Johan 'Pim' Kolff," in Ing, Rahman et al., eds., *Dialysis*; Eli A. Friedman and Don B. Olsen, "Memoriam and Tribute to Willem J. 'Pim' Kolff, Founder of Artificial Organs," ASAIO Journal (2009); and Phil Davison, "Dutchman Who Turned Nazi Debris into a Dialysis Machine," *Financial Times* (February 20, 2009).

40 **in wartime Sweden, Nils Alwall:** David Goldsmith, "Nils Alwall: The Quiet, Unassuming Swede," OUP blog (February 5, 2016) (https://blog.oup.com/2016/02/nils-alwall-dialysis-machine/); and Carl M. Kjellstrand, Birger Lindergård et al., "Nils Alwall, the First Complete Artificial Kidney

and the Development of Acute and Chronic Dialysis," in Ing, Rahman et al., eds., *Dialysis.*

41 **team led by John Merrill:** Regarding Merrill and his team, here and following, see Murray Epstein, "John P. Merrill," Clin J Am Soc Nephrol (2009); Eli A. Friedman, "John Putnam Merrill," in Ing, Rahman et al., eds., *Dialysis.*

41 **identified as a hantavirus:** James F. Winchester, "George E. Schreiner," Trans Am Clin Climatol Assoc (2013).

41 **Army medic, George Schreiner:** Winchester, "George E. Schreiner"; Paul E. Teschan, "Dialysis in Military Casualties with Post-traumatic Acute Renal Failure," in Ing, Rahman et al., eds., *Dialysis.*

42 **alongside Jean Hamburger:** Christophe Legendre and Henri Kreis, "A Tribute to Jean Hamburger's Contribution to Organ Transplantation," Am J Transplant (2010); Giorgina Barbara Piccoli, "Advice to the Medical Students in My Service," Philos Ethics Humanit Med (2013). For a broader look at transplantation and its relation to dialysis, see Renée C. Fox and Judith P. Swazey, *Spare Parts: Organ Replacement in American Society* (Abingdon, 2017).

42 **Joseph Murray had ideas:** Friedman, "John Putnam Merrill"; and Thomas E. Starzl, "Joseph E. Murray, MD, FACS, Opened Doors for Transplant Surgeons," Bull Am Coll Surg (2013).

43 **first successful kidney transplant:** On the dramatic story of this transplant, see Joseph E. Murray, "Richard and Ronald Herrick," in *Surgery of the Soul* (Sagamore Beach, MA, 2004); and Joseph E. Murray, "The Fight for Life," *Harvard Medicine* (2011).

43 **"The operating room fell silent":** Murray, "The Fight for Life."

44 **Belding "Scrib" Scribner:** There is an extensive bibliography on Scribner and his team in Seattle. See, for example, Renée C. Fox and Judith P. Swazey, *The Courage to Fail* (Abingdon, 2002); Christopher R. Blagg, *From Miracle to Mainstream* (Seattle, 2017); and Christopher R. Blagg, "Belding Hibbard Scribner— Better Known as Scrib," Clin J Am Soc Nephrol (2010). See also Scribner's own writings about the early years of dialysis in Seattle, including Belding H. Scribner, "A Personalized History of Chronic Hemodialysis," Am J Kidney Dis (1990); and Belding H. Scribner, "Ethical Problems of Using Artificial Organs to Sustain Life," Presidential Address to the American Society for Artificial Internal Organs (1964).

44 **"I cannot recall":** Quotations here and following, and the subsequent description of Scribner's invention of the shunt, in Fox and Swazey, *The Courage to Fail*, citing an unpublished manuscript by Scribner.

45 **rejoined after treatment:** P. B. Clark and F. M. Parsons, "Routine Use of the Scribner Shunt for Haemodialysis," BMJ (1966).

45 **system of cannulas:** Kjellstrand, Birger et al., "Nils Alwall, the First Complete Artificial Kidney."

45 **still developing his idea:** For accounts of the first dialysis patients treated by Scribner, Christopher Blagg and their team, see references in the earlier note

Belding "Scrib" Scribner. See also W. C. Heinz, "The Man Who Said 'They Don't Have to Die,'" *Today's Health* (1971).

46 **frontier of medical innovation:** For an overview of the pace of change and the conceptual and surgical breakthroughs over time that led to modern dialysis practice, in see Ing, Rahman et al., eds., *Dialysis*. For a historic paper on the fistula, see Michael J. Brescia, James E. Cimino et al., "Chronic Hemodialysis Using Venipuncture and a Surgically Created Arteriovenous Fistula," NEJM (1966).

46 **the "Mini-Monster," the "Pressure Cooker":** For descriptions of a range of early models of machines and filters, see Dialysis Machine Museum, Home Dialysis Central (https://homedialysis.org/home-dialysis-basics/machines-and-supplies/dialysis-museum).

46 **peritoneum as a blood filter:** See the overview of this modality at the NIDDK website, "Peritoneal Dialysis." For its history, see the section on "Peritoneal Dialysis," part VI of Ing, Rahman et al., eds., *Dialysis*. See also Angela Yee-Moon Wang, "Preserving Residual Kidney Function in Hemodialysis Patients," J Am Soc Nephrol (2016).

47 **girl of fifteen was denied:** See Blagg, "Belding Hibbard Scribner"; and Ing, Rahman et al., eds., *Dialysis*.

47 **John Agar's stint in Toronto:** John Agar, personal communication.

47 **Scribner and his team learned:** Here and following, see references in the earlier note Belding "Scrib" Scribner, particularly writings by Scribner and Blagg.

48 **"middle-molecule hypothesis":** For the formulation of this vital hypothesis, and its frequent neglect, here and following, see John K. Leypoldt, Lee W. Henderson et al., "Middle Molecules," in Ing, Rahman et al., eds., *Dialysis*; Belding H. Scribner and Dimitrios G. Oreopoulos, "The Hemodialysis Product (HDP): A Better Index of Dialysis Adequacy than Kt/V," Dial Transplant (2002); Bernard Charra, Belding H. Scribner et al., "The Middle Molecule Hypothesis Revisited," Hemodial Int (2002); and Raymond Vanholder, "Future Directions for Dialysis," Kidney Dial (2022).

48 **benefits of home dialysis:** For the Seattle group's championing of home dialysis, including the group's testimony in Washington, DC, see Christopher R. Blagg, "What Went Wrong with Home Hemodialysis in the United States and What Can Be Done Now?" Hemodial Int (2000); "Medicare End-Stage Renal Disease Program Amendments," hearing before the House Ways and Means Committee, Subcommittee on Health (April 25, 1977); and "Hospital Cost Containment and End Stage Renal Disease Program," hearings before the Senate Finance Committee, Subcommittee on Health (October 12, 13 and 21, 1977). See also Christopher R. Blagg, R. O. Hickman et al., "Home Dialysis: Six Years' Experience," NEJM (1970); John W. M. Agar, Katherine A. Barraclough et al., "Home Haemodialysis: How It Began, Where It Went Wrong, and What It May Yet Be," J Nephrol (2019); "End-Stage Renal Disease, Medicare Payment Refinements Could Promote Increased Use of Home Dialysis," report by the GAO (2015); and John D. Woods, Friedrich K. Port et al., "Comparison of Mor-

tality with Home Hemodialysis and Center Hemodialysis," Kidney Int (1996).
For the lack of familiarity with home dialysis and peritoneal dialysis among
US-trained nephrologists, see Nupur Gupta, Elizabeth B. Taber-Hight et al.,
"Perceptions of Home Dialysis Training and Experience among US Nephrology Fellows," Am J Kidney Dis (2021). Extensive analysis of and resources
on home dialysis can be found at Home Dialysis Central (https://home
dialysis.org).

49 **"If the treatment of chronic":** Belding H. Scribner, James J. Cole et al., "Why
Thrice Weekly Dialysis?" Hemodial Int (2004).

49 **September of 1959, Nancy Spaeth:** This section on Nancy Spaeth's life and
experiences on dialysis is based on Nancy Spaeth, personal communication;
Nancy Spaeth, "The Nurse, Mother of Two and Four Transplants—Nancy
Spaeth Tells Her Story," Nephrol Dial Transplant (2007); Lisa Hall, "Nancy
Spaeth's Story," J Nephrol Soc Work (2012); and Dori Schatell, "As Nancy
Hewitt Spaeth's Earthly Journey Ends, Her Inspiration Lives On," post on
Home Dialysis Central (2022).

50 **Belding Scribner described his own:** Scribner, "Ethical Problems of Using
Artificial Organs to Sustain Life."

50 **"Admissions and Policy Committee":** On this committee and its implications
for bioethics, see the discussion in Chapter 5, as well as the account in Fox and
Swazey, *The Courage to Fail.* See also Shana Alexander, "They Decide Who Lives,
Who Dies," *Life* (1962); Albert R. Jonsen, *The Birth of Bioethics* (Oxford 1998);
and David J. Rothman, *Strangers at the Bedside* (New Brunswick, NJ, 1991).

51 **$250,000 in 2022 dollars:** Estimated with the help of the Measuring Worth
website, using its consumer bundle metric (https://measuringworth.com/
datasets/consumer/), with additional advice from site owner Samuel H.
Williamson.

52 **Christopher Blagg . . . remarked:** Christopher R. Blagg, "Many Hemodialysis Patients in the 1960s Had Substantially Fewer Symptoms than Today's
Patients," Am J Kidney Dis (2009).

52 **drawn national media attention:** For a good overview, see Fox and Swazey,
The Courage to Fail. Media coverage and debates in Washington, DC, are discussed in Chapter 5.

5. MEDICAL MIRACLES, BIOETHICS AND DIALYSIS FOR ALL

54 **"I have decided to discuss":** Belding H. Scribner, "Ethical Problems of Using
Artificial Organs to Sustain Life," Presidential Address to the American Society for Artificial Internal Organs (1964).

55 **were transforming medicine:** Stanley Joel Reiser, *Technological Medicine*
(Cambridge, 2009), provides a useful review of the issues.

55 **Rothman and Albert Jonsen have identified:** David J. Rothman, *Strangers at
the Bedside* (New Brunswick, NJ, 1991); Albert R. Jonsen, *The Birth of Bioeth-*

ics (Oxford 1998); and Albert R. Jonsen, "The God Squad and the Origins of Transplantation Ethics and Policy," J Law Med Ethics (2007).

55 **the 1954 kidney transplant:** See the Chapter 4 note **first successful kidney transplant.** See also Joseph E. Murray, "The Kindest Cut," *Scientific American* (2004).

56 **rejected such acts:** Jonsen, *The Birth of Bioethics.*

56 **even thornier moral dilemmas:** For the account of the "Seattle experience" that follows, see the Chapter 4 note **Belding "Scrib" Scribner.**

56 **goods and services in a year:** Estimated with the help of the Measuring Worth website, using its consumer bundle metric (https://measuringworth.com/datasets/consumer/).

57 **"military-industrial complex":** See Farewell Address by President Dwight D. Eisenhower, January 17, 1961 (https://www.archives.gov/milestone-documents/president-dwight-d-eisenhowers-farewell-address); and the deft analysis of the speech and its historical context by James Ledbetter, *Unwarranted Influence* (New Haven, CT, 2011). For Fulbright's adaptation of the phrase, see J. Scott Turner, "The Military-Industrial-Academic-Political-Scientific Complex," blog of the National Association of Scholars (2022) (https://www.nas.org/blogs/article/the-military-industrial-academic-political-scientific-complex).

58 **the so-called Doctors' Trial:** Harvard Law School, Nuremberg Trials Project, NMT Case 1, U.S.A. v. Karl Brandt et al.: The Doctors' Trial (https://nuremberg.law.harvard.edu/nmt_1_intro); and the Holocaust Encyclopedia, "The Doctors Trial: The Medical Case of the Subsequent Nuremberg Proceedings." For the Nuremberg Code, see Herwig Czech, Christiane Druml et al., eds., "Medical Ethics in the 70 Years after the Nuremberg Code, 1947 to the Present," Wien Klin Wochenschr (2018).

58 **a Vienna-born Jewish doctor:** Alexander's seminal article, which is the source of the quotations and paraphrases of Alexander that follow, is Leo Alexander, "Medical Science Under Dictatorship," NEJM (1949). For a review of his life and work, see Ulf Schmidt, *Justice at Nuremberg: Leo Alexander and the Nazi Doctors' Trial* (Basingstoke, Hampshire, 2004); and Michael I. Shevell, "Leo Alexander's Contributions to the Nuremberg Code," Neurology (1998).

60 **the infamous Tuskegee Study:** On the study and its effects on public health among African Americans, see "The U.S. Public Health Service Syphilis Study at Tuskegee," The Tuskegee Timeline; and Ada McVean, "40 Years of Human Experimentation in America," McGill University, Office for Science and Society (2019).

60 **so with radiation:** On human radiation experiments in the United States, in addition to Eileen Welsome's magnificent, shocking *The Plutonium Files* (New York, 1999), see the Final Report of the Advisory Committee on Human Radiation Experiments (1995) (https://ehss.energy.gov/ohre/roadmap/achre/report.html); and William Moss and Roger Eckhardt, "The Human Plutonium Injection Experiments," Los Alamos Science (1995).

61 **article by Shana Alexander:** Shana Alexander, "They Decide Who Lives, Who Dies," *Life* (1962). On the committee, see references in the Chapter 4 note **"Admissions and Policy Committee."**

61 **the documentary *Who Shall Live?*:** The documentary is available at https://www.youtube.com/watch?v=FMay5zw1loA. Discussion of the patient selection process starts at 11:11; segment on Pim Kolff at 25:20; Melvin Laird at 35:33; Newman's summation at 49:39.

62 **a 1964 editorial:** J. Russell Elkington, "Moral Problems in the Use of Borrowed Organs, Artificial and Transplanted," Ann Intern Med (1964). This paper is discussed in Jonsen, *Birth of Bioethics*, where William Bennett is quoted.

62 **series of interdisciplinary conferences:** Conferences and other meetings during this revolution in medical ethics are described in Jonsen, *Birth of Bioethics*. For the details that follow, see Robert M. Veatch and Sharmon Sollitto, "Medical Ethics Teaching," JAMA (1976); Bernice L. Hausman, "Humanities at Penn State College of Medicine," website of the Penn State College of Medicine; and the websites of the Hastings Center and the Kennedy Institute of Ethics.

63 **cowritten by a lawyer:** David Sanders and Jesse Dukeminier, "Medical Advance and Legal Lag," UCLA L Rev (1968).

63 **Belding Scribner was startled:** Scribner's reaction is described in Renée C. Fox and Judith P. Swazey, *The Courage to Fail* (Abingdon, 2002).

64 **"life on the machine":** For an early account, see Harry S. Abram, "Survival by Machine," Psychiatry Med (1970). For current views on the psychological implications of life on dialysis, see Daniel Cukor, Scott D. Cohen et al., "Psychosocial Aspects of Chronic Disease: ESRD as a Paradigmatic Illness," JASN (2007); and Dora Zalai, Lilla Szeifert et al., "Psychological Distress and Depression in Patients with Chronic Kidney Disease," Semin Dial (2012). On the psychology of chronic illness more broadly, see Denise de Ridder, Rinie Geenen et al., "Psychological Adjustment to Chronic Disease," Lancet (2008).

64 **the phrase "therapeutic relentlessness":** Jean Hamburger, *La puissance et la fragilité* (Paris, 1972).

64 **"prototypically modern form of torture":** Paul Starr, *The Social Transformation of American Medicine* (New York, 2017).

64 **"Will These People Have to Die?":** Fox and Swazey, *The Courage to Fail*, which also devotes a section to the case of Ernie Crowfeather.

64 **One last ethical question:** Scribner, Blagg and other members of the Seattle team remained stalwartly in favor of nonprofit dialysis, as their extensive testimony before Congress, cited later, emphasizes. See also Christopher R. Blagg, A. Peter Lundin et al., letters to the editor at NEJM (1962) regarding "Profits and the End-Stage Renal Disease Program"; NMC's full-throated defense of for-profit medicine (discussed in detail later); and Christopher R. Blagg, "Belding Hibbard Scribner—Better Known as Scrib," Clin J Am Soc Nephrol (2010). In 1979, Scribner told *60 Minutes*, "I just don't think doctors should be involved in making profit on the same thing that they're doing as doctors. It's like doc-

tors owning drug stores and things like that. I'm against it." CBS television, *60 Minutes*, "What Price Medicine?" (1979).

65 **In Boston, the Harvard nephrology:** The fullest account of the Boston dialysis and transplant team, first at Harvard Medical School and then at National Medical Care (NMC), is Tim McFeeley, *The Price of Access* (Nashua, NH, 2001), which, though occasionally colored by McFeeley's former relationship with NMC and its executives (he represented NMC as an attorney), contains invaluable facts, anecdotes and insights. See also materials regarding NMC's early years in J. Michael Lazarus, "The Role of PBBH/BWH in the Development of Dialysis Therapy" (2013).

65 **debate about money in healthcare:** On the American medical profession's condemnation of fee splitting, and its struggle against for-profit medicine more generally, see Robert M. Veatch, "Ethical Dilemmas of For-Profit Enterprise in Health Care," in Bradford H. Gray, ed., *The New Health Care for Profit* (Washington, DC, 1983); and Arnold S. Relman, "Medical Professionalism in a Commercialized Health Care Market," JAMA (2007). Marc A. Rodwin's invaluable body of work on financial conflicts of interest in medicine includes *Medicine, Money, and Morals* (Oxford, 1995) and *Conflict of Interest and the Future of Medicine* (Oxford, 2011).

66 **founded National Medical Care (NMC):** McFeeley, *The Price of Access*; Gina Bari Kolata, "NMC Thrives Selling Dialysis," Science (1980); and James R. Hagerty, "Physician Saw Opportunity in Kidney Dialysis," *Wall Street Journal* (October 21, 2021).

66 **Shep Glazer, a traveling salesman:** Glazer's testimony is in "National Health Insurance Proposals," one of a series of hearings before the House Ways and Means Committee (November 4, 1971). For searching analyses of the legislative history and economic evolution of the ESRD Program under Medicare, see the many writings of Richard A. Rettig, the leading historian of the program, including: Richard A. Rettig, "Origins of the Medicare Kidney Disease Entitlement," in Kathi E. Hanna, ed., *Biomedical Politics* (Washington, DC, 1991); Richard A. Rettig and Norman G. Levinsky, *Kidney Failure and the Federal Government* (Washington, DC, 1991); Richard A. Rettig, "Special Treatment— The Story of Medicare's ESRD Entitlement," NEJM (2011); Richard A. Rettig, "The Social Contract and the Treatment of Permanent Kidney Failure," JAMA (1996); and Richard A. Rettig, "The Politics of Health Cost Containment," Bull NY Acad Med (1980). For the impact of Glazer's dialyzing on Capitol Hill, see also Richard D. Lyons, "When a Disastrous Illness Strikes," *New York Times* (October 22, 1972).

67 **George Schreiner:** James F. Winchester, "George E. Schreiner," Trans Am Clin Climatol Assoc (2013); and Robert J. Rubin, "A Tribute to George E. Schreiner," Clin J Am Soc Nephrol (2012).

68 **Stanley Joel Reiser:** "Commentary: Stanley Joel Reiser," in Hanna, ed., *Biomedical Politics*.

68 **financial implications of dialysis:** This and what follows is covered in detail in Rettig, "Origins of the Medicare Kidney Disease Entitlement"; and Rettig and Levinsky, *Kidney Failure and the Federal Government.*

68 **a long and contentious history:** For the historical evolution of American healthcare, in addition to Starr, *The Social Transformation of American Medicine,* and writings by Rettig, an essential source was personal communication with Max Fine, who lived through and participated in a significant part of this history. See also Max Fine Oral History, University of Virginia Miller Center, Presidential Oral Histories (2007) (https://millercenter.org/the-presidency/presidential-oral-histories/max-fine-oral-history); and Howard Markel, "69 Years Ago, a President Pitches his Idea for National Health Care," PBS News Hour (2014).

69 **"the swamp to the stars":** Ronald Reagan, "A Time for Choosing" (1964), in Alfred A. Bolitzer et al., eds., *A Time for Choosing: The Speeches of Ronald Reagan* (1983).

70 **Martin Luther King, Jr., stated:** See reference in the Epigraph note **"Of all the forms of inequality."**

70 **Throughout the 1960s:** Robert Baker and Matthew K. Wynia, "Living Histories of Structural Racism and Organized Medicine," AMA J Ethics (2021); P. Preston Reynolds, "The Federal Government's Use of Title VI and Medicare to Racially Integrate Hospitals in the United States," Am J Public Health (1997); and Jill Quadagno, "Promoting Civil Rights through the Welfare State," Soc Probl (2000).

70 **follow Jim Crow policies:** See references in the previous note, and Max Fine, personal communication.

71 **Calling the nation's skyrocketing medical:** Maggie Mahar, *Money-Driven Medicine* (New York, 2009); and Starr, *The Social Transformation of American Medicine.*

71 **comprehensive national health program:** Richard D. Lyons, "Americans Now Favor a National Health Plan," *New York Times* (August 9, 1971).

72 **Nixon signed Public Law 92-603:** Data in this section are presented and analyzed in detail by Rettig, particularly in his "Origins of the Medicare Kidney Disease Entitlement"; and by Rettig and Levinsky, *Kidney Failure and the Federal Government.*

72 **costs of transplants:** See Rettig and Levinsky, "Access to Kidney Transplantation," in *Kidney Failure and the Federal Government.*

72 **"time has come in America":** The American Presidency Project, Richard Nixon, "Special Message to the Congress Proposing a Comprehensive Health Insurance Plan" (February 6, 1974).

73 **"Nixon had proposed the best plan":** Max Fine, personal communication.

73 **supported a neoliberal agenda:** A recent overview of this massive topic, with updated bibliography, is Kevin Vallier, "Neoliberalism," Stanford Encyclopedia of Philosophy. See also David Harvey, *A Brief History of Neoliberalism* (Oxford,

2007); and Jonathan D. Ostry and Prakash Loungani, "Neoliberalism: Oversold?" International Monetary Fund, Finance & Development (2016). Specific to Reagan and Reaganomics, see David A. Stockman, "Premises for a Medical Marketplace: A Neoconservative's Vision of How to Transform the Health System," Health Aff (1981); and Lynn Etheredge, "Reagan, Congress, and Health Spending," Health Aff (1983).

73 **stream of tax dollars into dialysis:** For the data that follow, see references in the note above, **Shep Glazer, a traveling salesman,** especially Rettig and Levinsky, *Kidney Failure and the Federal Government;* and see Paul W. Eggers, Rose Connerton et al., "The Medicare Experience with End-Stage Renal Disease," Health Care Financ Rev (1984).

74 **nephrologists made their case:** See references in the Chapter 4 note **benefits of home dialysis.** Both Seattle and Boston nephrologists explained their rationales before Congress; see testimony by Scribner, Blagg, Lowrie, Schupak, Hampers, Merrill et al., in the following congressional hearings: "Medicare End-Stage Renal Disease Program Amendments," hearing before the House Ways and Means Committee, Subcommittee on Health (April 25, 1977); "Hospital Cost Containment and End Stage Renal Disease Program," hearings before the Senate Finance Committee, Subcommittee on Health (October 12, 13 and 21, 1977); and "Hospital Cost Containment and End Stage Renal Disease Program," hearing before the Senate Finance Committee, Subcommittee on Health (March 15, 1982).

74 **created financial disincentives:** Rettig and Levinsky, *Kidney Failure and the Federal Government;* and Rettig, "The Politics of Health Cost Containment." On the scarcity of donor kidneys, see the statement by Kevin Longino, chief executive officer of the National Kidney Foundation, "Congress Should Act on Living Donor Protection Act During Donate Life Month" (April 6, 2022).

75 **ESRD legislation of 1972:** Details of the maneuverings described here and below: Rettig, "Origins of the Medicare Kidney Disease Entitlement"; Rettig, "Special Treatment—The Story of Medicare's ESRD Entitlement," NEJM (2011); Kolata, "NMC Thrives Selling Dialysis"; Rettig, "The Politics of Health Cost Containment"; and "Hospital Cost Containment and End Stage Renal Disease Program," hearing before the Senate Finance Committee, Subcommittee on Health (October 21, 1977).

76 **"gutted the hell out of it":** Richard D. Lyons, "Concern Rising over Costs of Kidney Dialysis Program," *New York Times* (April 28, 1978).

76 **"I raise the question":** Blagg's and Scribner's statements are in "Hospital Cost Containment and End Stage Renal Disease Program," hearing before the Senate Finance Committee, Subcommittee on Health (October 21, 1977); and in "Medicare End-Stage Renal Disease Program Amendments," hearing before the House Ways and Means Committee, Subcommittee on Health (April 25, 1977).

76 **patients on home hemodialysis:** USRDS Annual Data Report 2021, ESRD,

Home Dialysis, figure 2.1a (https://adr.usrds.org/2021/end-stage-renal-disease /2-home-dialysis). An additional 11.2 percent of patients are dialyzing at home on peritoneal dialysis.

76 **among major industrial nations:** See the Chapter 2 note **"survival rate in the United States."**

76 **almost $38 billion:** USRDS Annual Data Report 2021, ESRD, Healthcare ExpendituresforPersonswithESRD,Highlights(https://adr.usrds.org/2021/ end-stage-renal-disease/9-healthcare-expenditures-for-persons-with-esrd). Total Medicare-related expenditures for ESRD patients was $51 billion.

6. THE ROLL-UP

77 **In April of 1983, Alonzo Plough:** Key sources throughout this section are Alonzo Plough, personal communication; and Plough's fascinating book, Alonzo L. Plough, *Borrowed Time* (Philadelphia, 1986), which chronicles his early research in dialysis and epidemiology and his run-in with Edmund Lowrie and NMC.

77 **writing an explosive article:** This article was eventually published as Alonzo L. Plough, Susanne R. Salem et al., "Case Mix in End-Stage Renal Disease," NEJM (1984).

78 **National Cooperative Dialysis Study (NCDS):** Edmund G. Lowrie, Nan M. Laird et al., "Effect of the Hemodialysis Prescription on Patient Morbidity: Report from the National Cooperative Dialysis Study," NEJM (1981).

78 Kt/V_{urea} **as the definitive measure:** For a basic understanding of Kt/V, its shortcomings, and how caregiver fixation on Kt/V often results in lack of attention to other vital aspects of treatment (such as volume and blood pressure control and clearance of solutes other than urea), see Björn Meijers and Raymond Vanholder, "HEMO Revisited: Why Kt/V(urea) Only Tells Part of the Story," J Am Soc Nephrol (2016); John W. M. Agar, "Kt/V(urea) Has Served Its Purpose, So Let Us Now Move On," Nephrol News Issues (2014); and Carl M. Kjellstrand, "My Addiction: The Artificial Kidney, The Rise and Fall of Dialysis," Artif Organs (2012), particularly the section entitled "The Fall of Dialysis." See also references in the Chapter 4 note **"middle-molecule hypothesis."** For contrary views, see John T. Daugirdas, "Kt/V (and Especially Its Modifications) Remains a Useful Measure of Hemodialysis Dose," Kidney Int (2015); and Edmund G. Lowrie, "The Kinetic Behaviors of Urea and Other Marker Molecules During Hemodialysis," Am J Kidney Dis (2007).

78 **importance of fluid balance:** For a startling review of the patient harm and mortality caused by lack of attention to fluid overload management, see Allan J. Collins, "Dialysis Can Create a Progressive Chronic Cardiovascular Disease State," presentation at the Annual Dialysis Conference in Orlando, Florida (2018).

79 **"nephrologists got themselves mired":** John Agar, personal communication.

79 **"self-proliferating giant"**: Drummond Rennie, "Nephrology Comes of Age," NEJM (1977).

79 **The population of patients**: For facts and statistics reported here, see Richard A. Rettig, "Origins of the Medicare Kidney Disease Entitlement," in Kathi E. Hanna, ed., *Biomedical Politics* (Washington, DC, 1991); Richard A. Rettig and Norman G. Levinsky, *Kidney Failure and the Federal Government* (Washington, DC, 1991); and Paul W. Eggers, Rose Connerton et al., "The Medicare Experience with End-Stage Renal Disease," Health Care Financ Rev (1984).

80 **Despite the recognized advantages**: Rettig, "Origins of the Medicare Kidney Disease Entitlement"; and Rettig and Levinsky, *Kidney Failure and the Federal Government*. See also Christopher R. Blagg, "What Went Wrong with Home Hemodialysis in the United States and What Can Be Done Now?" Hemodial Int (2000).

80 **patients represented only 1 percent**: USRDS Annual Data Report 2021, ESRD, Healthcare Expenditures for Persons with ESRD, Introduction (https://adr .usrds.org/2021/end-stage-renal-disease/9-healthcare-expenditures-for-persons -with-esrd).

80 **nation's leading dialysis firm**: Rettig and Levinsky, *Kidney Failure and the Federal Government*; Gina Bari Kolata, "NMC Thrives Selling Dialysis," Science (1980); and Tim McFeeley, *The Price of Access* (Nashua, NH, 2001).

80 **"National Medical Care is the largest"**: National Medical Care annual report (1976), cited in Maryam K. Saeed, Vivian Ho et al., "Consolidation in Dialysis Markets," Semin Dial (2020).

80 **"Government is not the solution"**: Ronald Reagan's inaugural address (January 20, 1981).

81 **period of "galloping socialism"**: Russell Roberts, "An Interview with Milton Friedman," EconTalk, EconLib Articles (2006). For Friedman's economic theories, Reaganomics and neoliberalism more generally, see the Chapter 5 note **supported a neoliberal agenda**. For more on Friedman, see his *Capitalism and Freedom* (Chicago, 1962), and the biography by Lanny Ebenstein, *Milton Friedman* (New York, 2007). Friedman called government healthcare "a socialist-communist system" here: Larry Arnn, "'Free to Choose': A Conversation with Milton Friedman," *Imprimis*, a publication of Hillsdale College (2006).

81 **NMC and its managers enthusiastically espoused**: See Edmund G. Lowrie and Constantine Hampers, "The Success of Medicare's End-Stage Renal-Disease Program: The Case for Profits and the Private Marketplace," NEJM (1981), which is discussed in detail in what follows. See also Kolata, "NMC Thrives Selling Dialysis"; McFeeley, *The Price of Access*; and Saeed, Ho et al., "Consolidation in Dialysis Markets."

81 **"prescription for gaining political power"**: Kolata, "NMC Thrives Selling Dialysis."

81 **the team that published**: See reference above in the note **National Cooperative Dialysis Study (NCDS)**.

81 **an influential NEJM editorial:** For Relman's arguments here and in what follows, see Arnold S. Relman, "The New Medical-Industrial Complex," NEJM (1980).

82 **In response, Lowrie and Hampers:** For Lowrie's and Hampers's contentions concerning for-profit medicine that follow, see Lowrie and Hampers, "The Success of Medicare's End-Stage Renal-Disease Program."

83 **practiced what they preached:** For NMC's approach to for-profit dialysis, see Kurt Eichenwald, "Death and Deficiency in Kidney Treatment," *New York Times* (December 4, 1995); Kurt Eichenwald, "At Big Kidney Chain, Deals for Doctors, Ruin for Rivals," *New York Times* (December 5, 1995); Kolata, "NMC Thrives Selling Dialysis"; McFeeley, *The Price of Access*; Rettig and Levinsky, *Kidney Failure and the Federal Government*; and Christopher R. Blagg, A. Peter Lundin et al., letters to the editor at NEJM (1962) regarding "Profits and the End-Stage Renal Disease Program."

83 **subsequent criminal and civil proceedings:** For summaries of alleged misconduct by NMC, see SEC, "Current Report on Fresenius Medical Care Holdings, Inc., Pursuant to Section 13 or 15(d) of the Securities Exchange Act of 1934" (January 18, 2000); the 1999 settlement agreement between the Department of Justice (both Main Justice and the US Attorney's Office for the Eastern District of Pennsylvania) and Fresenius Medical Care Holdings, NMC Diagnostic Services et al., regarding "Medical Director Compensation Conduct"; and Remarks of Eric H. Holder, Jr., Deputy Attorney General, "Announcement of Criminal Pleas and Civil Settlements *United States v. Fresenius* (National Medical Care) Boston, Massachusetts" (January 19, 2000) (https://www.justice.gov/archive/dag/speeches/2000/nmichaelhealthremarks.htm). See also McFeeley, *The Price of Access*; and Milt Freudenheim, "Dialysis Provider to Pay $486 Million to Settle Charges," *New York Times* (January 20, 2000). Additional observations by Steven Bander, personal communication.

83 **a 1980s financial swashbuckler:** Kenneth N. Gilpin, "A Tough Grace Insider Gets Even Tougher," *New York Times* (May 8, 1995); and John Burns, "NMC's Hampers Has History of Seizing Chances," *Modern Healthcare* (1995). An additional note of color in Hampers's career is his 1988 indictment, together with fellow NMC executive Edward Hager, on charges of illegally smuggling into the United States the skins of jaguars, ocelots, margays and other endangered cats, which the two doctors had shot in Mexico: "Two Charged with Smuggling Big-game Skins," UPI (April 29, 1988). I have not been able to determine how this case was resolved.

83 **allegedly poisoning local communities:** EPA Case Summary: W. R. Grace & Co. Bankruptcy Settlement (2007). See also Cass Peterson, "W. R. Grace Pleads Guilty to Lying on Chemical Use," *Washington Post* (June 1, 1988).

83 **Lowrie offered him coffee:** Details of this scene are from Alonzo Plough, personal communication, and from Plough's book *Borrowed Time*.

83 **fighting a running battle:** For material here and below, see Plough, *Borrowed Time*; Plough, Salem et al., "Case Mix in End-Stage Renal Disease"; and Richard A. Rettig, "The Politics of Health Cost Containment," Bull NY Acad Med (1980). See also Eggers, Connerton et al., "The Medicare Experience with End-Stage Renal Disease"; Lowrie and Hampers, "The Success of Medicare's End-Stage Renal-Disease Program"; and testimony by NMC executives and their Seattle opponents in the following congressional hearings: "Medicare End-Stage Renal Disease Program Amendments," hearing before the House Ways and Means Committee (April 25, 1977); "Hospital Cost Containment and End Stage Renal Disease Program," hearings before the Senate Finance Committee (October 12, 13 and 21, 1977); and "Hospital Cost Containment and End Stage Renal Disease Program," hearing before the Senate Finance Committee, Subcommittee on Health (March 15, 1982).

84 **"I was sitting there listening":** Alonzo Plough, personal communication.

84 **Plough had experienced medical hubris:** Plough's experiences in a New Haven, Connecticut, dialysis clinic, as described in what follows, are chronicled in his book *Borrowed Time*.

84 **"I saw how the central role":** Alonzo Plough, personal communication.

85 **"characteristic of a chronic disease":** Alonzo Plough, personal communication.

85 **one patient in particular:** Details of Mr. O's experiences on dialysis are in Plough, *Borrowed Time*.

86 **"Patients who spoke out":** Quotations here and below: Alonzo Plough, personal communication.

86 **his meeting at NMC headquarters:** Plough describes his exchanges with Lowrie, and Lowrie's apparent attempts to discredit his research, in Plough, *Borrowed Time*.

86 **did publish his paper:** Plough, Salem et al., "Case Mix in End-Stage Renal Disease."

86 **"an overly cautious (even deferential)":** Plough, *Borrowed Time*.

86 **The continued and expanded funding:** Plough, *Borrowed Time*; and Plough, personal communication.

87 **"They didn't stop my work":** Alonzo Plough, personal communication.

87 **Wall Street began to target healthcare:** See the explanation and analysis in Maggie Mahar, *Money-Driven Medicine* (New York, 2009); Paul Starr, *The Social Transformation of American Medicine* (New York, 2017); Bradford H. Gray, ed., *For-Profit Enterprise in Health Care* (Washington, DC, 1986); and Rosemary Stevens, *In Sickness and in Wealth* (Baltimore, 1999).

87 **the NEJM editorialist:** Drummond Rennie, "Nephrology Comes of Age," NEJM (1977).

87 **emphasis on financial metrics:** See annotations in the Chapter 5 note **debate about money in healthcare.** Perhaps the best introduction to the vast body of research on financial conflicts, in medicine and elsewhere, is *Conflicts of Interest* (Cambridge, UK, 2005), which is edited by four top authorities on the subject

(Don A. Moore, Daylian M. Cain, George Loewenstein and Max H. Bazerman), and includes four essays specific to medical conflicts. Further work that I found useful includes: Robert Whitaker and Lisa Cosgrove, *Psychiatry Under the Influence* (New York, 2015); Bernard Lo and Marilyn Field, eds., *Conflict of Interest in Medical Research, Education, and Practice*, National Academy of Sciences (Washington, DC, 2009); and Arnold Eiser, *The Ethos of Medicine in Postmodern America* (Lanham, MD, 2014).

On the broader psychology and impact of financial conflicts, see Max H. Bazerman and Ann E. Tenbrunsel, *Blind Spots* (Princeton, 2011); Sheldon Krimsky, *Conflicts of Interest in Science* (New York, 2019); and Michael Davis and Andrew Stark, eds., *Conflict of Interest in the Professions* (Oxford, 2001). See also extensive publications on medical and other professional conflicts by scholars at Harvard's Edmond & Lily Safra Center for Ethics, including the 2011 symposium titled "The Scientific Basis of Conflicts of Interest" (https://ethics.harvard.edu/event/scientific-basis-conflicts-interest-role-implicit-cognition).

87 **Giant hospital chains:** For information here and in what follows, see references in the Chapter 3 note **early for-profit hospital chains**. See also Starr, *The Social Transformation of American Medicine*; and Stevens, *In Sickness and in Wealth*. NME is further discussed below, in Chapter 8.

87 **often received large payouts:** Max Fine and Charlie Middleton, personal communication.

88 **removed from the doctors:** Roy Poses, personal communication. See also Mahar, *Money-Driven Medicine*; and Starr, *The Social Transformation of American Medicine*.

88 **a fast food business model:** See references in the Chapter 3 note **Thiry's fast food analogy**.

88 **ethics of healthcare changed:** See references in the Chapter 5 note **debate about money in healthcare**.

88 **Sister Irene Kraus:** John Paul Newport, "Health Care; Mission + Margin: The Nun as C.E.O.," *New York Times* (June 9, 1991); Monica Langley, "Money Order: Nuns' Zeal for Profits Shapes Hospital Chain, Wins Fans," *Wall Street Journal* (January 7, 1998).

88 **private healthcare industries emerged:** An early view of the phenomenon is provided in Relman, "The New Medical-Industrial Complex." More recent accounts include: Eileen Appelbaum and Rosemary Batt, "Private Equity Buyouts in Healthcare," Institute for New Economic Thinking Working Paper Series (2020); Richard M. Scheffler, Laura M. Alexander et al., "Soaring Private Equity Investment in the Healthcare Sector," report jointly produced by the American Antitrust Institute and the Petris Center at the UC Berkeley School of Public Health (2021); and Laura Katz Olson, *Ethically Challenged* (Baltimore, 2022).

88 **strip malls and industrial parks:** In addition to references in the Chapter 3

note **Thiry's fast food analogy**, see also Daryl Martin, Sarah Nettleton et al., *Architecture and Health Care* (Leeds, 2015); and David Charles Sloane and Beverlie Conant Sloane, *Medicine Moves to the Mall* (Baltimore, 2003).

89 **local and regional providers:** Rettig and Levinsky, *Kidney Failure and the Federal Government*; and personal communication with Steven Bander, Brent Miller and Leonard Stern.

89 **Mullin got her start:** Arlene Mullin, personal communication.

89 **Smith, a registered nurse:** "Betty Smith" is a pseudonym for one of the four former executives of the ESRD Networks system whom I interviewed, all of whom spoke on condition of anonymity.

89 **"Self-care was big back then":** "Betty Smith," personal communication.

89 **Veteran nephrologists tell horror stories:** Brent Miller, Steven Bander and Leonard Stern, personal communication.

89 **plenty of bottom feeders:** Brent Miller, personal communication.

89 **Steven Bander encountered:** This and the quote that follows: Steven Bander, personal communication.

90 **emerged to compete with NMC:** See the detailed review of the competitive environment in 1991 in Rettig and Levinsky, *Kidney Failure and the Federal Government*. Further information that follows, including quotations, is from Steven Bander and Brent Miller, personal communication.

90 **successive waves of consolidation:** See the analysis of this process in Saeed, Ho et al., "Consolidation in Dialysis Markets"; Paul Eliason, "Market Power and Quality: Congestion and Spatial Competition in the Dialysis Industry," NBER Working Paper (2017); Paul Eliason, Benjamin Heebsh et al., "How Acquisitions Affect Firm Behavior and Performance: Evidence from the Dialysis Industry," Q J Econ (2020); David Cutler, Leemore Dafny et al., "How Does Competition Impact the Quality and Price of Outpatient Service Facilities? A Case Study of the U.S. Dialysis Industry," NBER Working Paper (2012); and Nathan E. Wilson, "For-Profit Status and Industry Evolution in Health Care Markets: Evidence from the Dialysis Industry," Int J Health Econ Manag (2016).

90 **NMC was prosecuted:** See annotations in the earlier note **subsequent criminal and civil proceedings**, especially Remarks of Eric H. Holder, Jr., Deputy Attorney General, "Announcement of Criminal Pleas," in which Holder celebrated the event as "the largest health care fraud case in our nation's history."

91 **In 1997, Gambro bought:** Milt Freudenheim, "Swedish Holding Company to Buy U.S. Dialysis Provider," *New York Times* (May 6, 1997); and Stephen D. Moore, "Sweden's Incentive AB to Buy Vivra of the U.S. for $1.6 Billion," *Wall Street Journal* (May 6, 1997). For revealing background information on the purchase, see Robert L. Shook, "All for One and One for All," in *Heart & Soul* (New York, 2010).

91 **"a pig in a poke":** Steven Bander, personal communication.

91 **poor financial performance and crushing fraud:** See Bander's second amended complaint, United States ex rel. Steven J. Bander v. Gambro Healthcare US Inc.,

case number 4:01-cv-00553-DDN, US District Court for the Eastern District of Missouri (filed November 30, 2004); and "Gambro Healthcare Agrees to Pay Over $350 Million to Resolve Civil & Criminal Allegations in Medicare Fraud Case," Department of Justice press release (December 2, 2004) (https://www.justice.gov/archive/opa/pr/2004/December/04_civ_774.htm). Also Steven Bander, personal communication.

91 **"stealth consolidation":** Thomas G. Wollmann, "How to Get Away with Merger," NBER Working Paper (2020).

91 **Of the 6,900 clinics:** Clinic data were extracted from CMS Dialysis Facility Reports (Form CMS-2552-10) according to data dictionary attribute (F [AFS]: Facility Information—Number of all patients on 12/31/2020). The estimate for combined clinics as a percentage of total clinics in the industry was 78.65 percent. Net revenues estimates were extracted from CMS Dialysis Cost Reports (Form CMS-265-11), Statement of Revenues and Expenses section. The estimate for net revenues as a percentage of total industry net revenues was 78.73 percent.

92 **Grassley's Senate Subcommittee:** Information and quotations in this section, except as noted, derive from "Kidney Dialysis Patients: A Population at Undue Risk?" hearing before the Senate Special Committee on Aging (June 26, 2000). Video of the hearing, often fascinating, is available here: https://www.c-span.org/video/?157902-1/kidney-dialysis.

92 **driving force behind this hearing:** Personal communication with Arlene Mullin, Brenda Smith (sister of dialysis patient and witness Brent Smith) and Jamie Bays (widow of dialysis patient and witness W. Kenneth Bays). Mullin's written testimony is included in the published hearing record, though she says that Senate staffers did not allow her to testify in person.

93 **added their damning views:** "Oversight of Kidney Dialysis Facilities Needs Improvement," GAO report (2000); and compare "Problems Remain in Ensuring Compliance with Medicare Quality Standards," GAO report (2003).

96 **After testifying in Washington:** Details here and in what follows from Brenda Smith, personal communication; and Kerry Fehr-Snyder, "Dialysis Workers Under Fire: Certification Weighed as Mistakes Grow," *Arizona Republic* (February 25, 2002) (https://azcentral.newspapers.com/search/?ymd=2002-02-25), citing a 2001 Arizona state report.

7. ON THE BLOOD FLOOR

98 **Leonard Stern was raised:** The primary source for this section, including quotations, and except as noted below, is Leonard Stern, personal communication.

99 **attributed to Moses Maimonides:** For the text of the oath, see "Oath and Prayer of Maimonides," Resources for Education and Research on Bioethics, Dalhousie University. For its composition and provenance, see Fred Rosner, "The Physician's Prayer Attributed to Moses Maimonides," in *Medicine in the Bible and the Talmud* (New York, 1995).

101 **Miller experienced similar pressures:** Brent Miller, personal communication. Some parallels mentioned by Jeffrey Berns, personal communication.

103 **Stern explains how the consolidation:** Leonard Stern, personal communication. A good review of how conflicts of interest can affect nephrologists' decisions and the health of their patients is in Aaron Glickman, Eugene Lin et al., "Conflicts of Interest in Dialysis: A Barrier to Policy Reforms," Semin Dial (2020). There is a substantial literature on how quality of care degrades after a small and/or nonprofit dialysis unit is bought out by a large dialysis corporation; see, for example: Kevin F. Erickson, Bo Zhao et al., "Association of Hospitalization and Mortality among Patients Initiating Dialysis with Hemodialysis Facility Ownership and Acquisitions," JAMA Network Open (2019); Yi Zhang, Mae Thamer et al., "Organizational Status of Dialysis Facilities and Patient Outcome: Does Higher Injectable Medication Use Mediate Increased Mortality?" Health Serv Res (2013); Paul Eliason, Benjamin Heebsh et al., "How Acquisitions Affect Firm Behavior and Performance: Evidence from the Dialysis Industry," Q J Econ (2020); David Cutler, Leemore Dafny et al., "How Does Competition Impact the Quality and Price of Outpatient Service Facilities? A Case Study of the U.S. Dialysis Industry," NBER Working Paper (2012); P. J. Devereaux, Holger J. Schünemann et al., "Comparison of Mortality Between Private For-Profit and Private Not-For-Profit Hemodialysis Centers," JAMA (2002); and Pushkal P. Garg, Kevin D. Frick et al., "Effect of the Ownership of Dialysis Facilities on Patients' Survival and Referral for Transplantation," NEJM (1999). See also the discussion later in this chapter of research by economist Ryan McDevitt and colleagues, with annotations.

103 **"doctors get blackballed too":** Brent Miller, personal communication.

103 **"He's recruited a group of physicians":** Leonard Stern, personal communication.

103 **Miller blames his fellow MDs:** Here and following, Brent Miller, personal communication.

104 **Arlene Mullin founded Dialysis Advocates:** Here and following, Arlene Mullin, personal communication. On Mullin's experiences in her Portland clinic, see Nigel Jaquiss, "Whistle-blower," *Willamette Week* (March 24, 1999).

105 **bought out by Renal Care Group:** Arlene Mullin, personal communication; and see "Renal Care Group, Inc. Completes Joint Venture to Provide Dialysis Services in Portland, Oregon," *Business Wire* (1998). (The transaction was begun in 1997 and completed in 1998.)

106 **Betty Smith's nonprofit hospital:** Here and following, "Betty Smith," personal communication.

106 **Rosansky worked as a nephrologist:** Steven Rosansky, personal communication.

107 **A study from 2018:** Here and following, see Manjula Kurella Tamura, I-Chun Thomas et al., "Dialysis Initiation and Mortality among Older Veterans with Kidney Failure Treated in Medicare vs the Department of Veterans Affairs," JAMA Intern Med (2018); and Virginia Wang, Cynthia J. Coffman et al., "Sur-

vival among Veterans Obtaining Dialysis in VA and Non-VA Settings," J Am Soc Nephrol (2019).

107 **entering the for-profit dialysis arena:** This and the quotations below: Steven Rosansky, personal communication.

107 **"We're nothing but a number":** Cornelius Robbins, personal communication.

108 **"don't care about us":** Gregg Hansen, personal communication.

108 **the story of erythropoietin:** For good overviews of important aspects of the EPO story, see Jay B. Wish, "The Economic Realities of Erythropoiesis-Stimulating Agent Therapy in Kidney Disease," Kidney Int (2006); the judgment in United States ex rel. Coyne v. Amgen, Inc., case number CV 12-3881 (JMA)(AYS), before the US District Court for the Eastern District of New York (decided January 17, 2017); and "Ensuring Kidney Patients Receive Safe and Appropriate Anemia Management Care," hearing before the House Committee on Ways and Means, Subcommittee on Health (June 26, 2007).

108 **use of the drug shot up:** In addition to references in the previous note **the story of erythropoietin**, see: Marilyn Chase, "Amgen's Star Fades Amid Safety Questions," *Wall Street Journal* (April 10, 2007); and "Sacrificing the Cash Cow" [editorial], Nat Biotechnol (2007).

109 **paid Amgen consultants:** Daniel W. Coyne, "Influence of Industry on Renal Guideline Development," Clin J Am Soc Nephrol (2007); National Kidney Foundation, "KDOQI Clinical Practice Guidelines for Chronic Kidney Disease: Evaluation, Classification and Stratification," Am J Kidney Dis (2002); Madhuri Chengappa, Sandra Herrmann et al., "Self-Reported Financial Conflict of Interest in Nephrology Clinical Practice Guidelines," Kidney Int Rep (2021).

109 **"At no time was there ever":** Dori Schatell, "U.S. Dialysis Measures—Have We Set Up the Ladder Against the Wrong Wall?" Home Dialysis Central (2014).

109 **clinical practice guidelines in nephrology:** See National Kidney Foundation, "KDOQI Clinical Practice Guidelines for Chronic Kidney Disease"; and Nathan Levin, Garabed Eknoyan et al., "National Kidney Foundation: Dialysis Outcome Quality Initiative—Development of Methodology for Clinical Practice Guidelines," Nephrol Dial Transplant (1997).

109 **recommended a higher hematocrit target:** Dennis Cotter, Mae Thamer et al., "Translating Epoetin Research into Practice," Health Aff (2006); Jay B. Wish, "The Economic Realities of Erythropoiesis-Stimulating Agent Therapy in Kidney Disease"; and "End-Stage Renal Disease: Reduction in Drug Utilization Suggests Bundled Payment Is too High," GAO memorandum (December 7, 2012).

109 **adopted higher EPO doses:** For this and what follows, see Mae Thamer, Yi Zhang et al., "Dialysis Facility Ownership and Epoetin Dosing in Patients Receiving Hemodialysis," JAMA (April 18, 2007); Daniel W. Coyne, "Use of Epoetin in Chronic Renal Failure," JAMA (2007); Eliason, Heebsh et al., "How Acquisitions Affect Firm Behavior and Performance"; and "Ensuring Kidney Patients Receive Safe and Appropriate Anemia Management

Care," hearing before the House Committee on Ways and Means. See also "Amgen's Fourth Quarter 2006 Revenue Increased 17% to $3.8 Billion," Amgen press release (January 25, 2007) (https://www.amgen.com/newsroom /press-releases/2007/01/amgens-fourth-quarter-2006-revenue-increased-17 -to-38-billion-full-year-2006-revenue-increased-15-to-143-billion).

109 **A 2019 study found:** Eliason, Heebsh et al., "How Acquisitions Affect Firm Behavior and Performance."

109 **$40 billion on EPO:** For this and what follows: Mae Thamer, Yi Zhang et al., "Major Declines in Epoetin Dosing After Prospective Payment System Based on Dialysis Facility Organizational Status," Am J Nephrol (2014); "Update: Medicare Payments for End Stage Renal Disease Drugs," report by the HHS Office of the Inspector General (2014); Robin Fields, "Federal Grand Jury Probes Major Dialysis Provider," ProPublica (2011); "DOJ Drops Inquiry Against DaVita without Charges," Reuters (2012); Fresenius Medical Care v. United States of America, Appeal from the US District Court for the Eastern District of Missouri, appellate case number 07-2299 (filed May 16, 2008). See also United States ex rel. Coyne v. Amgen (2017).

110 **Several lawsuits were filed:** United States ex rel. Ivey Woodard v. Fresenius Medical Care, DaVita et al., case number 1:05-cv-00227-MAC, US District Court for the Eastern District of Texas, second amended complaint (filed March 22, 2005); and United States ex rel. Chester Saldivar v. Fresenius Medical Care, case number 1:10-CV-01614-AT, US District Court for the Northern District of Georgia (order of October 30, 2015). Further useful background at United States ex rel. George v. Fresenius Medical Care, case number 2:12-cv-00877-AKK, US District Court for the Northern District of Alabama, Southern Division (memorandum opinion of September 26, 2016); and "U.S. Renal Care Settles Billing Fraud Case Brought by Nurse," Nephrol News Issues (2013). Regarding the EPO biosimilar Aranesp, also manufactured by Amgen, see "Amgen Inc. Pleads Guilty to Federal Charge in Brooklyn, NY; Pays $762 Million to Resolve Criminal Liability and False Claims Act Allegations," Department of Justice press release (2012) (https://www.justice.gov/opa/ pr/amgen-inc-pleads-guilty-federal-charge-brooklyn-ny-pays-762-million -resolve-criminal); and "Amgen to Pay U.S. $24.9 Million to Resolve False Claims Act Allegations," Department of Justice press release (2013) (https:// www.justice.gov/opa/pr/amgen-pay-us-249-million-resolve-false-claims-act -allegations).

110 **In 2007, Kent Thiry declared:** Andrew Pollack, "The Dialysis Business: Fair Treatment?" *New York Times* (September 16, 2007).

110 **clinical evidence was accumulating:** Thamer, Zhang et al., "Dialysis Facility Ownership and Epoetin Dosing"; Coyne, "Use of Epoetin in Chronic Renal Failure"; and United States ex rel. Coyne v. Amgen (2017).

110 **major clinical trial of EPO:** The report on the trial is Anatole Besarab, W. Kline Bolton et al., "The Effects of Normal as Compared with Low Hemato-

crit Values in Patients with Cardiac Disease Who Are Receiving Hemodialysis and Epoetin," NEJM (1998). See the analysis in United States ex rel. Coyne v. Amgen (2017).

110 **FDA issued an alert:** The first FDA warning in 2006 is referenced in "Erythropoiesis Stimulating Agents (ESAs) For Non-renal Disease Indications," CMS alert, decision memo (2007) (https://www.cms.gov/medicare-coverage -database/view/ncacal-decision-memo.aspx?proposed=N&NCAId=203). Black box warning described in Andrew Pollack, "F.D.A. Warning Is Issued on Anemia Drugs' Overuse," *New York Times* (March 10, 2007).

110 **mounting medical concerns:** For this and what follows, see Thamer, Zhang et al., "Major Declines in Epoetin Dosing"; and "End-Stage Renal Disease: Reduction in Drug Utilization Suggests Bundled Payment Is Too High," GAO memorandum.

110 **Medicare eliminated reimbursement:** For this and what follows, see Thamer, Zhang et al., "Major Declines in Epoetin Dosing"; and USRDS Annual Data Report 2013, Volume II, Atlas of End Stage Renal Disease in the United States, ESRD Providers—Introduction.

111 **may not have been entirely:** See reference in the Chapter 3 note **"not about the patients."**

111 **role of the nephrologists:** On how nephrologists control patient prescriptions: personal communication with Brent Miller, Leonard Stern, Steven Bander and Jeffrey Berns.

111 **increase their usage of EPO:** United States ex rel. Alon J. Vainer and Daniel D. Barbir v. DaVita Inc. and Gambro Healthcare Inc., case number 1:07-cv-2509, US District Court for the Northern District of Georgia, Atlanta Division, fourth amended complaint (July 25, 2011); United States ex rel. Ivey Woodard v. Fresenius Medical Care, DaVita et al. (2005); United States ex rel. Coyne v. Amgen (2017); United States ex rel. Chester Saldivar v. Fresenius Medical Care (2015); and United States ex rel. George v. Fresenius Medical Care (2016). Regarding Snappy, see United States ex rel. Alon J. Vainer and Daniel D. Barbir v. DaVita Inc. and Gambro Healthcare Inc. (2011).

111 **"Dialysis providers realized":** Brent Miller, personal communication.

111 **"People who write the guidelines":** Steven Rosansky, personal communication.

111 **for patients and their families:** Rosansky also co-hosts DadviceTV, a YouTube show to educate patients on kidney disease and to explain how they can avoid starting dialysis earlier than is necessary and beneficial. See, for example, "Glomerular Filtration Rate: When Your Kidney Number, eGFR, Is the Wrong Thing to Focus On" (https://www.youtube.com/watch?v=_nfpFCwVILM); and "Kidney Disease Treatment in Older Adults—When Less Treatment Is More for Older Kidney Patients" (https://www.youtube.com/watch?v=_S5mjXWd9NU).

112 **In 2002, KDOQI established:** See references in the earlier note **clinical practice guidelines in nephrology.** See also Stein Ivar Hallan, Stephan Reinhold

Orth et al., "The KDOQI 2002 Classification of Chronic Kidney Disease," Nephrol Dial Transplant (2010).

112 **a frequent starting point:** See, for example, the National Kidney Foundation's web page, "Estimated Glomerular Filtration Rate (eGFR)."

112 **Rosansky and many other nephrologists:** Steven Rosansky and John Agar, personal communication. A trenchant analysis is provided in John W. M. Agar, "Starting Dialysis: When, How, Whether?" plenary presentation at the Annual Dialysis Conference in Atlanta (February 9, 2014).

112 **putting people on dialysis by rote:** Here and following, Steven Rosansky, personal communication.

113 **PowerPoint slides from presentations:** Steven Rosansky, personal communication. One presentation referenced in what follows is Steven J. Rosansky, "Renal Replacement Therapy Issues in the Elderly," presentation to Japanese nephrologists in Tsukuba, Japan (2015). Further sources include Steven J. Rosansky, William F. Clark et al., "Initiation of Dialysis at Higher GFRs: Is the Apparent Rising Tide of Early Dialysis Harmful or Helpful?" Kidney Int (2009); and Steven J. Rosansky, Paul Eggers et al., "Early Start of Hemodialysis May Be Harmful," Arch Intern Med (2011).

114 **"Here's the study by Crews":** Here and following, Steven Rosansky, personal communication. Deidra C. Crews, Julia J. Scialla et al., "Predialysis Health, Dialysis Timing, and Outcomes among Older United States Adults," JASN (2014).

114 **the case of Gerald Thompson:** Here and following, Sherry and Gerald Thompson, personal communication.

115 **"horrible end-of-life experiences":** Here and following, Steven Rosansky, personal communication.

115 **"a study by Kurella":** Manjula Kurella Tamura, Ann M. O'Hare et al., "Signs and Symptoms Associated with Earlier Dialysis Initiation in Nursing Home Residents," Am J Kidney Dis (2010).

115 **ESRD Quality Incentive Program:** See the two web pages by CMS, ESRD Quality Incentive Program, and ESRD Quality Incentive Program: Measuring Quality. For the 5-Star Quality Rating System, see CMS, Dialysis Facilities: Quality of Patient Care Rating.

116 **treatment duration and ultrafiltration rate (UFR):** See annotations in the Chapter 3 note **treatments are likely too short and fast.**

116 **CMS has debated internally:** Arbor Research Collaborative for Health and University of Michigan Kidney Epidemiology and Cost Center: Clinical and Data Technical Expert Panel Meetings Synthesis Report (2010) (https://www.cms .gov/Medicare/End-Stage-Renal-Disease/CPMProject/downloads/ESRD2010 TechnicalExpertPanelReport.pdf); and Arbor Research Collaborative for Health and University of Michigan Kidney Epidemiology and Cost Center: End Stage Renal Disease (ESRD) Quality Measure Development and Maintenance. Hemodialysis Adequacy Clinical Technical Expert Panel Summary

Report (2013) (https://www.cms.gov/Medicare/Quality-Initiatives-Patient
-Assessment-Instruments/MMS/Downloads/Hemodialysis-Adequacy-TEP
-Summary-Report-and-Addendum.pdf).

116 **in 2013, a technical expert panel:** See references in the previous note **CMS has debated internally.**

116 **to institute both metrics:** Arbor Research Collaborative for Health and University of Michigan Kidney Epidemiology and Cost Center: End Stage Renal Disease (ESRD) Quality Measure Development and Maintenance. Hemodialysis Adequacy Clinical Technical Expert Panel Summary Report.

116 **a noted nephrology researcher:** In 2018, Daugirdas received the American Society of Nephrology's Belding H. Scribner Award for his "significant contributions in patient care, research, and service to professional organizations." For his work on *Kt/V*, see, for example, John T. Daugirdas, "Kt/V (and Especially Its Modifications) Remains a Useful Measure of Hemodialysis Dose," Kidney Int (2015); and F. G. Casino, J. Deira et al., "Improving the 'Second Generation Daugirdas Equation' to Estimate Kt/V on the Once-Weekly Haemodialysis Schedule," J Nephrol (2021).

116 **criticized the vote:** 19-571 Releasable TEP emails, obtained from the University of Illinois under FOIA dated July 2, 2019, email from John Daugirdas to Aya Inoue (May 18, 2013).

116 **write public comments in opposition:** 19-571 Releasable TEP emails, obtained from the University of Illinois under FOIA dated July 2, 2019, email from John Daugirdas to Alfred Cheung (July 12, 2013).

116 **re-vote by the technical expert panel:** 19-571 Releasable TEP emails, obtained from the University of Illinois under FOIA dated July 2, 2019, email from John Daugirdas to Peter DeOreo (May 12, 2013).

116 **Time to Reduce Mortality in ESRD (TiME):** Laura M. Dember, Eduardo Lacson, Jr. et al., "The TiME Trial: A Fully Embedded, Cluster-Randomized, Pragmatic Trial of Hemodialysis Session Duration," J Am Soc Nephrol (2019).

117 **"The TiMe [*sic*] trial is designed":** 19-571 Releasable TEP emails, obtained from the University of Illinois under FOIA dated July 2, 2019, email from John Daugirdas to Aya Inoue (May 18, 2013).

117 **In a subsequent email:** 19-571 Releasable TEP emails, obtained from the University of Illinois under FOIA dated July 2, 2019, email from John Daugirdas to Peter DeOreo (May 21, 2013).

117 **this time both were rejected:** Arbor Research Collaborative for Health and University of Michigan Kidney Epidemiology and Cost Center: End Stage Renal Disease (ESRD) Quality Measure Development and Maintenance. Hemodialysis Adequacy Clinical Technical Expert Panel Summary Report. Ultimately, in 2020, CMS adopted the UFR measure, but only for reporting purposes, not as a clinical or safety metric that might lead to financial penalties for dialysis facilities. See CMS, ESRD QIP Summary: Payment Years 2016—2020.

117 **ultimately received $6.7 million:** Funding amount based on reported funds for project "Pragmatic Trials in Maintenance Hemodialysis," cooperative agreements UH2 AT007797 and UH3 DK102384, NIH Research Portfolio Online Expenditures and Results Reporting Tool (https://projectreporter.nih .gov/reporter.cfm).

117 **was discontinued early:** Dember, Lacson Jr. et al., "The TiME Trial."

117 **"poorly designed and executed":** Brent Miller, personal communication.

117 **large, granular data sets:** Information and quotations in this section are from personal communication with Ryan McDevitt, together with relevant publications by McDevitt and his colleagues. These include: Paul J. Eliason, Benjamin Heebsh et al., "The Effect of Bundled Payments on Provider Behavior and Patient Outcomes," NBER Working Paper (2020); Paul J. Eliason, Riley J. League et al., "Ambulance Taxis: The Impact of Regulation and Litigation on Health Care Fraud," NBER Working Paper (2021); Paul L. E. Grieco and Ryan C. McDevitt, "Productivity and Quality in Health Care: Evidence from the Dialysis Industry," Rev Econ Stud (2017); Riley J. League, Paul J. Eliason et al., "Variability in Prices Paid for Hemodialysis by Employer-Sponsored Insurance in the US from 2012 to 2019," JAMA Network Open (2022); and Eliason, Heebsh et al., "How Acquisitions Affect Firm Behavior and Performance."

117 **detailed yearly report card:** McDevitt learned this by reading the stories and materials from the seminal 2010 ProPublica project led by Robin Fields—see annotations in the Chapter 2 note **"survival rate in the United States."**

120 **researchers in a range of disciplines:** Herbert Kelman and V. Lee Hamilton, *Crimes of Obedience* (New Haven, CT, 1990), provide a useful framework for understanding certain psychological mechanisms—particularly obedience to authority, peer pressure, routinization of wrongdoing and derogation of victims—that enable good people who work and live within toxic organizational or societal cultures to perform, and rationalize, their harmful actions. Though Stanley Milgram's interpretations and scientific ethics have been criticized, his famous "shock experiments" remain powerful illustrations of some of these principles; see Stanley Milgram, *Obedience to Authority* (New York, 1974); and Thomas Blass, *The Man Who Shocked the World* (New York, 2004). See also Max H. Bazerman, *Complicit* (Princeton, 2022); Carol Tavris and Elliot Aronson, *Mistakes Were Made (but Not by Me)* (New York, 2007); J. Michael Wynne, "The Impact of Financial Pressures on Clinical Care: Lessons from Corporate Medicine" (https://documents.uow.edu.au/~bmartin/dissent/documents/ health/corpmed.html); and Dolly Chugh and Mary Kern, "A Dynamic and Cyclical Model of Bounded Ethicality," Res Organ Behav (2016). For broader context, see Elliot and Joshua Aronson's fascinating *The Social Animal* (New York, 2018).

121 **"Tone at the Top":** For an early formulation of the concept of "tone at the top," see the findings of the so-called Treadway Commission, titled "Report of the National Commission on Fraudulent Financial Reporting" (1987).

121 **"When the CEO of a large":** Robert Bear, personal communication.

121 **facilitated by graying them out:** Routinization, "slippery slope" and related mechanisms are discussed in references in the earlier note **researchers in a range of disciplines.** See especially Kelman and Hamilton, *Crimes of Obedience.*

122 **"goals gone wild":** Lisa Ordóñez, Maurice Schweitzer et al., "Goals Gone Wild," Harvard Business School Working Paper (2009) (https://www.hbs .edu/ris/Publication%20Files/09-083.pdf).

122 **DaVita's pay schemes:** See the firm's Schedule 14a (yearly notice of annual meeting and proxy statement) for recent years, particularly in the section concerning "Compensation Discussion and Analysis."

122 **Goals with threats:** Marianne M. Jennings, *The Seven Signs of Ethical Collapse* (New York, 2006); and Maggie Mahar, *Money-Driven Medicine* (New York, 2009).

122 **the "framing effect":** The original formulation of the effect is by Amos Tversky and Daniel Kahneman, "The Framing of Decisions and the Psychology of Choice," Science (1981). See also Daniel Kahneman, *Thinking, Fast and Slow* (New York, 2011). See the excellent analysis of and case studies illustrating the framing effect in business at "Framing," part of the Ethics Unwrapped website at the University of Texas at Austin McCombs School of Business.

122 **"continue to be dialysis practices":** Robert Bear, personal communication.

123 **or not placed—on transplant waitlists:** Literature on the disparity between for-profit and not-for-profit dialysis facilities in placing patients on transplantation waitlists includes: Laura J. McPherson, Elizabeth R. Walker et al., "Dialysis Facility Profit Status and Early Steps in Kidney Transplantation in the Southeastern United States," CJASN (2021); Divya Raghavan and Isaac E. Hall, "Dialysis and Transplant Access: Kidney Capitalism at a Crossroads?" CJASN (2021); and Pushkal P. Garg, Kevin D. Frick et al., "Effect of the Ownership of Dialysis Facilities on Patients' Survival and Referral for Transplantation," NEJM (1999). For economic analysis, see Eliason, Heebsh et al., "How Acquisitions Affect Firm Behavior and Performance." Oliver, *Last Week Tonight,* "Dialysis" contains a revealing segment on how some clinics discourage their patients from seeking a transplant.

123 **a kidney transplant in November 2021:** Here and following, Cornelius Robbins, personal communication.

123 **Medical researchers and economists:** See references in the earlier note **or not placed—on transplant waitlists.**

124 **classified by their clinic staff as "noncompliant":** Personal communication with patients including Cornelius Robbins, Gregg Hansen, Tangi Foster and Vanessa Winters.

124 **Brito was passed over:** Carrie Brito and William Sarsfield, personal communication.

124 **high-margin private payor patients:** Numerous patients and dialysis workers, including Megallan Handford and Emanuel Gonzales, and registered nurse and

dialysis spouse Marie DeFrancesco-Malviya, have told me about this phenomenon. Alonzo Plough already observed the derogation of public patients at the
New Haven dialysis facility he studied back in the 1980s: Alonzo Plough, personal communication, and his book *Borrowed Time* (Philadelphia, 1986). See also
the discussion below of whistleblower David Barbetta's experiences at DaVita,
and the special status of HIPPERs ("high-paying patients"); that is, patients
with a private insurance plan that reimburses dialysis treatments at a high rate.
Regarding HIPPERs, see also the I Hate Dialysis Message Board threads from
June 2006 (https://ihatedialysis.com/forum/index.php?topic=742.0) and May
2011 (https://ihatedialysis.com/forum/index.php?topic=23154.0).

124 **routinely steered by clinic staff:** See Teri Browne, PhD, dialysis social worker,
written comment to CMS Request for Information: Inappropriate Steering of
Individuals Eligible for or Receiving Medicare and Medicaid Benefits to Individual Market Plans (https://ffj-online.org/wp-content/uploads/2017/09/
Browne_response-3.pdf); "Why Are Dialysis Providers Paying Your Members'
Premiums?" a white paper by Renalogic, a firm that provides advice on containing the costs of dialysis treatment for members of employee health plans,
which alleges that the AKF arrangement with major dialysis companies represents a "'pay-to-play' scheme to steer dialysis patients"; and Peace Officers'
Annuity and Benefit Fund of Georgia, et al. v. DaVita Inc., Kent J. Thiry et al.,
case number 1:17-cv-00304, US District Court for the District of Colorado,
class action complaint (filed January 12, 2018).

124 **A 2018 letter:** Letter to Alex Azar, then secretary of the Department of Health
and Human Services, from America's Health Insurance Plans and fourteen
major insurance companies, decries the "inappropriate steering of individuals
with End Stage Renal Disease (ESRD) who are eligible for Medicare or Medicaid into commercial coverage" (April 16, 2018).

125 **report issued by J.P. Morgan:** J.P. Morgan, North America Equity Research,
"DaVita Inc." (October 9, 2017).

125 **AKF chief executive LaVarne Burton wrote:** "Statement from LaVarne A.
Burton, President and CEO of the American Kidney Fund," sent to me via
email on October 13, 2022.

125 **A subsequent letter:** Letter of November 15, 2022, from Donna M. D. Thomas,
attorney at the firm of Goodell, DeVries, Leech, & Dann, LLP.

125 **The advisory opinion mentioned by Burton:** Advisory Opinion No. 97-1,
issued by D. McCarty Thornton, Chief Counsel to the Inspector General of
HHS. Useful background information in United States et al. ex rel. David Gonzalez v. DaVita Health Care Partners, Fresenius Medical Care North America
and the American Kidney Fund, case number 1:16-cv-11840-NMG, US District
Court for the District of Massachusetts, first amended complaint filed September 8, 2016.

126 **opened the floodgates to donations:** See "American Kidney Fund: Funding
Growth," a report by The Bridgespan Group (February, 2007), which docu-

ments how, between 1996 and 2004, the Fund's revenues grew at a compound annual growth rate of 37 percent. For total revenues in 2021, the last year for which AKF financial information was available, see American Kidney Fund, Inc. audited financial statements, years ended December 31, 2021 and 2020, prepared by CliftonLarsonAllen LLP.

126 **now 54th on the Forbes list:** Forbes, "America's Top 100 Charities" (December 13, 2022).

126 **in a 2007 report:** "American Kidney Fund: Funding Growth" (February, 2007).

126 **the Fund's audited financial statements:** "American Kidney Fund, Inc. Audited Financial Statements, Years Ended December 31, 2021 and 2020."

126 **a shareholder class action lawsuit:** Peace Officers' Annuity and Benefit Fund of Georgia, et al. v. DaVita Inc., Kent J. Thiry et al., case number 1:17-cv-00304, US District Court for the District of Colorado, class action complaint (filed January 12, 2018).

127 **Another lawsuit, filed in 2019:** Blue Cross and Blue Shield of Florida, Inc. et al. v. DaVita Inc., case number 3:19-cv-00574-BJD-MCR, US District Court for the Middle District of Florida, Jacksonville Division, complaint filed May 14, 2019.

128 **a December 2016 article in the *New York Times*:** Katie Thomas and Reed Abelson, "Kidney Fund Seen Insisting on Donations, Contrary to Government Deal," *New York Times* (December 25, 2016). See also Reed Abelson and Katie Thomas, "Top Kidney Charity Directed Aid to Patients at DaVita and Fresenius Clinics, Lawsuit Claims," *New York Times* (August 2, 2019).

128 **a lawsuit filed in 2016:** UnitedHealthcare of Florida, Inc. et al. v. American Renal Associates Holdings, Inc. et al., case number 9:16-cv-81180-KAM, US District Court for the Southern District of Florida, second amended complaint filed March 13, 2017.

128 **a whistleblower lawsuit unsealed in 2019:** United States et al. ex rel. David Gonzalez v. DaVita Health Care Partners, Fresenius Medical Care North America and the American Kidney Fund (September 8, 2016).

128 **Representative Katie Porter wrote a letter:** Letter from Rep. Katie Porter to Joanne Chiedi, Acting Inspector General, HHS (July 23, 2019).

129 **a fact sheet and an interim final rule:** CMS Fact Sheet: Promoting Transparency and Appropriate Coverage for Dialysis Patients (December 12, 2016); and the Federal Register, Vol. 81, No. 240 (Wednesday, December 14, 2016), Rules and Regulations, pp. 90211-90228. See also Teri Browne, written comment to CMS Request for Information: Inappropriate Steering of Individuals Eligible for or Receiving Medicare and Medicaid Benefits to Individual Market Plans.

129 **"Our managers tell us":** This quote and what follows is from personal communication with dialysis workers in California (who spoke to me on condition of anonymity).

129 **"So long as I had a great insurance":** Cornelius Robbins, personal communication.

130 **culture of systemic fraud:** Described just below in the text (and the next note) as common practice by Joanne Bargman, and by other dialysis workers who spoke to me on condition of anonymity.

130 **"Buffing the Numbers":** Joanne Bargman, "Buffing the Numbers: The Decline and Fall of Dialysis Medicine," keynote address at the Annual Dialysis Conference in New Orleans (February 1, 2015). At the same conference, Bargman received the Gabor Zellerman Award for lifetime contributions to the science and practice of peritoneal dialysis and the next year was awarded the International Distinguished Medal of the National Kidney Foundation. See the commentary on Bargman's keynote and its reception by the audience in Mark Neumann, "Taken to the Woodshed . . . Again," Nephrol News Issues (March 17, 2015).

130 **received a standing ovation:** Neumann, "Taken to the Woodshed . . . Again."

130 **I've interviewed dialysis workers:** As mentioned earlier, these workers in California spoke to me on condition of anonymity.

131 **remembers how the nurses:** Cornelius Robbins, personal communication.

131 **"I always get a flood":** Arlene Mullin, personal communication.

131 **analysis by economist Ryan McDevitt:** Ryan McDevitt, personal communication; and "Strategic Patient Dropping," his preliminary report regarding comparisons of two QIP measures, URR and Kt/V, which McDevitt and colleagues extracted from USRDS data and are preparing for publication.

132 **to obscure their condition:** On this psychological process, see references in the earlier note **researchers in a range of disciplines,** especially Kelman and Hamilton, *Crimes of Obedience*; and Milgram, *Obedience to Authority*.

132 **"Patient harm in a for-profit":** Quotations here and in the rest of this section are from Steffie Woolhandler, personal communication. Woolhandler is a cofounder and board member of Physicians for a National Health Program (https://pnhp.org/). What follows is a small sampling of her numerous papers, often published jointly with her husband, David Himmelstein. Regarding patient harm, rising costs and degraded care caused by for-profit healthcare, see Steffie Woolhandler and David U. Himmelstein, *Bleeding the Patient: The Consequences of Corporate Health Care* (Monroe, Maine, 2002); Steffie Woolhandler with David Himmelstein and Adam Gaffney, "The Effect of Large-Scale Health Coverage Expansions in Wealthy Nations on Society-Wide Healthcare Utilization," J Gen Intern Med (2020); Steffie Woolhandler and David Himmelstein, "The High Costs of For-Profit Care," JAMC (2004); and Steffie Woolhandler and David Himmelstein, "When Money Is the Mission," NEJM (1999) (which ends with the lapidary remark: "Like blood, health care is too precious, intimate, and corruptible to entrust to the market"). Regarding national health and healthcare reform, see Steffie Woolhandler and David Himmelstein, "Public Policy and Health in the Trump Era," Lancet Commissions (2021); and Steffie Woolhandler and David Himmelstein, "Single-Payer Reform—'Medicare for All,'" JAMA (2019). Regarding COVID-19, see Steffie Woolhandler and David Himmelstein, "Intersecting U.S. Epidemics: COVID-

19 and Lack of Health Insurance," Ann Intern Med (July 7, 2020); and Steffie Woolhandler and David Himmelstein, "COVID-19's Lessons: Scientific and Social," Am J Public Health (2021).

133 **around 9 percent of its GDP:** Historical data from Nisha Kurani, Emma Wager et al., "How Has U.S. Spending on Healthcare Changed over Time?" Peterson KKF Health System Tracker.

133 **same as other member nations:** Emma Wager, Jared Ortaliza et al., "How Does Health Spending in the U.S. Compare to Other Countries?" Peterson KKF Health System Tracker. See also Manfred Huber, "Health Expenditure Trends in OECD Countries, 1970–1997," Health Care Financ Rev (1999). For broader context, see Austin Frakt, "Medical Mystery: Something Happened to U.S. Health Spending After 1980," *New York Times* (May 14, 2018).

133 **spent 17.6 percent of its GDP:** Kurani, Wager et al., "How Has U.S. Spending on Healthcare Changed over Time?" Kurani, Wager et al. also note that in 2020, healthcare spending rose sharply to 19.6 percent of GDP because of COVID-19.

133 **medical expenditures will grow:** CMS, NHE Fact Sheet (December 15, 2021).

133 **the bottom of the OECD:** Wager, Ortaliza et al., "How Does Health Spending in the U.S. Compare to Other Countries?"; Eric C. Schneider, Arnav Shah et al., "Mirror, Mirror 2021: Reflecting Poorly: Health Care in the U.S. Compared to Other High-Income Countries," report by the Commonwealth Fund; and America's Health Rankings, United Health Foundation, 2021 annual report.

134 **freestanding surgery centers:** Data on the industry are available in "Ambulatory Surgical Center Services," chapter 6 of the Medicare Payment Advisory Commission (MedPAC) March 2021 Report to the Congress: Medicare Payment Policy. See the investigation of patient harm at ambulatory surgery centers by Christina Jewett and Mark Alesia, "As Surgery Centers Boom, Patients Are Paying with Their Lives," Kaiser Health News (2018). The Ambulatory Surgery Center Association (ASCA), a lobbying group, stresses savings to government healthcare as one of the industry's primary aims and achievements: see ASCA's statement in Advancing Surgical Care, "Medicare Cost Savings."

134 **private equity (PE) firms are driving:** See references in the Chapter 6 note **private healthcare industries emerged.** For the further data and details that follow, see "Private Equity Firms Invest Record $150 Billion in Healthcare Sector," Consultancy.eu (March 28, 2022); Molly Redden, "Private Equity Is Gobbling Up Hospice Chains and Getting Involved in the Business of Dying," *HuffPost* (December 21, 2021); and John Summers, "As Private Equity Comes to Dominate Autism Services . . . ," *The Nation* (April 2, 2021).

134 **SEC officials have denounced:** Andrew J. Bowden, "Spreading Sunshine in Private Equity," speech at the Private Fund Compliance Forum (May 6, 2014); Andrew Ceresney, "Securities Enforcement Forum West 2016 Keynote Address: Private Equity Enforcement," (May 12, 2016); Gary Gensler, "Prepared Remarks at the Institutional Limited Partners Association Summit" (November 10, 2021);

and Henry Bregstein, Wendy E. Cohen et al., "SEC Staff Observes Practices of Private Fund Advisers That Raise Concerns," National Law Review (2022).

135 **Trends at hospices and nursing homes:** Details here and following, Steffie Woolhandler, personal communication. On hospices, see Joshua E. Perry and Robert C. Stone, "In the Business of Dying," J Law Med Ethics (2011); and Lynne Peeples, "Are For-Profit Hospices Cherry-Picking Patients?" Reuters (February 2, 2011). Regarding nursing homes, see Tanya Kessler, "Involuntary Nursing Home Discharges: A Fast Track from Nursing Homes to Homeless Shelters," a report by Mobilization for Justice (2021); Jessica Silver-Greenberg and Amy Julia Harris, "'They Just Dumped Him Like Trash': Nursing Homes Evict Vulnerable Residents," *New York Times* (July 23, 2020); and the ongoing investigation of nursing-home discharges by the HHS Office of the Inspector General (https://oig.hhs.gov/reports-and-publications/workplan/summary/wp-summary-0000541.asp). For a sampling of the considerable body of literature on involuntary discharges in other medical settings, see Paul J. Eliason, Paul L. E. Grieco et al., "Strategic Patient Discharge: The Case of Long-Term Care Hospitals," Am Econ Rev (2018); Paula Chatterjee, Mingyu Qi et al., "Association Between High Discharge Rates of Vulnerable Patients and Skilled Nursing Facility Copayments," JAMA Intern Med (2019); and Leigh Page, "Are More Doctors Cherry-Picking and Lemon-Dropping Patients?" Medscape (February 15, 2017).

135 **"There's no constitutional right":** Steffie Woolhandler, personal communication.

136 **$4.1 trillion annual medical bill:** Kurani, Ortaliza et al., "How Has U.S. Spending on Healthcare Changed over Time?" For falling US life expectancy and what economists Anne Case and Angus Deaton term "deaths of despair" in the white American working class, see Anne Case and Angus Deaton, *Deaths of Despair and the Future of Capitalism* (Princeton, 2020); Anne Case and Angus Deaton, "Life Expectancy in Adulthood Is Falling for Those without a BA Degree," PNAS (2021); and USRDS Annual Data Report 2021, ESRD, Mortality—for example, figure 6.1 (https://adr.usrds.org/2021/end-stage-renal-disease/6-mortality).

136 **And why life spans:** See references in the Chapter 2 note **"survival rate in the United States,"** especially Eric Weinhandl, "Troubling Health Trends in the New USRDS Annual Data Report," Nephrol News Issues (2018).

136 **Woolhandler stresses that this situation:** Steffie Woolhandler, personal communication.

136 **has reached similar conclusions:** Ryan McDevitt, personal communication.

8. MUSKETEERS

137 **A villain clad all in black:** DaVita in-house video, "Musketeer Skit" (no date). See also references in the Chapter 3 note **The atmosphere at a Nationwide**.

138 **Havian, a former federal prosecutor:** Eric Havian, personal communication.

138 **"The musketeers skit shows":** Quotations and details in this section, except

where otherwise noted, are from personal communication with David Barbetta, Eric Havian, Daniel Barbir and Alon Vainer (the latter two before their legal settlement with DaVita in 2015). See also United States et al. ex rel. David Barbetta v. DaVita Inc. and Total Renal Care Inc., case number 1:09-cv-02175-WJM, US District Court for the District of Colorado, first amended complaint (December 23, 2011); the United States complaint in intervention in the same case (October 22, 2014); and United States ex rel. Alon J. Vainer and Daniel D. Barbir v. DaVita Inc. and Gambro Healthcare Inc., case number 1:07-cv-2509, US District Court for the Northern District of Georgia, Atlanta Division, fourth amended complaint (July 25, 2011).

140 **In the Deal Depot:** Details about the Deal Depot, HIPPER compression and so on, are available in United States et al. ex rel. David Barbetta v. DaVita Inc. and Total Renal Care Inc.; and the United States complaint in intervention in the same case. Clarifications via personal communication with David Barbetta and Eric Havian.

141 **spelled out by Bryan Parker:** This exchange is reproduced in United States et al. ex rel. David Barbetta v. DaVita Inc. and Total Renal Care Inc.

141 **"shouldn't actually *do* anything wrong":** David Barbetta, personal communication.

142 **Deal Depot's "competitive hotspots":** David Barbetta, personal communication; and see United States complaint in intervention in Barbetta's case. All figures and the "bag of money" quotation are contained in the complaint.

143 **"winning practices":** United States complaint in intervention in Barbetta's case.

144 **noncompetition, nonsolicitation and nondisparagement clauses:** United States complaint in intervention in Barbetta's case.

144 **"We saw Kent Thiry's fingerprints":** Eric Havian, personal communication.

145 **"For years there were people":** Eric Havian, personal communication.

145 **seven full-time CFOs and six interim CFOs:** David Barbetta, personal communication. Turnover in the CFO position can be traced by examining the firm's 10-K and 10-Q financial statements, as well as its press releases.

145 **opened a grand jury investigation:** See Robin Fields, "Federal Grand Jury Probes Major Dialysis Provider, ProPublica (August 4, 2011).

145 **all civil and criminal charges:** "DaVita to Pay $350 Million to Resolve Allegations of Illegal Kickbacks," Department of Justice press release (2011) (https://www.justice.gov/opa/pr/davita-pay-350-million-resolve-allegations-illegal-kickbacks). The total settlement consisted of $389 million for the federal case, including legal fees, plus an additional $11 million settlement paid to five state Medicaid programs.

145 **David Barbetta continued to meet:** For this and what follows, David Barbetta, personal communication.

147 **records of recidivist wrongdoing:** For a good overview, see Maggie Mahar, *Money-Driven Medicine* (New York, 2009). Useful online resources include the Good Jobs First online Violation Tracker and the Federal Contractor Miscon-

duct Database of the Project on Government Oversight (POGO), where hospital companies, pharmaceutical companies, and medical device, biotech and other healthcare-related firms are amply represented. Recent litigation against pharmaceutical companies is neatly tallied in Sammy Almashat, Ryan Lang et al., "Twenty-Seven Years of Pharmaceutical Industry Criminal and Civil Penalties," report for Public Citizen (2018). On the rise of settlements, deferred prosecution agreements and nonprosecution agreements as tools to avoid the prosecution of defendant firms and individuals, see Brandon Garrett, *Too Big to Jail* (Cambridge, MA, 2014); and Jesse Eisinger, *The Chickenshit Club* (New York, 2017).

147 **"Certain very large healthcare companies":** Jacob Elberg, personal communication.

147 **paid large settlements for Medicare fraud:** Whistleblower law firms report that there has been an "onslaught of fraud in the kidney dialysis industry" (https://bergermontague.com/department-of-justice-combats-dialysis-ind ustry-false-claims); that "most of the major renal care facilities in the US have come under investigation for fraud in recent years, including Fresenius Medical Care America, DaVita Inc., Renal Care Group, Quest Diagnostics, and Bone Care International" (https://www.lawyersandsettlements.com/ legal-news/drugs-medical/gambro-00153.html); and that "horror stories" abound in the industry (https://www.daviscrump.com/blog/chapter-9 -horror-stories/). See also the further discussion below of allegations of wrongdoing by individual dialysis firms.

147 **receiving subpoenas and fending off lawsuits:** Jack Anderson, "Dialysis Clinics Probed by Government Auditors," *Alton Telegraph* (June 9, 1982) (archived at https://newspaperarchive.com/alton-telegraph-jun-09-1982-p-46), and references in the Chapter 6 note **practiced what they preached**.

147 **massive criminal and civil investigations:** See references in the Chapter 6 note **subsequent criminal and civil proceedings**.

147 **underwent fraud investigations:** Charlotte Snow, "Feds Probe Vivra: Investigation Relates to Dialysis Firm's Lab Practices," *Modern Healthcare* (January 6, 1997) (https://www.modernhealthcare.com/article/19970106/ PREMIUM/701060318/feds-probe-vivra-investigation-relates-to-dialysis -firm-s-lab-practices); "Vivra's Ex-Venture, Renal Unit Are Focus of U.S. Billing Probe," *Wall Street Journal* (December 30, 1996); "Gambro Healthcare, Inc. Agrees to Pay $53 Million for Overcharging Medicare, Medicaid & Tricare," Department of Justice press release (July 13, 2000) (https:// www.justice.gov/archive/opa/pr/2000/July/399civ.htm); and J. P. Bender, "Firm Pays $53 Million to Settle Fraud Case," *South Florida Business Journal* (August 7, 2000) (https://www.bizjournals.com/southflorida/ stories/2000/08/07/story3.html).

147 **several top Vivra executives:** Steven Bander, personal communication. See also references in the Chapter 6 notes **In 1997, Gambro bought** and **"a pig in a**

poke." See also Stephen D. Moore, "Sweden's Incentive AB to Buy Vivra of the U.S. for $1.6 Billion," *Wall Street Journal* (May 6, 1997).

147 **Gambro itself was:** See references in the Chapter 6 note **poor financial performance and crushing fraud.** Also Steven Bander, personal communication.

148 **bought up by DaVita:** See DaVita press releases "DaVita to Acquire Gambro Healthcare" (December 7, 2004), and "DaVita Closes Gambro Healthcare Acquisition" (October 5, 2005).

148 **$1.5 billion in legal settlements:** In 2014, David Barbetta's case regarding kickbacks settled for $400 million (David Barbetta, personal communication; and Department of Justice press release [https://www.justice.gov/opa/pr/davita-pay-350-million-resolve-allegations-illegal-kickbacks]). In 2015, the Vainer/Barbir case regarding drug wastage settled for $495 million (Tamara Chuang, "DaVita Will Pay $495 Million to Settle Atlanta Whistle-blower Case," *Denver Post* [May 4, 2015]). Also in 2015, kickback allegations were settled for $22.4 million (https://violationtracker.goodjobsfirst.org/violation-tracker/-davita-healthcare-partners). In 2017, a case regarding improper billing practices and unlawful financial inducements to federal healthcare program beneficiaries settled for $63.7 million (https://www.justice.gov/opa/pr/davita-rx-agrees-pay-637-million-resolve-false-claims-act-allegations). In 2018, the firm paid $270 million to resolve allegations of inflated Medicare payments (https://www.justice.gov/opa/pr/medicare-advantage-provider-pay-270-million-settle-false-claims-act-liabilities). Also in 2018, a federal jury in Colorado ordered DaVita to pay $383.5 million in three wrongful death lawsuits (https://www.reuters.com/article/us-davita-lawsuit-idUSKBN1JO1S4). Additional smaller settlements of $6 million, $3.4 million and $3.2 million were paid between 2014 and 2018 for lawsuits concerning various violations listed in the Good Jobs First Violation Tracker (https://violationtracker.goodjobsfirst.org/parent/davita-healthcare-partners).

148 **indicted two years later:** "DaVita Inc. and Former CEO Indicted in Ongoing Investigation of Labor Market Collusion in Health Care Industry," Department of Justice press release (July 15, 2021) (https://www.justice.gov/opa/pr/davita-inc-and-former-ceo-indicted-ongoing-investigation-labor-market-collusion-health-care). See also "Sherman Antitrust Act," Legal Information Institute, Cornell Law School.

148 **jury acquitted Thiry and DaVita:** "DaVita and Its Former CEO Acquitted of U.S. Antitrust Charges," Reuters (April 18, 2022).

148 **a variety of alleged civil and criminal misconduct:** See lawsuits brought against Fresenius for a range of alleged wrongdoing listed in the Good Jobs First Violation Tracker (https://violationtracker.goodjobsfirst.org/?company_op=starts&company=Fresenius&offense_group=&agency_code=). For the alleged Foreign Corrupt Practices Act (FCPA) violations, see "Fresenius Medical Care Agrees to Pay $231 Million in Criminal Penalties and Disgorgement to Resolve Foreign Corrupt Practices Act Charges," Department of Justice

press release (March 29, 2019) (https://www.justice.gov/opa/pr/fresenius
-medical-care-agrees-pay-231-million-criminal-penalties-and-disgorgement
-resolve).

148 **announced its latest whistleblower suit:** Department of Justice press
release, "United States Files Claims Alleging Fresenius Vascular Care,
Inc. Defrauded Medicare and Other Healthcare Programs by Billing for
Unnecessary Procedures Performed on Dialysis Patients" (July 13, 2022)
(https://www.justice.gov/usao-edny/pr/united-states-files-claims-alleging
-fresenius-vascular-care-inc-defrauded-medicare-and).

148 **other legal "contingencies":** Fresenius annual report 2021, under "Other
Notes—Commitments and Contingencies."

149 **drugs used for executions:** "German Drug Maker Sues to Halt Planned Execution in Nebraska," Agence France-Press via *The Guardian* (August 8, 2018); and
Rory Smith, "Judge Denies Effort by German Drug Maker to Block Nebraska
Execution," CNN (August 11, 2018) (https://edition.cnn.com/2018/08/09/
health/nebraska-lethal-injection-execution-lawsuit-intl/index.html).

149 **sent an internal memorandum:** Fresenius Medical Care, Internal Memo, Re:
Dialysate Bicarbonate, Alkalosis and Patient Safety (November 4, 2011). See
also Andrew Pollack, "Dialysis Company's Failure to Warn of Product Risk
Draws Inquiry," *New York Times* (June 14, 2012); and Andrew Pollack, "Dialysis
Equipment Maker Settles Lawsuit for $250 Million," *New York Times* (February
18, 2016).

149 **Fresenius claimed that the data:** Pollack, "Dialysis Equipment Maker Settles
Lawsuit for $250 Million."

149 **Scrushy, the flamboyant CEO:** See Mahar, *Money-Driven Medicine*; Milt
Freudenheim and Eric Lichtblau, "Former HealthSouth Chief Indicted by U.S."
New York Times (November 5, 2003); Kyle Whitmire, "Ex-Governor and Executive Convicted of Bribery," *New York Times* (June 30, 2006); and "Scrushy Ordered
to Pay Investors $2.9 Billion," Associated Press via *NBC News* (June 18, 2009).

149 **In December 2002, Columbia/HCA:** See the brief description of Scott's background on the "Team Rick Scott" website (https://rickscottforflorida.com/
meet-rick). Regarding the HCA fraud litigation, see "Largest Health Care Fraud
Case in U.S. History Settled: HCA Investigation Nets Record Total of $1.7 Bil-
lion," Department of Justice press release (June 26, 2003) (https://www.justice
.gov/archive/opa/pr/2003/June/03_civ_386.htm); Kurt Eichenwald, "HCA Is
Said to Reach Deal on Settlement of Fraud Case," *New York Times* (December
18, 2002); and Aaron Sharockman, "Rick Scott and the Fraud Case of Columbia/
HCA," PolitiFact (June 11, 2010). See also allegations by successful HCA whistleblower John Schilling in his book *Undercover* (Bloomington, IN, 2010), and
more recently in Mary Ellen Klas, "HCA Whistleblower Revives Claim That
Scott Knew of Fraud," *Tampa Bay Times* (October 6, 2014). More on Scott's management style at Columbia/HCA is found in Mahar, *Money-Driven Medicine*.

149 **One of the most graphic cases:** On the saga of NME, see references in the

Chapter 3 note **early for-profit hospital chains**. Another essential source was personal communication with James Moriarty, a plaintiff attorney who litigated against NME. Good background information is contained in Moriarty's brief account of his experiences, titled "National Medical Enterprises" (https://www .moriarty.com/Mass_Action_Case_Results/National_Medical_Enterprises); and in the appeals decision Morton v. National Medical Enterprises, Inc., District of Columbia Court of Appeals, appeal number 725 A.2d 462 (D.C. 1999) (decided February 11, 1999). See also "The Profits of Misery: How Inpatient Psychiatric Treatment Bilks the System and Betrays Our Trust," hearing before the Select Committee on Children, Youth, and Families, US House of Representatives (April 28, 1992); and Erica C. Hutchins, Richard G. Frank et al., "The Evolving Private Psychiatric Inpatient Market," J Behav Health Serv Res (2011).

150 **sweeping cost-cutting programs:** Personal communication with Jim Moriarty, supplemented by references in the previous note.

150 **"put heads on beds at any cost":** Personal communication with Jim Moriarty, quoting an internal memorandum that he produced in court papers, sent by a medical director at an NME facility in California to Richard Eamer himself.

150 **"In many ways," Richard Eamer:** Quoted in "Tenet Healthcare Corporation History," Funding Universe (no date).

151 **fêted by the business community:** See, as something of a curiosity, the February 13, 2013, resolution by the Los Angeles City Council, in which the council publicly "honors Richard K. Eamer and salutes him for his well-earned status in healthcare, law, animal welfare and wishes him continued success." For Eamer's 1991 earnings, see "Heinz Chief Tops Forbes' 1991 List of Highest Paid CEOS," *Deseret News* (May 11, 1992) (https://www.deseret.com/1992/5/11/18983380/ heinz-chief-tops-forbes-1991-list-of-highest-paid-ceos).

151 **"The corporate culture at NME":** For this and what follows, Jim Moriarty, personal communication.

151 **the video's theme song:** Also quoted by J. Michael Wynne, "The Impact of Financial Pressures on Clinical Care: Lessons from Corporate Medicine" (https://documents.uow.edu.au/~bmartin/dissent/documents/health/corpmed .html).

152 **Christy Scheck:** For information on Scheck's confinement and death, see Mahar, *Money-Driven Medicine*; David R. Olmos, "NME Admits Responsibility in Girl's Suicide," *Los Angeles Times* (July 26, 1994); and Calvin Sims, "Hospital Chain Said to Settle Fraud Case for $300 Million," *New York Times* (April 15, 1994). Also Jim Moriarty, personal communication.

152 **a $101 million settlement:** Jim Moriarty, personal communication.

152 **no senior managers were prosecuted:** Here and following, Jim Moriarty, personal communication; Stephen Klaidman, *Coronary* (New York, 2007); and Mahar, *Money-Driven Medicine*.

152 **eight of NME's original twelve:** "Grassley Investigates Tenet Healthcare's

Use of Federal Tax Dollars," letter from Chuck Grassley to Trevor Fetter, Acting Chief Executive Officer and President of Tenet Healthcare (September 5, 2003).

153 **"ethically and morally bankrupt"**: "Grassley Investigates Tenet Healthcare's Use of Federal Tax Dollars," letter from Chuck Grassley to Trevor Fetter.

153 **"Failure to remove or discipline"**: Jacob Elberg, personal communication.

153 **NME subsidiaries that spun off**: Subsidiaries included Hillhaven (https://www.latimes.com/archives/la-xpm-1989-01-06-fi-317-story.html); Recovery Centers of America (https://www.encyclopedia.com/books/politics-and-business-magazines/national-medical-enterprises-inc); and Medfield (https://www.company-histories.com/Tenet-Healthcare-Corporation-Company-History.html). Hillhaven later merged with Vencor. For their assorted brushes with the law, see, for example, Recovery Centers of America (https://www.statnews.com/2017/08/25/recovery-centers-of-america-addiction and https://www.wbur.org/news/2017/09/01/addiction-treatment-quality); Hillhaven/Vencor (https://www.leagle.com/decision/19841232687s w2d54511222, https://www.bmartin.cc/dissent/documents/health/vencor_fraud.html and https://law.justia.com/cases/california/court-of-appeal/4th/50/632.html); and Medfield (https://casetext.com/case/liles-v-pia-medfield-inc and https://casetext.com/case/gladwin-v-medfield-corp).

153 **Medical Ambulatory Care**: See details in "DaVita Inc.," the useful profile of the firm's genesis and early years at the Reference for Business website (https://www.referenceforbusiness.com/history/Ci-Da/DaVita-Inc.html).

153 **Total Renal Care**: See references in the Chapter 3 note **He calls his firm a "Village,"** especially Robert L. Shook, "All for One and One for All," in *Heart & Soul* (New York, 2010). See also "Dialysis Services Provider to Pay $25 Million in Fraud Case," Bloomberg News via the *Los Angeles Times* (July 26, 2000); Sharon Bernstein, "Total Renal Faces Lawsuit over Earnings," *Los Angeles Times* (February 24, 1999); and "Former Head of Total Renal Care Dies at 72," Nephrol News Issues (2014).

153 **Behind the jazzy new name**: See especially the earlier section on David Barbetta's experiences at DaVita, and references in the earlier notes **"The musketeers skit shows"** and **"We saw Kent Thiry's fingerprints."** See also references in the Chapter 3 notes **He calls his firm a "Village"** and **Success in the dialysis business**, the Chapter 7 note **high-margin private-payor patients**, and the earlier note **A villain clad all in black**. In particular, see United States et al. ex rel. David Barbetta v. DaVita Inc. and Total Renal Care Inc.; the United States complaint in intervention in the same case; and United States ex rel. Alon J. Vainer and Daniel D. Barbir v. DaVita Inc. and Gambro Healthcare Inc.

154 **"DaVita first mimicked"**: Jim Moriarty, personal communication.

154 **"They've lost control of their lives"**: "Betty Smith," personal communication.

154 **"We've sometimes had to choose"**: Sheldon Winters, personal communication.

155 **"I'm six foot seven"**: William Sarsfield, personal communication.

155 **"On any given day"**: Sherry Thompson, personal communication.

155 **"You sit next to someone"**: Gregg Hansen, personal communication.

156 **"Death is a constant presence"**: William Sarsfield, personal communication.

156 **"Nephrology is a terribly tough job"**: Steven Rosansky, personal communication.

156 **"When I started in this business"**: "Betty Smith," personal communication.

156 **involuntary discharges spiked**: "Betty Smith" and Arlene Mullin, personal communication. For further information on the practice of involuntary discharge, see Chapter 3 regarding the involuntary discharges of Carrie Brito, Justin Charles Evans and others, with associated references.

For the considerable literature on patient-provider conflicts in dialysis, "problem patients," blackballing, and so forth, see "Decreasing Dialysis Patient-Provider Conflict (DPC) Provider Manual" by the National Task Force Position Statement on Involuntary Discharge, particularly the executive summary (https://www.annanurse.org/download/reference/health/position/patientProviderConflict.pdf), as well as the task force's full report (https://media.esrdnetworks.org/documents/DPPCJune2005report.pdf). See also Adnan Hashmi and Alvin H. Moss, "Treating Difficult or Disruptive Dialysis Patients: Practical Strategies Based on Ethical Principles," Nat Clin Pract Nephrol (2008), mentioning that "For more than a decade, dialysis units have had to contend with an increasing number of difficult or disruptive dialysis patients"; Mark E. Williams and Jenny Kitsen, "The Involuntarily Discharged Dialysis Patient: Conflict (of Interest) with Providers," Adv Chronic Kidney Dis (2005); Stella L. Smetanka, "Who Will Protect the 'Disruptive' Dialysis Patient?" Am J Law Med (2006); "Barriers to Outpatient Dialysis Placement," ESRD Special Study, Final Project Report July 1, 2005—June 30, 2006; "Position Statement on Involuntary Transfer and Discharge of Dialysis Patients," ESRD Network 5 (October 27, 2006) (https://www.qirn5.org/Dialysis-Providers/Involuntary-Discharge.aspx); Amar A. Desai, Roger Bolus et al., "Is There 'Cherry Picking' in the ESRD Program?" Clin J Am Soc Nephrol (2009); J. Clint Parker, "Cherry Picking in ESRD: An Ethical Challenge in the Era of Pay for Performance," Semin Dial (2011); Edward R. Jones and Richard S. Goldman, "Managing Disruptive Behavior by Patients and Physicians," Clin J Am Soc Nephrol (2015); Danielle Janosevic, Aileen X. Wang et al., "Difficult Patient Behavior in Dialysis Facilities," Blood Purif (2019); Amber M. Borges, "Emerging Trends in Discharging Disruptive Dialysis Patients," J Nephrol Soc Work (2013); Christos Argyropoulos, "Involuntary Discharges from the Dialysis Unit," ESRD Network 15 Conference Call (May 13, 2019) (https://www.slideshare.net/chrisarg/involuntary-discharges-from-the-dialysis-unit); and "Involuntary Discharge (IVD) Process," presentation by the ESRD Network of Texas (August 24, 2017).

Excellent recent posts and videos concerning involuntary discharge, often with revealing responses from victims of discharge in the comments section, include: Beth Witten (a veteran social worker and dialysis industry expert),

"Involuntary Dialysis Clinic Discharges: Can More Be Avoided?" Home Dialysis Central website (April 14, 2022) (https://homedialysis.org/news -and-research/blog/483-involuntary-dialysis-clinic-discharges-can-more-be -avoided); "Involuntary Discharge from Dialysis: Has This Happened to You?" Urban Renal Talk, a show streamed live on July 17, 2020, that was hosted by Urban Kidney Alliance leader Tamika Ganues and by Steve L. Belcher, dialysis RN and Executive Director of the Urban Kidney Alliance (https://www .youtube.com/watch?v=YWu7KoB4fxk); Robert Bear, "Involuntary Discharge from Dialysis: A Health Care Practice Like No Other," KevinMD.com (January 9, 2017) (https://www.kevinmd.com/2017/01/involuntary-discharge -dialysis-health-care-practice-like-no.html); and Beth Witten, "Involuntary Discharge: What Happened to the Oath 'First, Do No Harm'?" Home Dialysis Central website (August 7, 2014). On the related question of so-called "behavioral contracts," see Beth Witten, "Is a Patient-Centered Dialysis Behavior Contract Possible?" Home Dialysis Central (November 9, 2017).

156 **watched the trend:** "Betty Smith," personal communication.

157 **an ongoing survey of violence:** Jane Kwatcher, "Staying Safe from Violence at Dialysis," *Kidney Citizen* (https://www.dpcedcenter.org/wp-content/ uploads/2020/06/staying-safe-from-violence-at-dialysis-english.pdf).

158 **"Some dialysis techs and nurses":** Personal communication with a longtime dialysis social worker, who spoke on condition of anonymity.

158 **noted the inherent authoritarianism:** Alonzo Plough, personal communication, and his book *Borrowed Time* (Philadelphia, 1986).

158 **"the prison camp guard" syndrome:** Leonard Stern, personal communication.

158 **"psychologically pushed into a corner":** "Betty Smith," personal communication.

158 **"In my opinion":** Robert Bear, personal communication.

159 **illegitimate as a motive for discharge:** This is explained in detail in the "Decreasing Dialysis Patient-Provider Conflict (DPC) Provider Manual"; and the post by Beth Witten, "Involuntary Discharge: What Happened to the Oath 'First, Do No Harm'?"

159 **Peter Laird, a retired doctor:** Peter Laird, personal communication. See Laird's valuable blog, "HemoDoc, From Doctor to Patient: Peter Laird, MD— A Doctor's Blog from a Patient's Perspective."

159 **Gerald and Sherry Thompson challenged:** For the events described in this passage, Gerald and Sherry Thompson, personal communication. Their contentions are supported by an extensive data file they have assembled over time, which contains documents from their clinic; claim details and explanations of benefits from Cigna; correspondence with Arlene Mullin and other potential allies; and memorializations of their experiences. The behavioral contract is "Agreement of Treatment Expectations," [Satellite] WellBound of Memphis, January 2, 2020. The termination letter is "Letter of Discharge," Satellite Healthcare WellBound, May 27, 2020.

161 **undocumented immigrants with kidney failure:** The study cited in what fol-

lows is Julianna West, Hei Kit Chan et al., "Insurance Status and Emergency Department Visits Associated with Hemodialysis in Texas," JAMA Network Open (2020). On this issue, see also Nathan A. Gray, "Cruel Carousel: The Grim Grind of 'Compassionate' Dialysis," AMA J Ethics (2018); Oanh Kieu Nguyen, Miguel A. Vazquez et al., "Association of Scheduled vs Emergency-Only Dialysis with Health Outcomes and Costs in Undocumented Immigrants with End-stage Renal Disease," JAMA Intern Med (2018); and Witten, "Involuntary Dialysis Clinic Discharges: Can More Be Avoided?"

161 **"a ludicrous waste of resources":** Henry Wang, personal communication.

162 **"If the CEO models":** Robert Bear, personal communication.

9. THE FOX IN THE HEN HOUSE

163 **an atypical dialysis patient:** Sources for this section on the dialysis-related experiences of Justin Charles Evans include personal communication with Justin Charles Evans, Arlene Mullin, Debbie Johnson and her sister Henrietta Johnson, together with the documents and recordings that Evans has compiled over time. Also see references in the Chapter 3 notes **Justin Charles Evans; letter to Johnny Isakson; discharged him and harassed; escorted him off the premises;** and **add the gun accusation.**

163 **began canceling treatments:** Justin Charles Evans's memorialization: "Spring and summer of 2017 patients routinely denied treatment due to staffing issues." See also form letter from DaVita Lake Hearn (August 1, 2017), referencing "a challenge with meeting our staffing needs."

164 **critical level of serum potassium:** Preliminary report from Northside Hospital in Atlanta dated July 25, 2017, referencing Evans's hyperkalemia (potassium of 7.5) and his immediate transfer "to the ICU for urgent hemodialysis."

164 **a letter he was drafting:** See reference in the Chapter 3 note **letter to Johnny Isakson.**

164 **passed the Atlanta Twelve's complaint letter to CMS:** Justin Charles Evans and Arlene Mullin, personal communication. This procedure fits the pattern noted by Kenneth Bays, Brent Smith and other patients who testified at the 2000 Senate hearing on dialysis—see references in the Chapter 6 note **Grassley's Senate Subcommittee.**

164 **the same ESRD group:** See references in the Chapter 6 note **Grassley's Senate Subcommittee.**

165 **several of the signatories:** Here and following, Justin Charles Evans and Arlene Mullin, personal communication; and recordings of select conversations between Evans and clinic staff. Also personal communication with Debbie Johnson and Henrietta Johnson.

165 **"tried to make me mad":** Justin Charles Evans, personal communication.

165 **"You should have seen Justin's face":** Arlene Mullin, personal communication.

165 **On the morning of December 29, 2017:** Sources for this scene include personal

communication with Justin Charles Evans, Arlene Mullin and the registered nurse involved (who spoke on condition of anonymity), as well as the police report, memorialization, recorded conversations and other documentation compiled by Justin Charles Evans (for which see annotations in the Chapter 3 notes **escorted him off the premises** and **add the gun accusation**).

166 **during the ambulance ride:** Justin Charles Evans and Arlene Mullin, personal communication.

166 **This produced no results:** Justin Charles Evans, personal communication.

166 **"hadn't followed any of the procedures":** Arlene Mullin, personal communication.

166 **Ceasar, a firebrand civil rights activist:** Personal communication with Ron Ceasar, Arlene Mullin and Justin Charles Evans.

166 **While speaking with staff members:** Here and following, Justin Charles Evans and Arlene Mullin, personal communication.

167 **ordeal began all over again:** For Evans's negative experiences at the new clinic, Justin Charles Evans and Arlene Mullin, personal communication. The termination letter from the nephrologist and the facility administrator at DaVita Northlake is dated October 12, 2021. It cites "missed treatments" and "nonadherent behavior" as the motivations for discharging Evans.

167 **clinic managers changed their story:** Arlene Mullin and Justin Charles Evans, personal communication; and a document of July 12, 2021, from a vascular surgery center reporting inadequate Medicare coverage as the reason for denying Evans an important procedure on his fistula.

167 **attended an advocacy meeting:** Here through the end of the section, Arlene Mullin and Justin Charles Evans, personal communication.

168 **Evans grew up in Lowndes County:** Justin Charles Evans, personal communication.

168 **aware of this kind of neighborhood:** Here and following: Alonzo Plough, personal communication; and Alonzo L. Plough, *Borrowed Time* (Philadelphia, 1986).

168 **Richard Rettig, the meticulous historian:** Richard A. Rettig, Keith Norris et al., "Chronic Kidney Disease in the United States: A Public Policy Imperative," Clin J Am Soc Nephrol (2008).

168 **"death by zip code":** Marcel Reid, personal communication.

169 **Plough is talking about Kaufman:** Xiaoxi Zeng, Jing Liu et al., "Associations Between Socioeconomic Status and Chronic Kidney Disease," J Epidemiol Community Health (2018); and—from the United Kingdom—Aminu K. Bello, Jean Peters et al., "Socioeconomic Status and Chronic Kidney Disease at Presentation to a Renal Service in the United Kingdom," Clin J Am Soc Nephrol (2008).

169 **"food deserts and food swamps":** Milda Saunders, personal communication.

170 **Hispanics as a group suffer kidney failure:** USRDS Annual Data Report 2021, ESRD, "Incidence, Prevalence, Patient Characteristics, and Treatment Modalities," figure 1.4, Race/Ethnicity tab (https://adr.usrds.org/2021/

end-stage-renal-disease/1-incidence-prevalence-patient-characteristics-and
-treatment-modalities).

170 **is genetically diverse:** Here and below regarding kidney disease among Hispanics, see Nisa Desai, Claudia M. Lora et al., "CKD and ESRD in US Hispanics," Am J Kidney Dis (2019); and Ana C. Ricardo, Matthew Shane Loop et al., "Incident Chronic Kidney Disease Risk among Hispanics/Latinos in the United States," J Am Soc Nephrol (2020).

170 **renal disease among Asian Americans:** USRDS Annual Data Report 2021, ESRD, "Incidence, Prevalence, Patient Characteristics, and Treatment Modalities," figure 1.4. For the kidney disease rate among Native Hawaiians and Pacific Islanders, see David Na'ai and Kalani L. Raphael, "Trouble in Paradise: CKD in Native Hawaiians and Pacific Islanders," CJASN (2019); and Jie Xiang, Hal Morgenstern et al., "Incidence of ESKD among Native Hawaiians and Pacific Islanders Living in the 50 US States and Pacific Island Territories," Am J Kidney Dis (2020).

170 **more than 570 different tribes:** See Federally Recognized Indian Tribes and Resources for Native Americans, at USA.gov.

170 **kidney failure among Native Americans:** USRDS Annual Data Report 2021, ESRD, "Incidence, Prevalence, Patient Characteristics, and Treatment Modalities," figure 1.4. Regarding the higher incidence of chronic disease among certain Native American populations, see Andrew S. Narva, "The Spectrum of Kidney Disease in American Indians," Kidney Int (2003); Ewan R. Pearson, "Dissecting the Etiology of Type 2 Diabetes in the Pima Indian Population," Diabetes (2015); and Leslie O. Schulz and Lisa S. Chaudhari, "High-Risk Populations: The Pimas of Arizona and Mexico," Curr Obes Rep (2015). Regarding the "thrifty gene" hypothesis, see "Stories from The Pima Indians: Pathfinders for Health," National Institute of Diabetes and Digestive and Kidney Diseases (NIDDK).

171 **exposure to uranium:** See "On Uranium Mining: Contamination and Criticality," a written statement of the Navajo Nation prepared for the House Committee on Natural Resources, Subcommittee on Energy and Mineral Resources (2019).

171 **linked to uranium poisoning:** Carrie Brito, personal communication.

171 **hardest hit by dialysis:** See "Race, Ethnicity, & Kidney Disease," NIDDK (https://www.niddk.nih.gov/health-information/kidney-disease/race-ethnicity).

171 **the APOL1 allele:** Milda Saunders, personal communication; David J. Friedman and Martin R. Pollak, "Genetics of Kidney Failure and the Evolving Story of APOL1," J Clin Invest (2011); and Parnaz Daneshpajouhnejad, Avi Z. Rosenberg et al., "The Evolving Story of Apolipoprotein L1 Nephropathy," Nat Rev Nephrol (2022).

171 **Before medical school:** Here and following, Milda Saunders, personal communication. For a small sampling of her numerous publications, see Milda R. Saunders, Ana C. Ricardo et al., "Neighborhood Socioeconomic Status and

Risk of Hospitalization in Patients with Chronic Kidney Disease," Medicine (2020); Milda R. Saunders, Haena Lee et al., "Racial Disparities in Reaching the Renal Transplant Waitlist," Clin Transplant (2015); Milda R. Saunders, Haena Lee et al., "Proximity Does Not Equal Access: Racial Disparities in Access to High Quality Dialysis Facilities," J Racial Ethn Health Disparities (2014); and Milda R. Saunders and Marshall H. Chin, "Variation in Dialysis Quality Measures by Facility, Neighborhood and Region," Med Care (2013).

172 **Even the estimated glomerular filtration rate:** Milda Saunders, personal communication; Milda R. Saunders with Chi-yuan Hsu, Wei Yang et al., "Race, Genetic Ancestry, and Estimating Kidney Function in CKD," NEJM (2021); and Lesley A. Inker, Nwamaka D. Eneanya et al., "New Creatinine- and Cysta-tin C-Based Equations to Estimate GFR without Race," NEJM (2021).

172 **removal of the race modifier:** Cynthia Delgado, Mukta Baweja et al., "A Unify-ing Approach for GFR Estimation: Recommendations of the NKF-ASN Task Force on Reassessing the Inclusion of Race in Diagnosing Kidney Disease," JASN (2021).

172 **improving access to transplants:** Milda Saunders, personal communication.

172 **"It starts with the Black diet":** Megallan Handford, personal communication.

173 **"By far the majority":** Arlene Mullin, personal communication.

173 **In financial terms, a racial bias:** For this demographic data, see Christa Fields, Juliette Cubanski et al., "Profile of Medicare Beneficiaries by Race and Eth-nicity: A Chartpack," Kaiser Family Foundation (2016); and "Poverty Rate by Race/Ethnicity," Kaiser Family Foundation.

173 **"You should be grateful":** Personal communication with Alonzo Plough and with several patients I've interviewed, including Eric Pickens, Corne-lius Robbins and Pacita Coats-Simpson. The industry bias in favor of private payors, and therefore against publicly insured patients, is widely acknowl-edged by patients and workers alike. See references in the Chapter 7 notes **high-margin private payor patients** and **routinely steered by clinic staff** and the discussions of HIPPERs ("high-paying patients") in Chapters 7 and 8.

173 **"drug-seeking behavior":** Vanessa Winters and Gerald Thompson, for exam-ple, were both accused of drug-seeking behavior.

173 **"A Black patient shows up":** Alonzo Plough, personal communication.

174 **disproportionately high number of COVID-19:** Latoya Hill Follow and Saman-tha Artiga, "COVID-19 Cases and Deaths by Race/Ethnicity: Current Data and Changes over Time," Kaiser Family Foundation (2022); and Anna M. Acosta, Shi-kha Garg et al., "Racial and Ethnic Disparities in Rates of COVID-19-Associated Hospitalization, Intensive Care Unit Admission, and In-Hospital Death in the United States from March 2020 to February 2021," JAMA Network Open (2021).

174 **"COVID-19 made clear":** Alonzo Plough, personal communication. See also Linda Villarosa, *Under the Skin* (New York, 2022).

174 **According to a 2016 study:** Kelly M. Hoffman, Sophie Trawalter et al., "Racial

Bias in Pain Assessment and Treatment Recommendations, and False Beliefs About Biological Differences Between Blacks and Whites," PNAS (2016).

174 **A 2019 article in *Frontiers*:** Xingyu Zhang, Maria Carabello et al., "Racial and Ethnic Disparities in Emergency Department Care and Health Outcomes among Children in the United States," Front Pediatr (2019).

174 **A 2022 paper in the *Journal*:** Yannis K. Valtis, Kristen E. Stevenson et al., "Race and Ethnicity and the Utilization of Security Responses in a Hospital Setting," J Gen Intern Med (2022).

174 **discharges from for-profit, long-term care:** Paul J. Eliason, Paul L. E. Grieco et al., "Strategic Patient Discharge: The Case of Long-Term Care Hospitals," Am Econ Rev (2018).

175 **insiders say that regulation:** My interviews with four former and current executives of ESRD Networks, who spoke on condition of anonymity, are described in what follows.

175 **Stark sent his urgent demand:** "Kidney Dialysis Patients: A Population at Undue Risk?" hearing before the Senate Special Committee on Aging (June 26, 2000).

175 **DeParle left government service:** "Nancy-Ann DeParle and William L. Roper Join DaVita Board of Directors," DaVita press release (June 4, 2001).

175 **employees often seem to have coached:** Many regional ESRD Networks offer online guides on the correct procedure for patient termination. See, for example, "Guide to Completing the Involuntary Discharge (IVD) Process," published by ESRD Networks 8 and 14 (2021).

175 **When Cornelius Robbins called:** Cornelius Robbins, personal communication, and his recording of the call.

176 **Networks routinely share information:** This practice, which was mentioned in the 2000 Senate hearings on dialysis chaired by Chuck Grassley ("Kidney Dialysis Patients: A Population at Undue Risk?"), was described to me by Arlene Mullin and a number of patients—including Vanessa Winters, Justin Charles Evans, Cornelius Robbins and Carrie Brito—as standard procedure.

176 **"chain of fools":** Sherry Thompson, personal communication.

176 **State agencies charged with surveying:** On underfunded, infrequent and inadequate inspection of dialysis facilities for the past quarter-century, see Nigel Jaquiss, "Whistle-blower," *Willamette Week* (March 24, 1999); the 2000 Senate hearing titled "Kidney Dialysis Patients: A Population at Undue Risk?"; "Dialysis Facilities: Problems Remain in Ensuring Compliance with Medicare Quality Standards," GAO report (2003); Robin Fields, "Led by California, Inspection Backlogs Weaken Dialysis Oversight," ProPublica (December 28, 2010); Sehee Kim, Fan Wu et al., "Comparative Effectiveness Analysis of Medicare Dialysis Facility Survey Processes," PLoS ONE (2019); and Duaa Eldeib, "They Were the Pandemic's Perfect Victims," ProPublica (2021).

176 **as Arlene Mullin discovered in Oregon:** Arlene Mullin, personal communication; and Jaquiss, "Whistle-blower."

176 **"Suddenly our workers":** Cass Gualvez, personal communication.

176 **Cornelius Robbins remembers:** Cornelius Robbins, personal communication.

177 **CMS, evidently recognizing that inspections:** See references in the earlier note **State agencies charged with surveying.** On the "Outcomes List," see End Stage Renal Disease Application & Survey & Certification Report (CMS-3427), Supporting Statement—Part A; and the memo to state survey agency directors titled "Revisions to the State Operations Manual (SOM)," Chapter 2, End Stage Renal Disease (ESRD) Program, Ref: QSO 18-22-ESRD (August 10, 2018). Refusal to release the Outcomes List under FOIA: personal communication with PhD healthcare researcher who consults for SEIU-UHW.

177 **Researchers have cross-checked the causes:** Thomas V. Pemeger, Michael J. Klag et al., "Cause of Death in Patients with End-Stage Renal Disease: Death Certificates vs Registry Reports," Am J Public Health (1993); and Simran K. Bhandari, Hui Zhou et al., "Causes of Death in End-Stage Kidney Disease: Comparison Between the United States Renal Data System and a Large Integrated Health Care System," Am J Nephrol (2021).

177 **After publishing *Sorrow's Reward*:** Here and following, Robert Bear, personal communication.

178 **interviewed four former executives:** All four executives spoke on condition of anonymity. I have referred to one of these executives as "Betty Smith" throughout my text. I will refer to the others as "ESRD Executive 2," "ESRD Executive 3" and "ESRD Executive 4."

178 **"a gloriously successful program":** ESRD Executive 2, personal communication.

178 **Formerly the strengths:** Personal communication with all four ESRD executives.

178 **a multimillion-dollar fund:** Personal communication with "Betty Smith," ESRD Executive 2 and ESRD Executive 3; and see "Summary of the ESRD Network Program," CMS memo dated January 27, 2006 (https://www.cms.gov/Medicare/End-Stage-Renal-Disease/ESRDNetworkOrganizations/downloads/ESRDNetworkProgramBackgroundpublic.pdf).

178 **Networks have been subsumed:** Personal communication with all four ESRD executives.

178 **"We bid to win":** Here and following, "Betty Smith," personal communication.

178 **arrival of Thomas Scully:** See reference in the earlier note **DeParle left government service.**

179 **$40 million annually:** ESRD Executive 2, personal communication; and USRDS 2021 Annual Data Report, figure 1.6 (https://adr.usrds.org/2021/end-stage-renal-disease/1-incidence-prevalence-patient-characteristics-and-treatment-modalities). The total tax was estimated as follows: there were 566,614 patients on dialysis in 2021 (the sum of patients on in-center hemodialysis, home hemodialysis and peritoneal dialysis, all of whom produced a $0.50 per-treatment tax for the Network program). Assume each patient received 140 treatments per year (estimated total treatments of 156 [3 treatments per

week times 52 weeks], minus 6 for 2 weeks' hospitalization each year, minus 10 for around one no-show per month = 140). 566,614 multiplied by 140, then multiplied by the per-treatment tax of $0.50, yields $39.66 million.

179 **When one of them asked:** ESRD Executive 2, personal communication. For more information on the CROWNWeb platform, see Oniel Delva, "CROWN-Web: What's in It for You," National Kidney Foundation (2012).

179 **"the gap between the aggregate":** This and the next sentence, ESRD Executive 2, personal communication.

179 **"The last contract that I signed":** "Betty Smith," personal communication.

10. THE WISDOM OF THE KIDNEY

180 **Emanuel Gonzales, a dialysis technician:** Except as noted in what follows, the source for this section is Emanuel Gonzales, personal communication.

181 **"So many of our members":** Cass Gualvez, personal communication.

181 **In 2018, 2020 and again in 2022:** See "Statewide Ballot Initiative Filed in California to Improve Dialysis Patient Care," SEIU-UHW press release (August 9, 2017); California Proposition 23, Dialysis Clinic Requirements Initiative (2020), Ballotpedia; and California Proposition 29, Dialysis Clinic Requirements Initiative (2022), Ballotpedia.

181 **SEIU-UHW brought patients and workers:** Personal communication with Cass Gualvez, Emanuel Gonzales and Megallan Handford.

182 **tears roll down Emerson Padua's face:** Emerson Padua and Amar Bajwa, personal communication.

183 **"four of our patient leaders":** Cass Gualvez, personal communication.

183 **"We realized that our dialysis workers":** Cass Gualvez, personal communication.

183 **began its initiative by documenting:** SEIU-UHW researchers performed an in-depth investigation of public health records, 9-1-1 call logs and other documents concerning dialysis facilities in California. The union has produced a number of press releases, briefing sheets and internal memoranda that cite the results of this research and analyze their implications. For poor conditions in dialysis facilities, see "Why Are There Roaches & Flies in This Clinic?" testimonial by California dialysis worker Roberto Acosta; and "Dialysis Industry Breaks National Record by Spending $110 Million to Oppose California Ballot Initiative, Protect Profits," SEIU-UHW press release (February 4, 2019). Also personal communication with Cass Gualvez, Emanuel Gonzales and Megallan Handford.

183 **revealed 5,190 deficiencies:** "YES on 23," SEIU-UHW briefing memo answering frequently asked questions about Prop 23; and "Protect the Lives of Dialysis Patients Act: Improving Quality of Care for Patients at Dialysis Clinics," SEIU-UHW briefing document on Proposition 23. For infections, see also "Dialysis Industry Breaks National Record," SEIU-UHW press release. The link between infections and time pressure at large dialysis corporations is also described by Paul Eliason, Benjamin Heebsh et al., "How Acquisitions Affect

Firm Behavior and Performance: Evidence from the Dialysis Industry," Q J Econ (2020).

183 **"Wiping bloodstains off the chair"**: California dialysis technician, who spoke on condition of anonymity.

184 **analysis of 9-1-1 calls**: "Los Angeles County 9-1-1 Data from Dialysis Facilities," SEIU-UHW internal memo.

184 **SEIU-UHW organized marches**: Cass Gualvez and Megallan Handford, personal communication.

184 **The first was Proposition 8**: "California Proposition 8, Limits on Dialysis Clinics' Revenue and Required Refunds Initiative (2018)," Ballotpedia. See also "Dialysis Industry Breaks National Record," SEIU-UHW press release. Additional context from Cass Gualvez, personal communication.

184 **"Dialysis Is Life Support"**: The coalition's aims and supporters are detailed on its website (https://dialysislifesupport.com/ab-290-fmc).

184 **threat to shut unprofitable facilities**: See references in the Chapter 6 note **fighting a running battle**.

185 **"When I started in the industry"**: For this incident, Emerson Padua and Cass Gualvez, personal communication. See also "DaVita Fires Employee One Day After Speaking at State Capitol in Support of Bill to Improve Patient Care, Reports SEIU-UHW," Cision PR Newswire (May 25, 2017).

185 **dialysis firms fired twenty-three workers**: Cass Gualvez, personal communication.

185 **Megallan Handford says he saw a video**: Megallan Handford, personal communication.

185 **Kent Thiry made video appearances**: California dialysis nurses and technicians, associated with the SEIU-UHW, who spoke on condition of anonymity.

185 **"That's $110 million that the industry"**: Cass Gualvez, personal communication.

185 **state assemblymember Jim Wood**: "Asm Jim Wood Introduces AB 290 to Prevent Dialysis Companies from Scamming the Health Care System," press release by Jim Wood, 2nd Assembly District (January 28, 2019). See extensive references in notes to Chapter 7, beginning with **routinely steered by clinic staff**. See also the letter to Senior Assistant Attorneys General Tania Ibanez and Nicklas Akers, Office of the California Attorney General, from Feinberg Jackson Worthman & Wasow, on behalf of their client SEIU-UHW, "Re: Complaint Regarding Unfair Business Practices and Charitable Trust Law Violations by the American Kidney Fund's Health Insurance Premium Program" (August 24, 2017); and Michael Hiltzik, "How Profiteering by the Same Dialysis Firms Trying to Kill Proposition 8 Almost Destroyed Obamacare," *Los Angeles Times* (October 11, 2018).

185 **Big Dialysis turned the issue**: Insightful commentary by Michael Hiltzik in the *Los Angeles Times*, including "Dialysis Firms' Profits Are Obscene. What Will Happen if California Tries to Cap Them?" (July 20, 2018); and "Dialysis

Firms Try to Strong-Arm Gov. Newsom into Vetoing a Bill Capping Their Profits" (September 24, 2019). For the injunction, see Jane Doe et al. v. Xavier Becerra et al and Fresenius Medical Care Orange County et al. v. Xavier Becerra et al., case 8:19-cv-02130-DOC-ADS, US District Court for the Central District of California (civil minutes filed December 30, 2019).

186 **industry spent another $105 million:** Samantha Young, "With 'a Lot to Lose,' Dialysis Firms Spend Big, Become California Power Players," *Los Angeles Times* (December 9, 2020), noting that between January 1, 2017, and November 30, 2020, large dialysis firms spent $233 million to defeat ballot initiatives and in lobbying and political contributions.

186 **Seventy-five thousand dialysis industry dollars:** On contributions to Alice Huffman's firm, see Laurel Rosenhall, "California NAACP Leader Resigns Amid Conflict-of-Interest Backlash," CalMatters (November 30, 2020); and Laurel Rosenhall, "California NAACP President Aids Corporate Prop Campaigns—Collects $1.2 Million and Counting," CalMatters (September 25, 2020).

186 **SEIU-UHW brought a third:** Cass Gualvez, personal communication, and California Proposition 29, Dialysis Clinic Requirements Initiative (2022), Ballotpedia.

186 **vigorous post-COVID-19 push:** Cass Gualvez, personal communication; and Michael Sainato, "California Dialysis Clinic Workers Push to Unionize over Short-Staffing and Low Pay," *The Guardian* (February 7, 2023).

187 **a direct legal challenge:** SEIU-UHW administrative complaint, "Re: High-Speed Hemodialysis Has a Disparate Impact on Latino and Asian American Patients" (https://healthlaw.org/wp-content/uploads/2022/01/2022-01-11-HHS-Complaint-final.pdf). See also "SEIU-UHW, NHeLP File Complaint Alleging CA Dialysis Providers Are Violating Civil Rights of Latino and Asian Patients," SEIU-UHW press release (January 11, 2022).

187 **One of the plaintiffs:** SEIU-UHW administrative complaint, "Re: High-Speed Hemodialysis Has a Disparate Impact on Latino and Asian American Patients"; and Roopa Bajwa, personal communication. (Roopa specified that Amar died on July 27, 2021, not in September 2021 as reported in the complaint.)

187 **Leonard Stern in New York City:** My source here and in what follows is Leonard Stern, personal communication, together with details supplied by dialysis technician Jonathan Longano, who has worked with Stern.

190 **Kjellstrand deplored the "unphysiology":** Carl M. Kjellstrand, Robert L. Evans et al., "The 'Unphysiology' of Dialysis: A Major Cause of Dialysis Side Effects?" Kidney Int Suppl (1975). Quote on "prevailing attitudes" in Carl M. Kjellstrand, "Dialysis in the USA," statement posted on a Home Dialysis Central forum (April 15, 1994) (https://forums.homedialysis.org/t/dr-carl-kjellstrand-akf/675). See also Carl M. Kjellstrand with Christopher R. Blagg, Todd Ing et al., "The History and Rationale of Daily and Nightly Hemodialysis," in Robert M. Lindsay, Umberto Buoncristiani et al., eds., *Daily and Nocturnal Hemodialysis*, Contributions to Nephrology (Basel, 2004).

190 **demanded the reform of US dialysis:** Speech at the 44th national symposium of the American Nephrology Nurses Association (ANNA), held in Las Vegas in 2013: "ANNA Hopes Ideas Delivered by Parker 'Catch Fire' with Nephrology Nurses at Annual Meeting," Nephrol News Issues (April 13, 2013) (archived at https://web.archive.org/web/20130520195728/https://www.nephrologynews .com/articles/109458-anna-hopes-ideas-delivered-by-parker-catch-fire).

190 **the HHS Civil Rights Office:** Vanessa and Sheldon Winters, personal communication. The existence of the investigation was confirmed during my personal communication with lead investigator Catherine Cushman, HHS Civil Rights Office. Citing the ongoing nature of the investigation, Cushman declined to provide further information about its scope and status.

190 **Law firms continue:** Personal communication with attorneys at several law firms, who spoke on condition of anonymity and confidentiality.

190 **A firm called Renalogic:** Personal communication with John R. Christiansen, executive vice president of Legal Risk and Strategy at Renalogic; and with Mary Stoll, a Seattle-based attorney who has done extensive outside legal work for Renalogic.

191 **DaVita filed five federal lawsuits:** John R. Christiansen, personal communication. The appeals court case is DaVita Inc. et al. v. Amy's Kitchen, Inc. Employee Benefit Health Plan, et al., case number 3:18-cv-06975-JST, US District Court for the Northern District of California, San Francisco Division, hearing on motion to dismiss (March 28, 2019). The US Supreme Court case is Marietta Memorial Hospital Employee Health Benefit Plan et al. v. DaVita Inc. et al., certiorari to the United States Court of Appeals for the Sixth Circuit, case number 20–1641 (argued March 1, 2022, decided June 21, 2022).

191 **"DaVita's stock price dropped":** John R. Christiansen, personal communication.

191 **seventeen House members:** Megan R. Wilson, "DaVita Helped Craft New Bill to Fix 'Loophole' Left by Supreme Court Ruling, Documents Show," *Politico* (August 9, 2022).

191 **"This law claims":** Kevin Weinstein, personal communication.

192 **hard-hitting investigations:** Ron Shinkman, "The Big Business of Dialysis Care," NEJM Catalyst (June 9, 2016); Duaa Eldeib, "They Were the Pandemic's Perfect Victims," ProPublica (2021); Carrie Arnold and Larry C. Price, "Kidney Dialysis Is a Booming Business—Is It Also a Rigged One?" part 1 of a series in *Scientific American* (https://www.scientificamerican.com/article/ kidney-dialysis-is-a-booming-business-is-it-also-a-rigged-one1); Oliver, *Last Week Tonight*, "Dialysis"; Trey Parker, Matt Stone et al., "Sassy Justice with Fred Sassy" (October 26, 2020)—appearances by ace dialysis salesman "Mark Zuckerberg" at 4:15 and 10:37. See also useful explainer by Ryan McDevitt, "Are Acquisitions Helping or Hurting the Healthcare Industry?" video of a LinkedIn Live broadcast (January 27, 2021).

Further recent publications on dialysis include "The Crusader Takes a

Closer Look: The Dialysis Hustle," a series by *The Chicago Crusader* (2021); and "First Came Kidney Failure. Then There Was the $540,842 Bill for Dialysis," *NPR Morning Edition* (July 22, 2019). Good podcasts include the hour-long segment in Freakonomics hosted by Stephen J. Dubner, "Is Dialysis a Test Case of Medicare for All?" (April 7, 2021); and Jeffery DelViscio and Carrie Arnold, "Science Talk: America on Dialysis," *Scientific American* (December 14, 2020) (https://www.scientificamerican.com/podcast /episode/america-on-dialysis). Finally, for a bit of historic trivia, watch *Star Trek's* Dr. McCoy call dialysis a treatment worthy of the Dark Ages (excerpt here: https://www.youtube.com/watch?v=UtllgbUiTto). Apparently the creator of *Star Trek*, Gene Roddenberry, had a relative on dialysis, and knew firsthand what an ordeal it was.

192 **a former pharma lobbyist:** David Lazarus, "Swamp Deepens as Trump Names Former Drug Industry Exec to Be Health Secretary," *Los Angeles Times* (November 15, 2017); and see the class action lawsuit against Eli Lilly and others, captioned In re Insulin Pricing Litigation, civil action number 3:17-cv-00699(BRM)(LHG), US District Court for the District of New Jersey, amended class action complaint (filed March 17, 2017).

192 **Azar had learned about:** Alex M. Azar II, remarks to the National Kidney Foundation in Washington, DC (March 4, 2019) (archived at https://web .archive.org/web/20190710222723/www.hhs.gov/about/leadership/secretary/ speeches/2019-speeches/remarks-to-the-national-kidney-foundation.html); Reed Abelson and Katie Thomas, "Trump Proposes Ways to Improve Care for Kidney Disease and Increase Transplants," *New York Times* (July 10, 2019); and "Azar: Outdated Medicare Payment System Hurting Kidney Care," Nephrology News and Issues (March 6, 2019).

193 **CMS issued a call:** See the proposed rule and call for comment at Medicare Program, End-Stage Renal Disease Prospective Payment System, a Proposed Rule by the Centers for Medicare & Medicaid Services on June 28, 2022, Federal Register.

193 **Several new bipartisan laws:** Five new laws were introduced in 2021 alone: the Improving Access to Home Dialysis Act; the Chronic Kidney Disease Improvement in Research and Treatment Act; the Coordination, Accountability, Research, and Equity (CARE) for All Kidneys Act; the Organ Donation Clarification Act; and the Living Donor Protection Act.

193 **"The law apparently":** Leonard Stern, personal communication. See Govtrack.us regarding the likelihood of the Improving Access to Home Dialysis Act of 2021 being enacted.

193 **becoming easier to obtain:** Here and following, Milda Saunders, personal communication. See also "Kidney Allocation System," Organ Procurement and Transplantation Network (OPTN); and details on the Organ Donation Clarification Act of 2021 at Congress.gov.

194 **Gerald Thompson continues to dialyze:** Gerald and Sherry Thompson, Justin Charles Evans, Carrie Brito and William Sarsfield, personal communication.

195 **Cornelius Robbins says he's grateful:** Cornelius Robbins, personal communication.

195 **"It is terrifying":** Sherry Thompson, personal communication.

196 **"What I've learned":** William Sarsfield, personal communication.

196 **Justin Charles Evans, too:** Justin Charles Evans, Arlene Mullin, Rev. Ronald Wright and Chili Most, personal communication.

196 **Arlene Mullin remains at the heart:** Arlene Mullin, Clem Johnson, William Summers, William Sarsfield and Sherry Thompson, personal communication.

197 **"For many years I fought":** Arlene Mullin, personal communication.

197 **Australia was passing:** John W. M. Agar, Charles R. P. George et al., "Dialysis in Australia and New Zealand," in Todd Ing, Mohamed Rahman et al., eds., *Dialysis* (Singapore, 2012); and John W. M. Agar, "The Success of Home Dialysis in Australia and New Zealand," Home Dialysis Central (August 18, 2016).

197 **a higher percentage of Australians:** The degree of urbanization in Australia (86.2 percent) vs. USA (82.7 percent) is reported by Statistica.com.

197 **his team of nurses trains patients:** Here and following, John Agar, personal communication.

198 **On Zoom with Darcy:** Dale Darcy, personal communication.

198 **"No one would believe me":** When John Agar heard this, he commented, "Nobody would believe him, indeed—including me!"

199 **Another of John Agar's patients:** John Agar, personal communication.

199 **died on home dialysis:** Finding into Death without Inquest, Andrew John O'Dwyer, Coroner's Court of Victoria at Melbourne, Court Reference COR 2015 4647 (https://www.coronerscourt.vic.gov.au/sites/default/files/2019-12/AndrewODwyer%20findiing%202015%204647.pdf).

199 **Agar remembers Edna Kent:** John Agar, personal communication.

200 **"What is freedom, you ask?":** Seneca, *Moral Letters to Lucilius*, Epistle 51, "On Baiae and Morals"; and Walter Englert, "Seneca and the Stoic View of Suicide," *Society for Ancient Greek Philosophy Newsletter* (1990).

200 **Mental integrity is a sine qua non:** Homer W. Smith, "Evolution of the Kidney," in *Lectures on the Kidney* (Lawrence, KS, 1943).

201 **Alcmaeon of Croton:** Carl Huffman, "Alcmaeon," Stanford Encyclopedia of Philosophy.

INDEX

Abel, John Jacob, 38–39
Abelson, Reed, 128
"Advancing Kidney Health" (2019), 192
African American healthcare. *See* Black
    healthcare
Agar, John
    background of, 10–12
    on "bazooka dialysis" treatments,
        24–25, 187
    home dialysis and, 197–200
    nocturnal home hemodialysis and, 47
    on solute clearance, 79
    treatment philosophy of, 197
AKF (American Kidney Fund), 124–29,
    185
AKI (acute kidney injury), 114
AKS (Anti-Kickback Statute), 124–29,
    140, 144
Alcmaeon of Croton, 201
Alexander, Leo, 58–61
Alexander, Shana, 61
ALS (amyotrophic lateral sclerosis), 213n
Alwall, Nils, 40–41, 45, 47, 89
AMA (American Medical Association)
    civil rights movement and, 70
    interdisciplinary conferences and, 62–63
    on money in healthcare, 65
    national health insurance plans and,
        68–69, 71
    on practicing medicine, 80, 88

American Antitrust Institute, 135
amino acids, 8
ancestral ocean, 6, 38
Animal Farm (Orwell), 145–46
antitrust laws, 134, 148, 190
antitrust watchdogs, 91
ARA (American Renal Associates), 128
Aristotle, 35
arteriovenous fistulas, 14, 16, 46, 198
artificial kidney, 39, 40, 43, 44–46, 47,
    56–57, 80
Asian healthcare, 170, 172, 174, 187
ASN (American Society of Nephrology),
    103
Atlanta Twelve, 164–65, 166, 167
autoimmune diseases, 8
Azar, Alex, 124–25, 192, 193

Babb, Les, 47
Bajwa, Amar, 182–83, 187
Bajwa, Roopa, 187
Bander, Steven, 89–90, 91, 147, 195
Barbakow, Jeffrey, 152, 153
Barbetta, David, 21, 138, 139–42, 143,
    145–46, 247n
Barbir, Daniel, 31, 32, 214–15n
Bargman, Joanne, 22, 130, 242n
Bays, Kenneth, 92, 93, 94–95, 107, 164,
    175, 177
Bazerman, Max, 122

"bazooka dialysis," 24–25, 116, 187, 191–92

Bear, Robert, 19, 24, 121, 122, 158, 161–62, 177

Bedrosian, John, 150

behavioral contracts, 17, 160, 175

Bennett, William, 62

Bernard, Claude, 6, 36–37, 38

Berns, Jeffrey, 195

Big Dialysis

  "bazooka dialysis" treatments, 24–25, 116, 187, 191–92

  business model of, 24, 27, 195

  closing facilities and, 184

  fraud and, 147–49, 246n

  history of, 88, 89–91

  industry expectations and, 118

  lobbying and, 181, 184, 185–86, 191

  media coverage, 192

  normal kidney function definitions and, 111–12

  policy/regulation and, 194

  profit priorities of, 91, 105, 124, 191

  public accountability and, 147, 191

  public investigations of, 110, 191–92

  transplant inequities of, 123–24, 195

  union legal challenges to, 183, 184, 187, 191–92, 259n

  whistleblower dismissals, 185

  whistleblowing investigations and, 190

bioethics, 1

  American economic calculus and, 58–60

  field beginnings, 54–57

  for-profit medicine and, 64–66, 81–82, 88, 120, 135–36, 221–22n

  politics of dialysis eligibility, 66–73

  Seattle experience and, 60–65, 221–22n

Bismarck, Otto von, 69

Black healthcare, 70, 168–69, 170, 171

  See also racism

Blagg, Christopher, 52, 74, 76, 221n

Book of the Dead, 34

Borrowed Time (Plough), 86

Brescia, Michael, 46

Brito, Carrie

  current dialysis care and, 194

  environmental etiology and, 171

  on ESRD diagnosis, 156

  high speed dialysis and, 14–18, 19

  as involuntary discharge/blacklisting victim, 26

  on racism, 14

  too early dialysis treatments and, 113

  transplant waitlist exclusion and, 124

Brown, Frank, 95

Brown, William, 26, 124

Buddha, 31

Buffett, Warren, 28

"Buffing the Numbers: The Decline and Fall of Dialysis Medicine" (Bargman), 130

Burton, LaVarne, 125, 126

Callahan, Daniel, 63

CA Proposition 8 ballot initiative (2018), 184

CA Proposition 23 ballot initiative (2020), 186

Carey, James, 67

Carlos, Jose, 26

Ceasar, Ron, 166

Ceauşescu, Nicolae, 32

Chili Most, 20, 196

Christiansen, John R., 191

Cimino, James, 46

Civil Rights Act (1964), 70, 71

civil rights movement, 70–71, 133, 190, 192

CMS (Centers for Medicare & Medicaid Services)

  AKF funding and, 126–27

  Atlanta Twelve complaints and, 164–65

  dialysis center financial penalties and, 130

  dialysis politics and, 86

facility tax and, 179, 258–59n
as federal healthcare agency, 2–3, 94
for-profit vs. non-profit kidney
  treatments, 129–30
low bid contracts and, 178
medical expenditures growth and, 133
missing critical measures and, 116–17
"Outcomes List," 177
oversight programs of, 2–4, 89, 115,
  130, 175, 177–79
policy changes and, 193
whistleblower hotline and, 106
See also 5-Star Quality Rating System;
  ESRD Networks; Quality
  Incentive Program
Coats-Simpson, Pacita, 26
Cody, William Frederick (Buffalo Bill), 8
Cohen, Leonard, 150
Cold War human radiation experiments,
  60
corporate culture
  dialysis centers and, 26–28, 30–32, 86,
    122–23, 137–42, 146, 156–58
  fraud and, 122–23, 151
  malignance in, 120–22, 146, 151–53,
    238n
corporate dialysis centers, 2–4
  corporate culture and, 26–28, 30–32,
    86, 122–23, 137–42, 146, 156–58
  false accusations filed by, 21–23, 24,
    159–60, 173
  market consolidation of, 90–91, 93,
    118–19
  as neoliberal rent-takers, 132–33
  nephrologist practice joint ventures
    and, 140–44
  oversight of, 175–79
  patient blacklisting and, 19, 22–23, 26,
    157, 160, 190, 195
  patient-staff ratios in, 106–7
  physician blacklisting and, 103
  poor patient outcomes in, 105–7,
    118–19

private payors and, 23, 102, 124, 129–
  30, 141, 184, 256n
profit motives of, 24–25
retaliation campaigns and, 15–18,
  23–24, 84–86, 159–60, 166
supply rationing/reusing, 105
transplant options and, 123–24
workers in, 25–26, 93, 104–5, 130, 166,
  182
See also DaVita; fraud; Fresenius;
  involuntary discharges; National
  Medical Care; ultrafiltration rates
COVID-19, 9, 36, 114, 160, 174, 190
Coyne, Daniel, 195
Crafoord, Holger, 41
"cream skimming," 77–78, 81–82, 83–84,
  86, 129–30
Crowfeather, Ernie, 64
CROWNWeb, 179
"crush syndrome," 39
Cuban kidney failure, 171
cytokine storms, 36

Daniels, Leonard Polak, 39
Darcy, Dale, 198–99
Daugirdas, John, 116–17
DaVita
  board members of, 175, 178–79
  CEO. *See* Thiry, Kent
  corporate culture of, 26–28, 30–32,
    137–42, 146
  criminal investigations and, 144–45
  Deal Depot and, 139, 140–44
  dialysis consolidation outcome and, 91,
    100, 119
  EPO overuse and, 110–11
  high-speed dialysis in, 15
  HIPPER compression and, 141, 144–45
  history of, 29–31
  joint ventures and, 102, 103, 104,
    143–44, 190
  lawsuits/settlements and, 126–27, 128,
    148, 191–92, 215n, 247n

DaVita (*continued*)
  lobbying groups and, 184
  market dominance of, 1, 13, 26, 126
  nephrologists and, 100–102, 103
  PAC campaign donations and, 191
  pay schemes of, 122
  private health plan lawsuits by, 191
  specific responses to author, 2–4
  union legal challenge to, 186, 187
  university revenue streams and, 104
  whistleblowing retaliation and
        blacklisting, 165–67, 185, 254n
DaVita v. Marietta Memorial Hospital
  (2022), 191
DeParle, Nancy-Ann, 94, 175
Depner, Thomas, 52
diabetes, 9, 29
dialysis
  COVID-19 and, 9, 36, 114, 160, 174, 190
  early machine manufacturing and, 41
  early tools of, 38–39
  hemodialysis origins, 44–46, 47
  historical conceptual framework for,
        36–38
  in-center vs. home treatment, 74–76
  as medical entitlement, 1–2, 29, 72, 213n
  as new technology, 9–12, 84
  original dialysis machines, 39–41
  patient advocates and, 18–19, 20–21,
        22, 195
  patient costs of, 56, 64, 67, 68, 75–76,
        167, 185
  patient loss of agency and, 84–86, 93,
        154, 195
  quality industry benchmarks, 81
  quality measures of, 78–79, 131
  recovery time and, 2, 15, 25
  screening processes and, 50–51, 63
  side effects of, 2, 15, 48, 52, 110
  standards of care, 78
  techno-centric character of, 84
  treatment duration and, 55, 116–17, 118
  types of, 44–46, 47, 48, 208n

  See also bioethics; end-stage renal
        disease; fast food healthcare
        business model; home dialysis;
        ultrafiltration rates
Dialysis Advocates, 19, 104, 106, 161, 165,
  196, 197
"Dialysis for All," 2, 73–76, 82
dialysis industry, 1–4
  American early-start dialysis patients,
        112–14, 192
  anticompetitive structure of, 119–20
  calls for reform of, 189–90, 192
  evaluation metrics within, 115–17
  financial conflicts and treatment, 108–
        11, 123–24
  for-profit centers cream skimming, 77–
        78, 81–82, 83–84, 86, 129–30
  for-profit vs. non-profit treatment,
        74–76, 79–80, 81–82, 129–30
  market consolidation of, 90–91, 93,
        103, 118–19
  oversight of, 2–4, 89, 115, 130, 175–79
  progressive deregulation and defunding
        of oversight, 94–95, 176, 179
  racially segregated marginalized
        communities and, 168–74
  racism in, 14, 70, 165, 171–74, 193–94
  as reflection of American values, 133,
        201–2
  systemic harm documentation and,
        190–91
  university revenue streams and, 90, 104
  unsanitary clinic conditions and,
        183–84
  See also Big Dialysis; corporate dialysis
        centers; *specific companies*
dialysis technicians, 2, 16, 20, 25, 158, 180
dialyzers, 38
  disposable hollow-fiber, 46, 101
  Kiil, 44, 51
  Skeggs-Leonards plate, 44
DiCaprio, Leonardo, 30
disposable hollow-fiber dialyzers, 46

doctor-entrepreneur, 83, 88
Doctors Trial, 58
Dominican healthcare, 170, 189

Eamer, Richard, 122, 150–51, 152, 249n
Eisenhower, Dwight D., 57
Elberg, Jacob, 147, 153
electrolytes, 5, 8
Eliason, Paul, 118
emergency healthcare, 2
    COVID-19 and dialysis patients, 36, 160
    dialysis clinic requests for, 184
    dialysis outcomes and, 96, 155, 186
    as dialysis outlet, 19, 21, 157, 161
    dialysis survival rates and, 19
    as for-profit industry, 88, 134
    racial biases in, 174
end-stage renal disease (ESRD)
    chronic dialysis, 154, 159
    long-term management and, 161, 193
    marginalized communities incidence of,
        170–71
    renal failure treatments, 39, 41, 43, 44,
        45, 50–52, 123
    See also kidney transplants
"Energizing a Firm with Mission & Values"
    (Thiry), 26–27
Enola Gay, 42
Enron, 120
EPO (Epogen), 108–11
erythropoietin, 108
ESRD legislation (1972), 75
ESRD Networks
    as CMS dialysis oversight body, 2–3, 89
    complaints registered with, 21, 160,
        164, 166
    complicity of, 175, 176, 178
    data honor system of, 95, 178–79
    geographic diversity of, 178
    involuntary discharges racial bias, 173
    national task force formation, 156–57
    priorities of, 94–95, 175–76, 177
    suspected malfeasance of, 179

ESRD Quality Incentive Program (QIP),
    3–4, 115, 130, 131, 193
Ester, Dale, 95
ethics. *See* bioethics
euthanasia movement, 58
Evans, Justin Charles, 21–22, 26, 163,
    164–67, 168, 194, 196, 254n

fast food healthcare business model
    changing economics and ethics, 88–89
    economics and, 118
    expansion/consolidation of, 89–91
    framing effect and, 122–23
    history of, 27, 212n
    human costs and, 105
    lobbying and, 243n
    medical expenditures/outcomes, 133–34
    physicians profits and, 65
    private equity firms and, 134–36
    private payors and, 124–29
    See also fraud
Fetter, Trevor, 153
Fine, Max, 69, 70–71, 73
Fischer, Bobby, 8
fistulas, 14, 16, 46, 198
5-Star Quality Rating System, 115, 130
Foreign Corrupt Practices Act, 148
for-profit medicine
    bioethics and, 64–66, 81–82, 88, 120,
        135–36, 221–22n
    history of DaVita and, 29
    patient harm and, 131–32
fraud, 1
    Big Dialysis and, 147–49, 246n
    corporate culture and, 122–23, 151
    EPO overuse and, 110–11
    impunity and, 146–47
    laboratory practices and, 130–31
    Medicare and Medicaid and, 147, 247n
    NME case, 150–54
Fresenius
    AKF funding and, 128
    corporate structure, 207n

Fresenius (*continued*)
  dialysis consolidation outcome and,
      90–91, 119
  dialysis workers and, 25, 105, 186
  EPO overuse and, 110
  false accusations and, 21, 23
  high-speed dialysis in, 14–15
  involuntary discharges and, 17, 21, 23
  lawsuits against, 128, 147, 148, 246n
  lobbying groups and, 184
  market dominance of, 1, 13, 126
  nephrologists and, 101, 103
  union legal challenge to, 187
  university revenue streams and, 104
  whistleblowing retaliation and
      blacklisting, 159, 160
Friedman, Milton, 80–81
Frontiers in Pediatrics, 174
FTC (Federal Trade Commission), 91
Fulbright, William, 57

Galen, 34
Gambro, 90, 91, 99, 101, 147–48, 215n
Gawande, Atul, 212n
Gaylin, Willard, 63
Gentry, Harvey, 46
GFR (glomerular filtration rate), 112–13,
      172, 193
Gidey, Tirsit, 26
Glazer, Shep, 66, 67–68, 71–72
glomerulonephritis, 14, 49
glomerulus, 7, 8, 14
God Committee, 50–51, 57, 60–61, 63
Goldman, Jesse, 22–23
Golper, Thomas, 195
Gonzales, Emanuel, 180–81, 182, 183, 195
Gonzales, Vince, 180, 181
Gonzalez, David, 128
Gordon, Dexter, 8
Gottschalk, Carl, 62, 68
Gottschalk Report, 68
Grace, W. R., 83
Graham, Thomas, 38

GranuFlo, 149
Grassley, Chuck, 92, 95, 97, 153, 164, 175
Great Depression, 68, 73
Great Society, 69, 73
Grieco, Paul L. E., 118
Gualvez, Cass, 26, 176, 181, 183, 185

Hager, Edward, 42, 65, 66, 227n
Hamburger, Jean, 42, 62, 64
Hamilton, Joseph G., 60
Hampers, Constantine, 42, 65, 66, 74,
      82–83, 118, 227n
Handford, Megallan, 25–26, 172–73, 185,
      195
Hansen, Gregg, 26, 108, 155
hantavirus, 41
Harris, Kenneth, 26
Harrison, J. Hartwell, 43
Hart, Kevin, 163
Hastings Center, 63
Havian, Eric, 138, 144–45
HCFA (Health Care Financing
      Administration), 175
healthcare system
  debates about, 2
  dialysis companies systemic harm to,
      190–91
  dialysis involuntary discharge cost of,
      161–62
  expansion of, 87–88
  federal funding of, 68–69, 71, 117–20
  health inequity and race-based
      disparities, 169–74
  high-margin private payor patients and,
      23, 102, 124, 129–30, 141, 184,
      256n
  medical ethics and, 27, 52–53, 55,
      81–82, 120, 144, 201
  neoliberalism and, 132–36
  private equity business model and,
      134–36
  privatization and consolidation, 88–89,
      90–91, 118–19

racial justice reforms and, 70
services as commodity, 88
structural/systemic racism in, 171–74, 193–94
unions, 181–87, 190, 191–92, 259n
See also fast food healthcare business model; for-profit medicine; fraud
Health Security Plan, 71
Heebsh, Benjamin, 118
Hegel's principle, 58
Heming, Rollin, 46
hemodialysis. *See* dialysis
Herrick, Richard, 10, 43, 44
Herrick, Ronald, 10, 43, 55–56
HHS Office of Civil Rights, 187
high-speed dialysis, 14–15, 209n
HIPPER bus, 141
HIPPER compression, 141, 144–45
HIPPERs (high-margin private payor patients), 23, 102, 124, 129–30, 141, 184, 256n
Hippocratic Oath, 55, 56, 57, 84, 99, 120
Hispanic healthcare, 174
Holmes, Elizabeth, 122
home dialysis
    assisted, 187–89, 193
    Australia and, 197–200
    benefits of, 48–49
    executive order for, 192
    federal funding and, 74–76, 80
    for-profit pay schemes, 122
    involuntary discharges and, 159–61
    nocturnal dialysis, 11, 47, 51, 52
    peritoneal children's method and, 46–47
    racial biases and, 171–72
homeostasis, 6–7, 33, 201–2
House Ways and Means Committee dialysis, 66–67
Huffman, Alice, 186
human experimentation ethics, 57–58
human plutonium experiments, 60
hypertension, 9, 29

ibuprofen, 9
immunosuppression, 42–43, 44
International Military Tribunal, 58
involuntary discharges
    authoritarian tendency driven, 24, 158
    as blacklisting component, 19, 157
    clinic oversight and, 175–77
    costs to healthcare system, 161–62
    dialysis workers and, 22–23, 130
    ESRD Networks taskforce and, 156–58
    false accusations and, 26
    financially driven, 23, 158
    home dialysis and, 159–61
    patient advocates and, 195–96
    potential lethal outcomes of, 21
    quality incentive driven, 131
    racial biases in, 173–74
    whistleblower testimony and, 95–96
Isakson, Johnny, 21, 164

Jim Crow policies, 70–71
Johns Hopkins School of Medicine, 7
Johnson, Clem, 20–21, 197
Johnson, Debbie, 164, 167
Johnson, Lyndon B., 68, 69, 70
Jonsen, Albert, 55
Journal of Internal Medicine, 174

Kasiewicz, James, 21
Kaufman, David, 13
KDOQI (Kidney Disease Outcomes Quality Initiative), 104, 109, 111–12, 113
Kennedy, Edward, 71, 72
Kennedy, John F., 69
Kennedy Institute of Ethics, 63
Kent, Edna, 199–200
"Kidney Dialysis Patients: A Population at Undue Risk," 92
kidneys
    artificial, 39, 40, 43, 44–46, 47, 56–57, 80
    biochemical tasks, 6

kidneys (*continued*)
  blood and, 7–8, 108
  failure of, 8–9, 29, 35–36, 41, 111–12
  genetic disease factors, 171
  historical underappreciation of, 33–35
  homeostasis and, 6–7, 33, 201–2
  human physiological role of, 48–49, 200
  necessity of, 5–6, 201
  odor receptors of, 7
  preventive medicine and, 192–93, 194
  See also kidney transplants
kidney transplants
  advances in, 46
  donor allocation policies and, 193
  eligibility/waitlists, 89, 123–24, 172
  financial disincentives and, 74–75, 76
  history of, 9–10, 41–44
  medical ethics and, 55–56
  organ procurement system, 75
  patient advocates and, 195
  policy mandates and, 192
Kiil, Fred, 44
Kiil dialyzer, 44, 51
King, Martin Luther Jr., 70, 190
Kjellstrand, Carl, 190
Kogod, Dennis, 137–38
Kolff, Willem "Pim," 39–40, 41, 44, 46, 62, 63
Kolff-Brigham dialysis machine, 41, 42, 43, 44
Korean War, 41
Kraus, Irene, 88
Kt/V, 78, 79, 116, 131, 187
Ku Klux Klan, 71

Laird, Melvin, 62
Laird, Peter, 159
Lake, Veronica, 8
Learn the Facts About Kidney Disease (Rosansky), 111, 115
Lectures on the Phenomena Common to Animals and Plants (Bernard), 37
Lee, Terry Thermutis, 26
Liberty Dialysis, 91

Lincoln, Abraham, 71
Living Donor Protection Act (2021), 193
lobe-finned fish, 5
Lockridge, Robert, 195
Lombardi, Vince, 31
"Lookin' for Love" (Johnny Lee song), 151
Lowrie, Edmund
  dialysis quality industry benchmarks and, 81
  dialysis standards of care and, 78
  early kidney transplant advances and, 42
  free-market, for-profit medicine manifesto of, 79, 82, 118
  in-center dialysis and, 74, 75–76
  as NMC senior vice president, 77
  Plough's article and, 83–84, 86

Mahone, Richard, 164, 167
Maimonides, Moses, 99
Man in the Iron Mask, The, 30
Massey, Jack, 27, 88
McCain, John, 97
McDevitt, Ryan, 117–20, 131, 136
medical ethical dilemmas, 54–57, 58, 63
medical malpractice, 16
"Medical Science Under Dictatorship" (Alexander), 58
"Medicare for All," 1–2, 29, 72, 213n
Medicare and Medicaid
  commercial exchange plans and, 125, 129
  creation of, 69–70
  dialysis for all, 72–76, 80
  End-Stage Renal Disease (ESRD) Program, 52, 80
  for-profit policies and, 136
  fraud and, 147, 247n
  Friedman on, 81
  medical expenditures/outcomes, 133
  new medical-industrial complex and, 82, 108, 134
  reimbursement, 111, 115
  Wall Street investment opportunity and, 87–88

Mehta, Chet, 141
Mengele, Josef, 99
Merrill, John, 41, 42–43, 44, 46, 55–56,
    62, 65
mesonephros, 6
metabolic wastes, 5, 6
metanephros, 6
middle-molecule hypothesis, 48
Milgram, Stanley, 238n
milieu intérieur (internal environment), 6,
    37–38, 201
military-industrial complex, 57
Miller, Brent
    background of, 101–2
    on corporate dialysis patient care, 103–4
    on dialysis center revenue streams, 90, 104
    as dialysis patient-centered care
        advocate, 195
    on dreadful dialysis care, 89
    on EPO boom, 111
    HIPPER treatment priority and, 141
    on NIH TiME trial, 117
    physician blacklisting, 103
Mills, Wilbur, 67, 69, 71
Moore, Jessica, 138
moral injury, 25
Moriarty, Jim, 151, 152, 154
Mozart, Wolfgang Amadeus, 8
Mullin, Arlene
    as Dialysis Advocates founder, 104–5
    as dialysis worker, 89
    as full-time private dialysis advocate,
        18–22, 161, 165–66, 196
    inspection preparations and, 176
    on quality ratings, 131
    on racism in dialysis, 165, 173
    as Senate subcommittee hearing driving
        force, 92
    whistleblowing dialysis workers and, 26
Murray, Joseph, 42, 43, 55, 56, 65

NAACP, 186
National Health Insurance Partnership
    Act, 71

National Health Law Program, 187
Native American healthcare, 170–71, 174
Nazi Germany, 57–58, 120
NCDS (National Cooperative Dialysis
    Study), 78, 81
neoliberal economic theory, 66
neoliberalism, 132–36
nephrology, 2, 9, 10, 11, 46–48, 109
nephrons, 7, 8, 9
New Deal, 68, 69–70, 73, 133
Newman, Edwin, 61–62
Newsom, Gavin, 184, 186
NIDDK (National Institute of Diabetes and
    Digestive and Kidney Diseases), 194
Nixon, Richard, 71, 72, 73
Nixon White House, 120
NKF (National Kidney Foundation),
    103–4, 172, 193
NMC (National Medical Care)
    applying financial management
        methods/metrics and, 80
    assembly line approach of, 84
    business model of, 74, 90
    criminal and civil investigations of, 147
    ethical/psychological implications in,
        77–78
    Friedman ideology and, 81
    investor owned medicine, 83–84
    lobbying of, 75–76
    as nation's largest dialysis firm, 66
    nephrologist founded and managerial
        control of, 106
    prosecution and purchase of, 90–91
NME (National Medical Enterprises),
    150–54
Nuremberg Code, 58
Nutcracker, The, 163

obesity, 9
O'Brien, Flann, 200
O'Cain, Trina, 26
O'Dwyer, Andrew, 199
Oliver, John, 192
OPEC oil embargo, 73

Ordóñez, Lisa, 122
Organizaţia Pionierilor (Pioneers), 32
Organization for Economic Co-operation
    and Development (OECD), 133
organ procurement system, 75
Outcomes List, 177
outpatient dialysis centers, 83

Pacific Islanders kidney failure, 170
Padua, Emerson, 182–83, 185, 195
Parker, Bryan, 141
Parker, J. Clint, 195
Parker, Thomas, 190
Parker, Trey, 192
Parks, Rosa, 190
Peace, Breon, 148
Peña, Jaime, 142
peripheral neuropathy, 47, 48
peritoneal dialysis, 46–47, 48, 208n
PHS (Public Health Service), 57, 70
Pickens, Eric, 26
Pierratos, Andreas, 47
Pius XI, 56
Pius XII, 56
Plough, Alonzo
    background of, 168–69
    corporate nephrology and, 79
    ethical/psychological implications
        dialysis research, 77–78
    for-profit, free-market, Wall Street–
        fueled medicine and, 83–87
    on healthcare racial bias, 173
    patient-caregiver relationship and,
        158
    on preventative care, 193
    on structural racism, 174
Pluznick, Jennifer, 7
Porter, Katie, 128–29
prison camp guard syndrome, 158
private equity (PE) firms, 134–36
Proceedings of the National Academy of
    Sciences, 174
pronephros, 6

Public Law, 72, 92–603
Puerto Rican kidney failure, 171
Purdue Pharma, 120

QIO (Quality Improvement
    Organizations), 178
QIP (Quality Incentive Program), 3–4,
    115, 130, 131, 193
Quinton, Wayne, 45
Quinton-Scribner shunt, 45

racism, 13–14, 60, 70, 165, 171–74, 193–94
    See also Black healthcare
Reagan, Ronald, 69, 75, 80, 133
Reaganomics, 80–81
Reid, Marcel, 21, 168
Reilly, Pat, 20
Reiser, Stanley Joel, 68
Relman, Arnold, 81–82
renal disease. *See* kidneys
Renalogic, 190–91
"Restore Protections for Dialysis Patients
    Act" (2021), 191
Rettig, Richard, 168
Robbins, Cornelius
    on assembly-line patient care, 107–8
    early start dialysis and, 113
    ESRD Networks and, 175–77
    on falsifying lab tests, 131
    as involuntary discharge/blacklisting
        victim, 26
    as kidney transplant recipient, 123–24,
        195
    private payor vs. federally funded care,
        129–30
Roberts, Jimmy, 118
Roosevelt, Franklin Delano, 68
Roper, William, 175
Rosansky, Steven, 106–7, 111, 112–15,
    156, 195
Rothman, David, 55
Roy, Don, 126
Ruiz, Abelinda, 26

Sarsfield, William, 16–18, 155, 156, 196, 197
Satellite Healthcare, 114, 187
Saunders, Joe, 44, 45, 50
Saunders, Milda, 169, 171, 172, 193
Schafstadt, Sofia, 40
Schatell, Dori, 109
Scheck, Christy, 152
Schilling, John, 149
Schreiner, George, 41, 46, 62, 63, 67
Schupak, Eugene, 42, 65, 74
Scott, Rick, 122, 149
Scribner, Belding "Scrib"
    advances in uremic care, 50
    artificial kidney challenges and, 47
    artificial kidney treatments and, 56–57
    care screening committee and, 50–53, 62
    corporate dialysis abuses and, 189–90
    defining kidney's role, 48
    dialysis as rehabilitation, 196
    dialysis vascular access and, 44–45
    as home dialysis advocate, 48–49, 74, 76
    on medical ethics, 54–55
    modern technology/professional ethics and, 57–58
    not-for-profit care and, 65, 221–22n
    patient selection, 63
    "Seattle experience" and, 60–61
    university medical center innovator, 46
Scrushy, Richard, 122, 145, 149
Scully, Thomas, 175, 178
Sears, John, 75
"Seattle experience," 61–62, 63
SEC (Securities and Exchange Commission), 134
self-care dialysis programs, 106
Seneca, 200
Shaldon, Stanley, 47
Shaw, George Bernard, 8
Shields, Clyde, 45, 47, 56, 61
Skeggs-Leonards plate dialyzer, 44
Smith, Betty, 89, 106, 154, 156, 157, 158, 178–79

Smith, Brenda, 96, 97
Smith, Brent, 92–93, 95, 96, 175
Smith, Homer, 33, 200, 201
Smith, W. Randolph, 152
Snappy, 111
socialism, 66
Social Security, 69
social welfare programs, 73
Sorrow's Reward (Bear), 177
Spaeth, Nancy, 49, 50, 51–52
Stark, Pete, 94, 95, 175
Stark II law (1993), 83
Starr, Paul, 64
Stern, Leonard
    assisted home dialysis and, 187–89, 193, 197
    background of, 98–101
    on corporate dialysis patient care, 24, 158
    dialysis evolution, 11
    modernist art and, 196
    as nephrologist dialysis program founder, 10
    on nephrologist's patient responsibility, 103
    as patient-centered care advocate, 195
    on Thiry's dramatics, 28
stoicism, 200
Stone, Matt, 192
Stravino, James, 26
Summers, Bill, 197
systemic racism, 14, 60, 70, 165, 171–74, 193–94

Taylor, Bill, 28
technological ambivalence, 57
technology-driven medical ethics, 64, 84
Tenet, 153–54
"They Decide Who Lives, Who Dies" (Alexander), 61
Thiry, Kent
    antitrust lawsuit indictment and, 148
    approach to medical business and, 26–30, 153–54

Thiry, Kent (*continued*)
  company investigations and, 145
  corporate dialysis consolidation and, 90
  creating corporate culture and, 31
  DaVita business plan and, 144
  on EPO overprescribing, 110–11
  fast food business comparisons by, 26–27
  historical fraud allegations and, 147
  nephrologists and, 103
  on patient clinic dependence, 119
  on regulator board appointments, 175
  roll-up acquisitions and, 91
  unions and, 185
See also DaVita

Thomas, Katie, 128
Thomas, Louis, 26
Thomas, Sherry, 196
Thompson, Gerald, 23–24, 26, 114, 155, 159–60, 194, 195–96
Thompson, Sherry, 23–24, 114, 155, 159–60, 176, 194, 195–96
Thoreau, Henry David, 63
Three Musketeers, The (Dumas), 30
Time to Reduce Mortality in ESRD (TiME) trial, 116–17
Tone at the Top, 121
totalitarianism, 32
Total Renal Care, 90, 95, 153
transplants. *See* kidney transplants
transplant specialists, 62
Truman, Harry, 69
Trump, Donald, 192
Tuskegee Study, 60

Uldall, Robert, 47
ultrafiltration rates (UFR)
  dialysis speed and duration and, 14–15, 116–17, 167, 187
  kidney glomerulus function, 7–8, 40
  low rates and, 24–25
  quality/quantity measurements and, 79
  See also "bazooka dialysis"

undocumented immigrants, 99–100
Unetaneh Tokef, 61
unions, 181–87, 190, 191–92, 259n
universal healthcare programs, 69, 72, 107
university medical centers, 46, 90, 102
uranium mining, 171
urea, 8, 38, 39, 40, 48, 78–79, 190
urea reduction ratio (URR), 131
uremia, 39, 41, 49–50
USRDS (United States Renal Data System), 118, 170
US Supreme Court, 191
utilitarianism, 59, 60–61

VA (Veterans Administration), 57
Vainer, Alon, 215n
Vivra, 90, 91, 147
Vlchek, Doug, 28

Wallach, Jeffrey, 195
Wang, Henry, 161
Warsaw Ghetto, 98
Watergate, 73
water-salt balance (pH), 5
Watson, Antonia, 26
Weinstein, Kevin, 191
whistleblowing
  accounting fraud and, 149
  advocates/activists and, 20–21, 92, 168
  CMS hotline and, 106
  corporate culture malignance and, 120–22, 146, 151–53
  dialysis center lawsuits and, 190
  dialysis treatment center workers and, 1, 147–48
  on involuntary discharges, 95–96
  lawsuits and, 128, 138–39, 190
  medically unnecessary procedures and, 148
  retaliation for, 165–67, 185, 254n
  Senate Subcommittee testimony retaliation, 95
  Tuskegee Study and, 60

Who Shall Live (Edwin Newman documentary), 61–62
Wilde, Oscar, 200
Winstead, Edwin, 142
Winters, Sheldon, 154–55
Winters, Vanessa, 26, 154–55, 190
Winterscheid, Loren, 45
Wish, Jay, 94
Wollmann, Thomas G., 91
Wood, Jim, 185
Woolhandler, Steffie, 132–36
world's national health systems, 82
World War II
   German medicine critics, 58

post-war group psychological tools research, 120–21
post-war medical research/technology, 55
post-war renal advances, 9, 41
renal failure treatment necessity from, 39
transplant immunosuppression theories, 42–43
trauma of, 98
universal healthcare programs and, 69
uranium mining, 171
Wright, Ronald, 20, 196
Wyden, Ron, 94

xenotransplantation, 11